Equal Partners – Go

CW00548148

Friendship is a desired state for couples today, but friendship is limited in marriage by the interaction of rigid sex roles and traditional views about the sharing of power. While all couples are influenced by the changing roles of men and women, marriage lags behind the workplace in achieving equality for women. *Equal Partners – Good Friends* examines the connection between inequality in marriage and marital distress. In today's relationships partners demand fairness as well as intimacy, and marital therapists have to be prepared for this change.

The essential nature of equality is examined through the comparison of couples attempting to share equally in three different cultures: UK, USA and Israel. This cross-cultural view has resulted in the creation of a model for equality in marriage that has direct relevance to all couple relationships in a world of changing sex roles. It creates a new vision of what equality in marriage can look like and ways it can be achieved.

By looking at case studies of marital therapy, the book examines the effects of inequality on marriage and offers a vision for therapists of an equal relationship that can encompass diverse lifestyles. Therapeutic methods are offered which help couples move towards equality in their relationships.

This book proposes that there is real therapeutic benefit in bringing issues related to social change in gender roles into therapy sessions. It offers a clinical treatment model based on empirical research. Offering numerous clinical case examples, the author suggests practical tools for couples therapy. Implications of this therapy model for training and supervising therapists working with couples are explored.

Claire Rabin, D.S.W. is a teacher and supervisor of family and couples therapy at the Bob Shapell School of Social Work, Tel Aviv University and a therapist in private practice.

ood Friends

Equal Partners – Good Friends

Empowering couples through therapy

Claire Rabin

London and New York

First published 1996
by Routledge
11 New Fetter Lane, London EC4P 4EE

Simultaneously published in the USA and Canada
by Routledge
29 West 35th Street, New York, NY 10001

Routledge is an International Thomson Publishing company

© 1996 Claire Rabin

Typeset in Times Ten by Florencetype Ltd, Stoodleigh, Devon
Printed and bound in Great Britain by
TJ Press (Padstow) Ltd, Padstow, Cornwall

British Library Cataloguing in Publication Data
A catalogue record for this book is available from the British Library

Library of Congress Cataloguing in Publication Data
Rabin, Claire Low
    Equal partners – good friends: empowering couples through
    therapy/Claire Rabin.   Includes bibliographical references and index.
    1. Marital psychotherapy.   2. Man–Woman relationships.   3. Sex role.
    4. Dominance (Psychology).   5. Communication in marriage.
    6. Equality.   7. Friendship   8. Marriage – Psychological aspects.
    I. Title.
    RC488.5.R33 1996
    616.89'156 – dc20   95–42247
                                                         CIP

ISBN 0–415–11614–7 (hbk)
ISBN 0–415–11615–5 (pbk)

To my husband Yossi
and my children, Noa,
Omri and Shani.

In memory of Professor
Naomi Gottlieb,
mentor and friend.

Contents

Acknowledgements

The seeds of this book germinated while I was on leave at the School of Social Work, University of Washington, Seattle. The nurturing environment created for me by the staff, through the generous support of the Head of the Department, Professor Nancy Hooyman, was crucial in getting the research project off to a good start. Professor John Gottman, of the Department of Psychology, gave freely of his time for numerous challenging talks over Seattle's famous coffee. Professor Bob Kohlenberg, also of the Department of Psychology, and his wife, Mavis Tsai, were important in giving me new ways of understanding therapy with couples. Professor Pepper Schwartz, of the Department of Sociology, contributed her immense knowledge of 'peer marriages' and introduced me to equity theory, as well as helping me apply this thinking to clinical cases. Dr Ellen Olshansky, of the Department of Nursing, contributed to the qualitative methodology and helped me develop the themes of the research. All these and others demonstrated collegial support and caring way beyond the call of duty.

I would also like to thank friends and colleagues in Israel who generously took up the slack while I was busy writing. Professor Yossi Katan especially has my gratitude for taking over many tasks to free me up for this work and Professor Shimon Spiro helped me take time off from teaching. Dr Ayala Pines and Dr Fredda Ronen read the final draft of this book and contributed their thoughtful comments and careful editing. It is hard to imagine ever having finished without all this support.

This book is based on ideas gained from my teachers, the couples I interviewed in Seattle, Washington, Israel and the UK. These very busy people took time they did not have to share their lives with me. Their honesty and commitment to the equal partnership lifestyle was a source of continual inspiration. And the beauty I witnessed in their lives, flowing from cooperation and love, will never, never be forgotten. To all of these people, who appear in this book under pseudonyms, I send my deep appreciation. In addition, I thank my clients. They reaffirmed my awe in the human capacity to change and transform, creating new relationships in front of my eyes.

In the final analysis, this project would never have happened, and the book would never have been written, if it weren't for my egalitarian husband, Yossi. The first to introduce me to equal partnership, he supported me all along the way to complete this work. In addition to hours of listening, and talking, he shared doing the interviews with me, took care of the children and kept house while I wrote, and co-led couples groups with me, teaching me by example what friendship in marriage is all about.

Introduction

A change in perspective

It happened towards the end of an exhausting, intense but seemingly helpful second session with a couple in a midlife crisis. Sharon and Tom sat closely together on the same couch, despite the fact that they were discussing ending their marriage. Sharon had initiated therapy when she discovered that Tom was having an affair. Between the first and second session with me, Tom had revealed that he had been unfaithful regularly for the twenty years of their marriage. Their dependable homelife, based on traditional religious values and center to five children, seemed to be crumbling in the face of his lies, and betrayal.

And yet, the sessions offered them hope. They both wanted to stay together, and it did appear that perhaps for the first time in their marriage the prospect of honest communication arose. Sharon, a frustrated homemaker wanting to work, had been influenced by Tom to stay home. Tom, who worked long hours in a family business, liked the security of having her home. Now, in light of the recent discoveries, she decided to get a job and realized that she had been 'asleep for years in a fantasy of marital bliss'. Tom reported that he had been frustrated sexually from the start of their marriage; he had worked it out for himself that since their need for sex was irrevocably different, he would 'protect' their marriage by taking care of his sexual needs elsewhere. However, recently his double life had become compounded as his lover insisted on a commitment.

They appeared engaged in therapy and both wanted to continue to work. Then it happened.

As we tried to set up the next session, Tom mentioned that for the next three weeks he would be very busy at work. He preferred to wait three weeks and then to make the appointment. He said this casually, and reasonably, and I was at first caught off guard – after all, people did have busy times at work; I could certainly understand that. Sharon gazed down, and remained silent. My internal warning light went off in the form of a tightening of my stomach muscles.

I turned to Sharon and inquired how she felt about this. Staring at me intensely, she said 'I knew he would run away ... I just knew it.' It was apparently up to me to react. Sharon and Tom were both replaying their basic marital dynamics (the only dance they knew) in my presence.

Important gendered interactional patterns can be revealed around a seemingly small and technical issue. In this case, Tom was avoiding confronting the next session. In their relationship as well, Tom evaded emotional conflict in a male sex-role stereo-typed way. His work was regarded as vital to both partners and seldom had Sharon demanded that he put her needs before work. They both labeled the business as contributing to the whole family, and thus not meeting his needs, but 'their needs'. In her sex-role stereotyped way, Sharon became a victim to this mutually agreed upon definition, and therefore did not protest or assert her own needs. If I had not asked her, I think that Sharon would have allowed the meeting to be scheduled in three weeks' time, despite the fact that she was not sleeping, was taking tranquilizers and needed immediate support during her search for work. Significantly, Sharon did not ask for a session alone when Tom said he was going to be busy.

I decided to support Sharon and challenge Tom, stating in as assertive manner as I could summon:

> I understand that you Tom are probably very busy right now at work, and I am sure that being in the midst of all this conflict isn't helping you concentrate on that either. However, I really don't think that I can continue working with you both as a couple if you cannot commit yourself coming regularly to the session. Imagine that I was a medical doctor and you were just diagnosed as having a serious infection that required antibiotics. Could I treat you if you said that you would start the course of medication in three weeks' time? I certainly would understand if you decided not to continue with me in light of my position – and would not be hurt or upset if you decided to get help elsewhere.

Tom laughed and said that he saw my point. He tested me a bit more and saw that I was serious, that I really would not take on the therapy of this couple without a commitment from him to arrive regardless of workload issues. He decided to make the next appointment in a week's time, and actually looked relieved. He then asked for a session for himself as well. Work with the couple continued productively, with Sharon showing relief that Tom had accepted responsibility for their problems.

To Sharon, I had presented a model of a respectful but empowered woman who was willing to forfeit the couple in therapy rather than back down from what I considered imperative. For Tom, I displayed that I saw effects of his 'decisions' about how to spend his time and energy. I requested that he be more aware of his choices and the responsibility they entail, and though I would respect his choices, I would not deny their impact. I was willing to use my position as therapist to correct an imbalance of power. While the ultimate goal is to help both partners be mutually empowered, the path towards shared power can result in the therapist taking sides to unbalance in strategic ways.

Thinking about my reaction to Sharon and Tom, I realized that my entire way of looking at marital therapy had undergone a important paradigm shift. Whereas in the past I might have missed this incident as crucial to the 'politics' of therapy (I rarely thought about the politics of therapy), I now had recognized that our therapeutic system had entered the territory of gender and power, and that my reaction could determine the outcome of the treatment. *I knew that not to react would be a type of reaction, supporting a marital system, in which all the emotional responsibility is up to Sharon.* Theirs was a marriage in which Tom had the power to leave when things got uncomfortable. In my view, the potential for both partners to achieve any type of enduring intimacy relied on finding a new balance of power and division of responsibilities.

Starting with my research on egalitarian couples, in the USA, Israel and in England, I now recognize power and gender as at the heart of intimate relationships and thus at the heart of marital therapy. This shift in vision has caused much personal and professional change. My response was the result of my own growth as a woman, as a therapist and as a researcher who was increasingly aware of how society impacts on the couple. To confront Tom was hard for me as a woman – I had been socialized to be polite, to accept men's work as an extremely serious matter, and certainly not to challenge their authority in such a direct manner. As a therapist, I had been trained in acceptance and empathy. Understanding Tom's need for a pause was almost instinctive for me. I had been trained not to side with one partner against the other, and here was a dilemma that demanded siding with one person at a precariously early stage in therapy. The research underlying the writing of this book has opened my eyes to the need for working strategically around these issues with contemporary couples.

AN EMPIRICALLY BASED TREATMENT FOR COUPLES

This book will show the ways that power and gender interact, limiting couples' ability to be friends. It will demonstrate how inequality is at the root of most marital distress today and how remedying this inequality has to be the major thrust of our intervention with couples. I will be taking the reader through a journey in feminist consciousness which has redefined my vision of what marriage can be, and certainly what marital therapy is. Devitalized relationships can be renewed, as a quantum leap towards becoming friends is realized.

However, I also know that addressing these issues so directly challenges basic assumptions as to rights of clients to 'choose' their lifestyles and their power structure. Choice is inherent in empowerment, a major theme in this book. I will establish that in our obsession to protect client choice, we are actually colluding in the limitation of choices through permitting the continuation of sex roles and power imbalances. My experiences have resulted in an increasing responsibility to make the implicit underlying structure of gender and power more explicit. I have come to the conclusion that there are real therapeutic benefits obtainable in daring to bring issues related to social change in sex roles into therapy sessions.

This book will apply relationship principles discovered in an interview study of equal partnership couples in the USA, Israel and England to therapy with couples. When I first started interviewing equal partnership couples in Seattle, Washington, I was rather astounded by the differences between them. I put up an advertisement in the University of Washington, saying that I wanted to interview 'equal partner couples who were attempting to live a non-sexist lifestyle'. Other than that, I did not define equality for the couples, but explained to each that I wanted them to be my teachers; I wanted to learn what equality meant for them. Couples varied by race, class, income, age, education, years married, number of children, number of marriages and of course their own unique personal histories.

Many couples came forward, most with a clear conviction that they had equal partnerships. Many divulged that they wanted to be interviewed because they felt they had found the secret of marital happiness and wanted to share it. Each couple had a story: a rich tapestry of individual stories interwoven in their relationship story. It was fascinating, but bewildering. The only initial similarities were these couples' enthusiastic willingness to be interviewed, and the fact that all were raising or had raised children together.

Like a developing print in a darkroom, patterns slowly began to emerge. Interviewing these couples together with my husband, we thoroughly discussed each interview in depth. I wrote up summaries, and then transcribed the interview, analyzing each, line by line, for content themes. Categories were identified and then used as the basis for further interview questions.

Over the next few years I continued this work, interviewing in Israel and in England and using each interview as the basis for further probing in future interviews. Students working with me at the Tel Aviv University School of Social Work contributed their ideas, assisted in analyzing transcripts and helped move towards the following conceptualization. This model is the distillation of hundreds of hours of interview analysis and constant comparison between seventy couples in these three cultures.

As a therapist, I wanted to uncover interactional processes between the partners, as well as the emotions, attitudes and behaviors of both individuals, that constitute the interlocking system underlying equal sharing. When this system is firmly in place, issues relating to who does what become relegated to the background and serve to support the overall maintenance of the couple as friends.[1]

When I began this work in 1990, my own view of equal partnership was based on two major sources: my perception of the current social reality, and my own life experiences. I had developed two antithetical and seemingly contradictory notions. The first was that most couples today want to have an equal partner relationship where the wife works and is an autonomous and self-actualized person. After a quarter century of feminism, it seemed self-evident that most contemporary couples aim to treat both partners as equal human beings, without the prejudices and limitations imposed by gender. Certainly this appears the goal for middle-class, educated couples, and appears to be an emerging goal in the entire Western world. It is related to an increasing desire to improve the quality of life in general, as opposed to primarily ensuring survival.

Support for this rather optimistic view came in the form of reactions to my intended research, with comments such as: 'What is there to study? Everyone believes in equality for women, so what is there to say?' This notion was also bolstered by the rather large number of couples who immediately applied to be interviewed as equal partners. There appeared to be a great number of people out there who believed they had egalitarian marriages.

I also assumed that I had an equal partnership with my own husband of twenty years. Having three children, we have always known that without this kind of cooperation, there was no way we could both combine full-time careers with raising children. But I had never really scrutinized exactly how my partner and I had achieved this state in our marriage. In hindsight, we underwent many of the processes I discovered in the interview study. But, as with many other equal partnership couples, our egalitarianism was so taken for granted that it faded into the background of other more outstanding issues: whether we felt close enough, how to survive upsetting quarrels, how many children to have, scheduling, how to manage to have a sex life though exhausted from work and the demands of small children, and all the other myriad problems of the typical dual-career marriage. My failure to examine closely our partnership had promoted the notion that sharing equally is a simple thing.

I also managed to hold an opposing view that there are in fact very few couples who truly achieve an equal partnering lifestyle. My observation of women friends showed them to be compromising their careers for homelife while their husbands seemed to have both. I had noticed how my friends deferred to their husbands in my presence and yet alone with me were assertive and vibrant. The couples I knew had conventional sex-role division of roles at home in many areas, even if the wife was working full time and even if she was earning more than her husband. At parties, it was inevitably the wife who kept getting up to serve the guests. It was the wife who attended to all the couples' social contacts (including the care of *his* mother), and at the playground and supermarket I generally noticed the presence of women.

This pessimistic view was reinforced by other reactions to my search for egalitarian couples. 'Oh, I knew a couple like that once – they're divorced now' (USA). 'Equality in marriage – there is no such thing!' (England). 'You are going to need a flashlight to find a really egalitarian relationship around here' (Israel). One Israeli equal partner husband said, 'Why are your studying us? We are not exactly your average couple.'

Colleagues who heard I was taking a year off to study egalitarian couples while my husband was undertaking full-time child-care reacted as if he were a true prince. I didn't remember the wives of male professors in my department being so congratulated for taking a year off for their husbands' sabbatical. Equal sharing seemed like a strange mutation.

It later became clear from my work with couples, both in research and in therapy, that a transitional world of rapidly changing sex roles fosters this kind of inconsistent thinking. Ambivalence, contradictions and internal psychological splits related to gender are the rule today. Since we learn to accept everyone's right to chose their own lifestyle, we learn not to scrutinize too much; perhaps we would rather not think about how unequitable most modern relationships still are for women.

Many couples believe in equality while playing out sexist interactional patterns at home. Few couples have a clear vision of how true equal sharing would be. There may be an idealized and vague notion of equal partnership without a game plan, so that no matter what they are doing, each feels that they give more than they get back. There is the potential for great damage to relationships as unrecognized and unarticulated inconsistencies generate confusion and eventually bitterness.

Turmoil about these issues also extended to my therapeutic work with couples. I maintained my own feminist beliefs and attitudes but never attempted to impose them on my clients, accepting some blatant sexism in couples' lives without comment. This went along with the prevailing professional conviction concerning values in therapy. We are encouraged to be aware of our values, in order *not* to bring them into the therapy room. It never occurred to me that *not* taking a stand on issues related to sex-role stereotyping, or the unfair burden on women, is taking a stand to uphold the status quo.

Equality is more than a slogan, or a political preference. It is a core organizing principle linking the social, dyadic and psychological levels of human behavior. Whether any social system is an equitable one touches on the basic issue of whether there is an equal place for all members in the system. It asks whether each individual can maximize his or her potential while attending to the needs of the other members of the system.

This is a question that cannot be ignored in therapy with couples today. However, it is often misunderstood. Many envision equality as meaning 'similar to'. This book will show that equal does not mean 'the same' and that attempts to foster equality through measurement of similar benefits or contributions is actually a destructive process. It is actually by understanding and honoring gendered differences that the drive to equality can become a beneficial force for couples.

Equality for many conjures up a dual-career lifestyle, and an abandonment of all familiar gendered roles. Seen in this way, it is understandable that therapists would hesitate to impose one kind of lifestyle on couples. However, the dual-career life does not at all guarantee equality, and may be actually unfairly enticing women into doing a second shift, including full-time work and full-time home responsibilities. My study demonstrated that some of the most egalitarian couples had rejected the 'fast track' with both partners wanting to stay home with children as much as possible.

This book will elaborate the definition of equality to go beyond who does the dishes or stays home with a sick child. Such issues will be located as part of a holistic gestalt relating to the level of fairness in the relationship and the way couples can be helped to attain and keep a high level of fairness. When partners struggle to maintain their subjective appraisal of their relationship as a fair one, conflicts between the needs of each of the individuals are constantly being balanced and continually readjusted with the needs of the marital system. This sense of fairness can be maintained in the context of a variety of lifestyles, including dual career, part-time work and even homemaking/primary-provider structures. It has more to do with fostering a sense of choice than imposing any role behaviors of any kind.

Often during my interviews I heard husbands state that equal sharing is actually highly practical in that it leads to their wives' happiness and thus ultimately to their own. These men were acutely aware that their own happiness was tied to their wives' happiness. In an era and environment where women are increasingly demanding equal rights in the home as well as at work, equality, as defined by egalitarian couples, offers us a conceptual model to help achieve marital happiness for both partners.

This approach shares a great deal with a sociological orientation to the family,[2] and applies this thinking to therapy with couples. The research underlining the therapeutic model focused on heterosexual couples with children. While an egalitarian model may well have implications for same-sex relationship counseling as well, this book focuses on marriage and cohabitating heterosexual relationships. Hopefully this work will stimulate thinking about applying the model to other relationship forms.[3]

CHAPTER PREVIEW

Chapter 1 will look at the ways that a focus of equality, power and gender enriches our understanding of contemporary relationship distress. It will take up the results of neglecting issues related to power and gender, and some unintended outcomes of ignoring these concerns in relationship therapy. The chapter targets the individual, dyadic and societal level of interaction and proposes several key ways in which gender and power impact on these various levels.

Chapter 2 examines the role played by definitions of equality in marriage, and the ways in which disagreement about interpreting the concept are instrumental in creating marital distress. This chapter will examine different meanings of equality in marriage, the resulting confusion that has prevailed, and the effects on couples. Research results on equality in marriage will be reviewed and my cross-cultural research will be introduced.

Chapter 3 introduces the process-model definition of equal partnering based on cross-cultural research. Interviews in three different cultural settings, USA, UK and Israel generated universal process themes which underlie the advancement towards equal partnership. Other processes were found to hinder progress to equal sharing, and their presence alerts us to problematic interactions in couples in treatment. This chapter focuses on friendship, a central theme of the interviews and of this book.

Chapter 4 looks at another major theme of egalitarian couples, their ability to share power, leading to mutual empowerment of both partners.

Chapter 5 finishes up the major themes learned from the interviews by looking at equal partners' ability to recognize and overcome gendered communication patterns. These couples also highlight the importance of shared values and the development of a coherent ideology. This chapter will sum up the four major themes (friendship, empowerment, overcoming gendered communication and ideology) and preliminary discussion on couples in therapy will link the interview themes with the demarcation of therapy goals.

Chapter 6 links themes with a focus on assessment of the level of equality in the couple relationship. Within a social climate of changing sex roles for women, the pervasiveness of egalitarian ideals, as well as ambivalence about achieving these ideals, couple tension today can generally be related to problems touching on this shifting social context. Assessment aims to locate barriers in the couple relationship that hinder further progress towards an equal relationship.

Chapter 7 establishes the position of the relationship on a continuum of changing sex-role patterns; couples are more or less traditional, transitional or egalitarian, with each type evidencing typical problem areas and concerns.

Chapter 8 focuses on the establishment of an egalitarian relationship between the therapist and both partners. Establishing an equal partnership with the couple in therapy is assumed to be a necessary condition for helping them assimilate these ideas in their relationship. This chapter will locate barriers to the creation of teamwork with the clients and propose methods for overcoming these obstacles.

Chapters 9 and **10** introduce the overall treatment model. Three treatment components are offered:

1 Modifying dominant/subordinate roles, and education towards equality.
2 Developing intimacy through individual focus in couples.
3 Conjoint preparation for sharing through couple interaction.

Examples from different couples' therapy sessions introduce the different components. Gender and power influences can be discerned as they are enacted between therapist and client. Throughout therapy, and especially in work alone with individual partners, gender and power revealed in interaction with the therapist are offered as primary instruments to heighten awareness and further the process of change.

Couples differ greatly in their level of gender inequality and their awareness about, or desire to deal directly with these issues. **Chapters 11** and **12** illustrate therapy with two different types of couples. Traditional couples, while not identifying equality issues in their complaints, especially suffer from the consequences of rigid sex-role stereotyping in both partners. Examining the problems of these couples helps in grasping the connection between symptoms and the mostly unconscious power and gender issues. Transitional relationships show more movement towards an egalitarian lifestyle. This results in some typical issues that arise in treatment, mostly related to ambivalence around changing sex roles and power reversals. The two case examples describe treatment methods and reactions of the partners in these two different types of couple.

Gender and power are both the most central and yet the least openly discussed variables in treatment of relationships. **Chapter 13** focuses on training and supervision in gender and power as direct targets for change. The therapist's use of self to further equal relationships models is explored. The therapist is continually confronted with his/her own sex-role beliefs, current life situation and any contradictions that may exist between the two. The interaction between the therapist's and client's gender impacts on the process of intervention. The female therapist especially confronts her own life in work with client couples, and in dealing with the male partner. This chapter looks at the types of changes that women therapists often undergo when attempting to target gender and power for change.

The chapter will explicate how the egalitarian themes located in the research emerge on the level of teamwork between supervisor and students, and ways that supervisors can use the themes to model egalitarian relationships as a tool for learning. The potential for using the notion of equal partnership as an 'umbrella' framework for the combination of other approaches is explored.

THE LENS OF GENDER: SOME PROBLEMS IN REFOCUSING

There is a well-known axiom in the world of family therapy that 'there is no such thing as not communicating'. Silence, or refusal to attend a session are communications; our responses to these communications are also communications.

I would here add that there is no such thing as not dealing with gender and power. All heterosexual couple relationships have these interlocking issues. From birth, male and female gender socialization histories are different, generating gender differences in communication styles, expectations and self-concept which are more or less a source of dissension in any relationship.

The second point revolves around the fact that the larger social system treats men and women differently. Unless the couple choose to live on a desert island (in which case they still would take their gendered socialization histories with them), the fact that women and men have different opportunities will have an impact on the relationship. More often than not, this effect results in more power within the relationship for the husband.

Many couples attempt to deal with these difficult and thorny issues the way I did: somewhat unconsciously living with the contradictions, splits and ambivalence inherent in gender and power, and getting on with daily life. Regardless of whether we as therapists are prepared to deal directly with these issues, they have a bearing on couples' interactions. Couples who deal satisfactorily with these issues can put them to rest. It is exactly those couples who do not cope constructively with gender and power who have to handle them more. And these are the couples we see in relationship therapy.

This book hopes to help therapists in taking up gender and power in a productive way. Sorely lacking in books on this subject has been the 'nuts and bolts' of how to help couples with these sensitive issues. Readers may find themselves focusing on gender and power in a rather uncomfortable way; it is at first not natural to integrate this way of observing with more familiar ways. This appears to be a necessary stage in allowing gender, power and equality to take their rightful place among the relationship variables which therapists assess and treat. This book's intense focus on gender and power is meant to right the balance, to encourage perceiving these issues more explicitly. Therapists must of course combine this approach with other orientations. Focusing *only* on gender and power would probably be as limited as ignoring these issues.

A source of resistance that many of us have to analyzing cases according to gender and power is a reluctance to admit how much our behavior is actually socially determined. We all like to think of ourselves as free agents and as overcoming sex-role stereo-typing. Moreover, speaking about 'men and women' makes it seem as if all men and all women behave the same way. The egal-itarian couples I interviewed seemed to detest speaking about their differences as gender differences. Many chose to see obvious gender differences as personality differences. Dedicated to fighting gender stereotypes, they certainly did not want to see themselves as constricted by them. People resist cultural norms and exercise some freedom in creating their lifestyles. But it is by examining the repercussions of social impingements that we can learn to minimize limitations and maximize personal choice. I find that the benefits of tapping into these crucial issues outweigh the discomfort inherent in putting on the 'lens of gender'.

Chapter 1

Gender, power and contemporary relationship tension

Therapy to improve a relationship is undertaken within a specific social context. This context defines what a good relationship is and thus impacts on the goals of therapy. Today the context involves gender roles in transition: elements of traditional roles coincide with egalitarianism in varying degrees within each person and thus within each relationship. Men and women today face a changing and confusing world. Men experience the expectation to continue providing for the family, but at the same time the expectation to incorporate elements of the 'new man', including emotional expression of vulnerability, nurturing behavior and the ability to sustain emotional intimacy. Women face expectations to continue their maternal homemaker and emotional nurturer roles, but to incorporate a focus on self-fulfillment and individual achievement.[1]

Never have expectations from the marriage relationship been so high, nor so contradictory. The traditional desire for stability, homelife and responsibility to the extended family coincides with anticipation of personal individuation and growth. Each partner is expected to take responsibility for his or her own growth and yet also foster the other's happiness. Marriage itself is moving from an institution based on predesignated roles stressing duty and obligation, to a more spontaneous, individualistic relationship almost resembling therapy for the members.

Progress is uneven in any social transition, for the society and for the couple. Some social institutions (i.e. schools, churches) may reinforce the traditional, while others (i.e. movies, television) may encourage change. Or it might be the media (i.e. commercials and advertising) which promote a return to 'the good old days' of rigid and clear sex-role distinctions, while social institutions (i.e. the university) foster change.

Moreover, individual couples show elements of change over time, including progression and regression at different stages in the lifecycle. Couples stress individual growth before the birth of children, return to a more traditional model based on obligation and roles while raising small children, and move later towards a focus on individual growth when the children begin to leave home. A common problem for couples who stay together throughout the family lifecycle is that wives' sense of injustice may be nurtured during the childrearing period, but only verbalized during the empty nest period when the demands of young children are no longer compelling. Paradoxically, it is just then that husbands are more willing to be involved in the home, but discover that their wives are angry and on their way out, emotionally and possibly physically.

The two partners are rarely at exactly the same place with regard to these important social changes, and rarely agree on all issues related to gender. Within each partner is a unique and particular combination of ambivalence and contradictions about these issues, based on individual history, attitudes, and changing current experiences.

Given all this, conflict is to be expected as the norm in marriage today. Yet conflict is still perceived by the majority of couples as a sign of trouble, indicating that something is wrong with the marriage, rather than intrinsic to marriage itself today. As such, marriage is at high risk of failure despite the fact that most people wish to marry and the majority remarry after divorce.

Most marital therapy is initiated by women. Women appear to perceive their marriages as more problematic, and most divorces today are initiated by women. The view taken here is that women's anger and disillusionment is the major universal dynamic underlying marital distress. Women's continued attempts to make things right, their frustration at their partners' avoidance of conflicts and their increasing sense of having other options to marriage is the major predicament brought to relationship therapy.

Thus I found that in talking to counselors in the USA, the UK and Israel, they all seemed to be treating the same couple. In this universal archetype, the wife brings the complaints and is viewed by her husband as making too much out of nothing. He does not know why she is unhappy, and thinks that her unhappiness is the cause of the couple's problems. He thinks she should stop complaining. She sees him as withdrawing, not expressing enough emotion and cold. She feels very much alone; she goes to sleep crying, he seems to sleep very well.

The fact that the presenting dynamics are often similar, does not make the treatment easy. Since gender differences are deeply embedded in a mighty social transition, therapists are at the front line of social change. Therapists have to sort through and respect the details and stories in order to honor each person's individuality. Identifying universal unifying concepts is the first step in any treatment plan and knowing how to create the linkage between idiosyncratic details and overall common themes is a major therapeutic task.

Couples rarely come to counseling with presenting complaints, such as 'I am confused about my gendered sex role', or 'I have no idea how to cope with this new fad that we share power'. Of course, people do not usually directly identify any therapeutic construct. Rarely has a client been known to announce at the door 'I have a problem with separation/individuation', or 'I am having a hard time maintaining a comfortable balance between emotional closeness and distance'. The closest clients and therapists might get initially to having a common language is 'we have a communication problem', but usually they mean different things by this catch-all phrase.

Therapeutic assessment relabels symptoms, such as 'we no longer have sex', 'we fight all the time', or 'there is no more romance in our lives' through a more functional conceptual lens. Gender and power issues offer a potential way to link current social issues, relationship problems and individual concerns. Using these concepts we have a way of looking at problems that normalizes universal problems and alleviates guilt. Couples are relieved when they begin viewing their problems as reflecting difficulties in navigating the transition towards more flexible gender roles. Paradoxically, the more we are aware of what we did not cause, the more we can identify what is within our power to change.

The problem is that much of the dynamics of gender and power occurs out of awareness of the partners in treatment, as well as the therapist. Gender and power are like the air we breathe. We rarely think of how our behavior is conditioned by our sex. Nor do we note the pervasive way that power hierarchies constrain our behavior. These are issues so basic to our daily lives that we have all learned to ignore them. Since there is little going on between people that is not touched by gender or power issues, we naturally let them influence us in an unconscious manner.

THE CEILING EFFECT: GENDER–POWER AS LIMITING FACTORS IN THERAPY

The two cases presented here highlight how a lack of attention to gender and power limited my capability as a therapist to go beyond superficial change. Today, I would deal differently with both situations. I present here a re-analysis based on hindsight, and some creative liberty, using information gathered after termination. I believe that we learn the most from our failures. Consciousness is a constantly developing process, with new insights changing our interventions, which lead to additional new insights and increased understanding.

Case 1 The triangle

Monica, aged 47, came to therapy in crisis, with her marriage falling apart. Her husband Ron had recently revealed a three-year affair with a younger woman, declaring that he no longer loved Monica and planned to continue the affair. He also had no intention of leaving his family, saying that he saw no reason for him to give up a situation that was comfortable for him. Monica was desperate. Showing numerous signs of stress and depression, she wasn't eating, hardly slept at night and had frequent anxiety attacks which kept her housebound. A housewife with four children, she had devoted the last twenty-five years to her family, had no independent source of income and no job prospects.

The family had moved to a new town three years prior to her request for therapy and for this period Monica had been cut off from previous friends and family support. Also, having moved from a farming community to town, she was having difficulty adjusting to the city. Since their move, Ron had increasingly ignored her, coming home later and spending less time with the children. He refused to come to therapy.

Therapy alone with Monica went very well at first and I was surprised how quickly she pulled herself together. We reinforced strengths she revealed to me, including her running a family farm and her competent handling of all family affairs during her marriage. Within weeks Monica realized that she wanted to confront Ron with an ultimatum. For the first time in her marriage, she put her foot down. After years of following Ron, of accepting his handing over all the parenting and housework to her, Monica started thinking about her own needs.

Monica told Ron he needed to decide between her and his lover, and she even initiated a talk with the other woman in which she declared her willingness to fight for her marriage. When Ron decided to give up his lover, she told him that if he wanted to continue the marriage, he would have to enter marriage therapy.

Ron agreed and together with me they began to explore their marriage. She asked for help around the house, for shared parenting and for Ron to speak to her with more respect. To her surprise, he was not only willing but seemed relieved. Ron had been turned off for years by Monica's subservient behavior and had wanted someone he felt he could really talk to. He said that one of the main things that attracted him to his younger lover was her ability to talk with him as an equal. As Monica demonstrated her ability to stand up to him, he appeared more interested in her than ever before. Monica decided that she wanted to go back to school, and started looking at local community college programs.

About five months after starting therapy, Ron and Monica canceled their therapy session. A week later, Monica asked for a session alone, saying that Ron had decided to hire his lover to work in his office. Monica felt that she was not willing to confront him about this. She felt that the marriage was better than it was before therapy. They were now going out together as a couple and were sharing more of family life. But Ron was again in daily contact with his lover and Monica just hoped it would be temporary. She suggested a break from therapy as she felt she did not want to pressure Ron in any way. Ron was willing to take her up on the offer, saying that he was getting more busy at work.

Having seen real changes in Monica and improvement in their marriage, I was convinced that Ron's attachment to his lover signaled a regression to their previous status quo, and that any gains they had made would soon be lost. Therapy had stalled, and while both partners were flattering about our work together, I was rightly worried. Monica seemed to be protecting the relationship by slowing down the process of change, but it seemed difficult to envision how the status quo would not regress into more tension.

The second case involves a couple in their late twenties who jointly requested marital counseling:

Case 2 The successful wife

Jackie and David are a 'cross-cultural' couple; she is an American who settled in Israel and he a native-born Israeli. Their marriage of six years was continually stormy as Jackie found life in Israel difficult, and was especially unhappy since the birth of their year-old son. Jackie had met David in the USA where they attended the same college. Their relationship was established with the agreement that both would have careers. Jackie had been eager to start her own business in Israel and was becoming more successful than David, who had difficulties getting customers for his store.

Sessions with David and Jackie revealed very similar models of family life in their families of origin. David was an only son, and had not only seen a traditional marriage but had been explicitly told that a husband is the 'Jewish prince' and could expect his wife to serve his needs. His exposure to American college life and feminist values convinced him that he did not want a marriage with traditional roles.

Jackie had been exceptionally close to her parents and felt cut-off from them living in Israel. Her mother, a housewife, had wanted Jackie to marry well and both parents never understood her need for her own career. They were so outraged at her independent decision to marry a foreigner and live abroad that for the first years of her marriage they refused to visit.

Both partners stated that since they believed that they each needed their own career, only by sharing childcare could they achieve their goal. David said that he was proud of Jackie's accomplishments and that he firmly supported her advancement. Three months of conjoint therapy resulted in a marked decrease in fighting and in improved communication. On her own initiative, Jackie arrived one week to a session with the following list, saying she felt more confident about being able to communicate her needs to David. This list summarized her requests for change from David:

1 Common courtesy: clean up after self, favors, help out, advance notice, do not say certain things in 'mixed company', keeping secrets, maintaining discretion, being sensitive, asking before committing.
2 Express yourself: needs, desires, dissatisfaction, fair/unfair, fears, ambitions, frustration, etc.
3 Division of domestic responsibilities: especially during crisis and being with the baby.
4 Dedicate family time: just for the three of us; time alone with me, without other friends.
5 Initiate activity in the relationship: share creative ideas of things to do, places to go and people to meet.
6 Show me the respect you show others: when I do not understand, when others take advantage of me, when I have a problem/display weakness, when others insult me or show me a lack of respect.

David said that the list made a lot of sense to him. I requested that he think of a list of his own and bring it to the next session.

During the following week, Jackie called to say that David wanted to stop therapy. He said that he needed a break, and that if he ever went back to therapy, he would only see a male therapist. At present talking to his male friends was enough, and that perhaps Jackie should visit her parents in the States. Jackie wanted to continue therapy but knew that coming alone might result in terminating her marriage. She wanted to remain with David, so she reluctantly agreed to stop.

Therapy was terminated prematurely, with David stonewalling further change and Jackie feeling compelled to acquiesce.

THE LENS OF GENDER

These cases differ in significant respects. The first couple are middle-aged 'sabras' (native-born Israelis) with older children. The second couple are in the early stages of marriage, with American and Israeli cultural mixing. The severity of their presenting problems was different; the first couple at the brink of divorce and the second experiencing the typical struggles of early married life. Yet a re-analysis in light of gender and power shows that therapy was derailed on similar grounds. In both cases, issues relating to sex-role identity and the power balance of the relationship were not adequately dealt with, nor were gender differences addressed.

A homeostatic reaction led to both couples' resistance to further change. This was based on the degree to which the husband resisted further change, and the degree to which the wife perceived herself as powerless to cope with his resistance. Ironically, in trying to remain neutral about gender and power, I had ignored this common couple dynamic. Often in therapy, the wife experiments in increasing her power and demands on her husband. However, neither partner (or therapist) may be prepared for the degree of change this entails for *both*. I passively reacted as a bystander to a process I later was able to harness as a source of relationship change.

A re-analysis of both cases will highlight the multi-level interaction of society, marital and individual factors making increased wife power a potential source of discomfort to both partners. It is then easy to see why both partners might opt for a homeostatic return to the status quo, in light of the far-reaching effects of increased wife power and of the potential threat involved in gender role change.

Gender–power analysis of Case 1: persistence of a triangle

Monica is 47 years old. As a woman aging in a youth-oriented society, she is anxious about decreasing attractiveness. In the past she was considered extremely beautiful, but no longer feels this holds true. Ron is also aware of time slipping away, wondering if he will be able to attract young women anymore. The thought that he is no longer a sexy man panics him. His sense of masculinity is shaken further as he looks at his aging wife and sees a mirror of his own increasing age. His lover, aged 35, reassures him that he is indeed potent and exciting.

As Monica gains self-confidence in therapy, she begins to play with the idea that she might be capable of making it on her own and could end the marriage. These thoughts give her the power to confront Ron with an ultimatum: give up either her or his lover. Choosing her, he is unconsciously humiliated by having 'caved in' to pressure from his wife, supported by a female therapist. His dependency on Monica revealed, he now needs even more reassurance about his masculinity. All this when his sense of security is shaky! Turning to Monica, he finds little comforting intimacy in their relationship. He has no language for opening up to her about his anxieties and fears of aging. For twenty-five years, Monica has devoted herself to the children, and he to his work. They have never talked about their fears, upsets or disappointments. Whenever Ron had a problem in the past, he prided himself on the fact that he was able to solve problems on his own, sparing Monica the worry. She had no experience in dealing with her husband's vulnerable feelings, never having discussed them with him. Sensing his upset, she tries to help by preparing nice meals and by pressuring him to talk, neither of which seems to help him.

Sexually, Ron has always taken the role of the initiator in the marriage. In sex, Monica continues to play the passive role she views as feminine, and cannot help him regain confidence, as the pressure remains on him to perform. He wants her to initiate. To her, nice girls don't show too much interest in sex. She is instinctively afraid of reducing his self-security even further by becoming more sexually active. Yet, Monica has no idea what to do about her own anxieties about attractiveness. Self-help books she reads tell her to be more sexually active and suggest new positions. She is ambivalent, swinging between pursuing him and waiting passively for him to take the initiative. Feeling more pressured than aroused, she makes love to reassure herself that she is still sexy to him and not because she wants to. Wanting her to initiate, Ron feels stressed to perform when she does make advances.

Sex became forced for both of them. His response is to avoid her. He starts coming home later, and stays up watching television, coming to bed after she has gone to sleep. Ron's withdrawal reduces the tension and is a relief for both of them. The pressure is off, the fears temporarily subside and both return to a more familiar and comfortable state than when they were attempting to be intimate. Ron finds reassurance from his lover. He is only able to be with her once a week for a few hours, so the sense of pressure he has with Monica is absent.

When Monica hears that Ron wants to hire the lover, she is very angry and worried, and considers using the previous method of giving him an ultimatum. However, having inquired into the possibility of returning to college, she now knows that the program she wanted is filled with young people and her chances of getting back to the field she has envisioned for herself are poor. Her self-confidence is lowered as she hears from friends how tight the job market is for unskilled re-entry women of her age. She compares herself to working men and women of her age. She looks at what will happen to her in case of a divorce, in contrast to what will happen to Ron. Her situation seems hopeless to her. Monica worries about what lies ahead for her when the last child leaves home. Perceiving her lack of opportunities, her options seemed better at home.

This is the context in which the couple reached their 'ceiling' for change. Personal insecurities about gender identity interact with issues about aging and sexual appeal. Couple dynamics result in a sudden increase in demands for intimacy, and male withdrawal from the conflicts this engenders. The lack of options for Monica outside the home, compared to Ron's options for a younger lover, reduces her power further. Monica settles for the status quo, by rationalizing that perhaps he will hire his lover but won't have an affair with her. Ron continues to have both his lover and his family, seeing no reason to modify this arrangement. For both, the status quo appears more rewarding than change.

As I look back on my work with this couple, I realize how I had underestimated the degree of *threat* the therapy entailed. I was also unaware of the extent of underlying ambivalence in both partners about gender roles. Ron and Monica hid their anxieties from themselves, from each other and from me. Unused to open expression of feeling in the presence of the partner, they presented a front in therapy that served to mask the degree to which each one was terrified – about their gender identity, the new pressure to be intimate and their insecure self-esteem.

Gender–power analysis of case 2: the successful wife

Jackie and David stopped therapy abruptly after Jackie came to therapy with a list of demands, a sign of increasing entitlement and power. In attempting to be gender neutral, I had disregarded the intimidation a man might feel by the demands of a woman. As a woman, I felt proud of Jackie for being so assertive and ignored the fact that an assertive woman can look pretty aggressive to a man who feels coerced. I also miscalculated the degree of competition David felt with Jackie about her success at work. It was easy to ignore these issues as David played the role of enlightened and progressive husband. His belief in a feminist ideology masked deep ambivalence about his wife's working when there was a small child at home, and about his own masculinity. The stronger Jackie felt, the worse David felt. Not only was he not 'providing' better than her for the family, but she was feeling better about herself than he did about himself. David could not admit to himself that he was angry, but instead avoided shared housework, and discussions about sharing with Jackie. The more he 'passively–aggressively' forgot promised tasks, the more Jackie assertively presented him with her increased demands, and the more pressured and competitive he felt. His father had always said 'when you give a woman a finger, she wants the whole hand.' David started thinking he had given in too much from the start. His father's wisdom was also that if you don't control your woman, she will end up controlling you. David decided father knows best.

David was also competitive and threatened by me. As professional career woman, I represented a 'liberated woman'; if Jackie would be influenced by me, she might not need David. Her success could mean that she might eventually leave him. So in addition to uncomfortable competitive feelings, David also felt fear of abandonment. As a man, he had been brought up not to acknowledge fear and automatically to translate this vulnerability into feelings of anger. However, he did not know what he was angry about. He vaguely experienced the therapy as two women against him.

Seeking support from male friends with homemaker wives, he received reinforcement for his feeling that he was a 'sucker' for having to clean the house and diaper the baby. Increasingly David found himself at work, where he was the boss, feeling more comfortable there than with Jackie and her demands.

In this case, the couple's stated egalitarian ideology made it unsuitable for David to admit to himself how humiliating it was for him to be taking orders from a woman. David, coming from a patriarchal Middle Eastern background (his parents immigrated to Israel from Iraq), was deeply conflicted about the role of women. His exposure during college to the American culture made him want to be more modern than his parents.

Both partners yearned to believe that David had left his 'primitive' background behind. David believed in open communication; but now he had a real dilemma. At least when Jackie nagged and criticized, he had a good reason for his discomfort. What reason did he have now that she was assertive? Thus, the better the communication, the worse David felt. The literature on communication training hardly prepared us for the possibility that increased skill competency might threaten gender identity. The therapist's own female gender, and the model the therapist offers can contribute to this dynamic if the husband is already feeling unsure about his masculinity. But just as David could not show Jackie his vulnerable feelings, his worries and fears, neither could he show these feelings to a female therapist.

Elements common to both cases

To think systemically means to envision the interplay of societal pressures, couple interaction, and partners' feelings and behaviors. Therapists tend to feel comfortable emphasizing one or two levels in conceptualizing, such as thinking about individual functioning or about couple dynamics. However, thinking about gender and power challenges us to conceptualize on as many as four different levels, since society, dyadic and individual dynamics interact in a feedback loop with the therapeutic system.

Gender identity, self-esteem and androgyny

Gender role identity, or one's sense of masculinity or femininity, contributes significantly to self-concept in general and self-esteem in particular. Social psychologists have addressed the relationship between self-esteem and equitable outcomes in relationships (Creek and Hogan, 1982). Research demonstrates that self-esteem has significant effect on what is expected from a relationship. Persons of high self-esteem expect more equal relationships. Especially in women, lowered self-esteem may result in settling for a less equitable relationship.

Men face a struggle in establishing a secure masculine identity. Different writers have proposed that since men must differentiate early on from their primary maternal caretakers, they are never truly secure about being 'man' enough, needing to prove their maleness throughout their lives. Thus masculinity is intricately tied to performance, something constantly to be achieved but never quite secured. Masculine identity has to be continuously confirmed through steady achievements.[2] Difficult as this is, a man's masculinity poses ready access to self-esteem; the equation is simple – achieve and you get to feel good about yourself.

Women have a more confusing job of establishing feminine identity and thus of gaining access to self-esteem. Femininity may not be tied to performance, but women have to handle society's confusing messages about feminine traits. While an overly idealistic view of femininity is promoted by advertising and the media, femininity is essentially devalued in our society. Women are at the same time 'madonnas and whores', both the 'pot of gold at the end of the rainbow', and the source of all evil.[3] Sanford and Donovan differentiate between self-concept and self-esteem and tie these into the problems of feminine identity:

> The self-concept ... is a set of beliefs and images we all have and hold to be true of ourselves. By contrast, our level of self-esteem (or self-respect, self-love, or self-worth) is the measure of how much we like and approve of our self-concept ... self-esteem is the reputation you have with yourself.
>
> (1984:7)

Research makes it clear that androgyny, or the flexible combination of feminine and masculine traits in each person, predicts increased mental health and marital satisfaction in both men and women (Marsh and Byrne, 1991). In both men and women, it is the feminine traits (the more the better in both partners) that are associated with marital satisfaction (Antill, 1983), while at work, more masculine traits such as assertiveness and self-competence are related to success. Research shows that men and women alike should strive to broaden their range of competencies, leading to the ability to bring forth the needed traits in various situations. Androgyny also means that each person could freely express whatever personality traits do exist, instead of trying to become someone they are not. And self-esteem would be tied into being more oneself than trying to be a prototype of a societal image or meet society's confusing expectations. Few of us are programmed by empirical studies. In reality, people cope with society's discrepant messages the best they can.

Gender role identity is also a relational concept as well as a building block of personal identity. We 'do gender' in that the degree to which we feel masculine or feminine changes in relation to the degree of our perceived partner's gender role identity. A woman feels more feminine when her partner earns more, is older, smarter and stronger than she. A man feels more masculine when his female partner depends on him, emotionally and economically.

Similarly, gender identity is intricately bound to the power discrepancy between the sexes. Men will feel more masculine when in control, while women will feel more feminine when controlled. Both partners find considerable comfort playing familiar roles, knowing what to expect in their customary positions.

However, women pay a price in self-esteem. While the dominant controlling position embraces personal power, the controlled position results in submissiveness. Thus women who attempt to preserve their femininity are less equipped to fight back, to try to convince, to assert, to take risks or to negotiate their needs. People of lower status do not command respect. This is often evident in the interactions of traditional couples. The husband may cut off his wife in the middle of a sentence, may put her down in public, may not listen to her with real attention, may take little interest in her life, may be impatient with her, or patronize her. In caring for the more powerful partner, women lose touch with their own needs, feel their partners are selfish and nurse a great deal of resentment.

This dynamic can be seen in the young career-oriented couple, David and Jackie. Hidden behind their shared egalitarian attitudes is their shaky and uncertain gender identity. They are a transitional couple, moving away from traditionalism but not having firmly established their egalitarianism. Jackie wants her career. However, if she is too successful she is aware of threatening David. His unspoken competition with her means that he feels less masculine as she increases her competency as a wage-earner, which in turn threatens her sense of femininity. Unlike Monica, Jackie is less clear what it is exactly that makes her feel feminine. On the surface she rejects the homemaker role. But she also needs it to reassure herself that her career success does not diminish her sense of being an attractive female. Her confusion is deep and unfocused; does she have to sacrifice a good relationship in order to be successful? Is she less of a woman when she is more successful than her husband? There are unsettling questions and few answers.[4]

The gender-tension line

In what ways do the issue of status difference and its relationship to gender identity and self-concept, translate into daily life? Rapoport and Rapoport (1975) suggest a useful concept of the 'gender-tension line' to explain how far marriage partners will go in changing their gendered behaviors. This line is the point at which a sense of uncomfortableness comes up for an individual and at which traditional values kick in.

A man might find diapering a baby to be more than he can take. Refusal to take on this task would result from a threat to his sense of masculinity. Status threat may be one reason that he reached his gender-tension line; diapering the baby made him feel subservient, less powerful, more dependent or simply more female. He may find himself trying to learn, but somehow never becoming competent in taking care of the baby. His wife just cannot fathom why a man, head of a company and able to learn complicated computer programs, cannot seem to master the simple art of diapering. However, this same man may be quite able to nurture an adolescent at a different stage in his life. Perhaps caring for the older child might not be perceived as indicating lower status, or a different lifecycle stage results in reduced demands at work, more maturity, and more overall flexibility; an increased tolerance for change follows.

Having reached their gender-tension line, women find ways of undermining attempts to share. Criticism, insisting tasks be done a certain way and showing no appreciation for what is done are all common. For the feminine women the most likely strategy is that she will simply do it herself; complaining, feeling victimized but at least secure that she is a true woman.

For Monica and Ron, intimacy was unusual and increasing intimacy through therapy pushed them towards their gender-tension line. Neither were particularly prepared for a closeness impeded by their traditional gender roles. Monica's feminine identity dictated her being extremely sensitive to Ron's well-being, making her less able to challenge him or allow him to expose his fears and vulnerabilities. For her to feel feminine, he had to be the strong and secure partner. For Ron, intimacy increased the potential that he would reveal his mid-life crisis, his sexual insecurities and fears about aging. For them, intimacy was not as comfortable as their traditional separate sphere lives, and neither knew how to overcome the gendered inhibitions that blocked the closeness they wanted.

Power and the pursuer–distancer syndrome

Empirical studies confirm that while women clearly appreciate receiving help and are more satisfied with their marriages when their husbands share, men experience an increased sense of dissatisfaction and reduced attraction to their wives. When men perceive their wives as wanting more help, their perception of their marital happiness suffers.[5]

Women intuitively sense that increased requests would harm the quality of their significant attachment. And since women's well-being is intricately tied to their relationships, they retreat from increasing tension. Women care if their marriages are not harmonious. Women who want to preserve their marriages have to care; they may lose their partners. Husbands have been found to withdraw from marital conflict (Gottman and Levenson, 1988; Gottman, 1979). As women become more demanding of equity in their relationship, and as tension around these issues increases, withdrawal of their partners may also increase.

Longitudinal findings show the potential long-term harm to women if their husbands withdraw from conflict. Women whose husbands were found to withdraw and avoid conflicted marital discussions, were found three years later to have poorer immune system functioning. Interestingly, Gottman and Levenson also found that husbands who shared housework had better health themselves in the long-term. Unfortunately, those long-term benefits don't show up immediately.

Research also shows that when men withdraw from marital conflict and refuse to discuss painful issues, wives tend to escalate their demands and have been found to become more aversive (Raush et al., 1974), as well as far more emotional and critical (Christensen, 1988). Lerner (1985) has proposed that women's anger is extremely intimidating to men. It is a rare husband who has the ability or the motivation to cope with the increasing anger and negativeness that demands for equality entail. Gottman and Krokoff (1989) show that men experience more emotional arousal during conflict than women, and that they have the harder time regulating their emotions. This runs counter to the stereotype of the 'hysterical female' as it posits the male partner as more excitable during conflict. Gottman proposes that men withdraw from conflict in order to regulate the unpleasant effect resulting from overall emotional arousal.

While a physiological explanation is certainly possible, and even comforting (perhaps there is some medication men might take, or relaxation training that might help), it ignores the role of power in couples interactions. If men were to stay engaged in marital conflict, they might have to change. Men who deal directly with their wives' anger may have to compromise, changing their roles at home.

Clinicians working with couples have identified the 'pursuer–distancer' syndrome, in which the more one partner withdraws, the more the other pursues. In an increasingly vicious cycle, increased pursuing results in increased withdrawal, etc. This is one of the most common and stubborn problems couples experience. Marital therapists admit that in many cases it is the wife who pursues, while it is the husband who withdraws.

It is important to note here that while women tend to be the pursuers, it is not at all clear that women are better prepared for true marital intimacy than men. Schnarch (1991) has proposed two different views of intimacy: self-validated and other-validated intimacy. In self-validated intimacy, a high level of emotional autonomy allows for continued closeness and self-expression, without overreactivity to the partners' behaviors. Other-validated intimacy is generated more by neediness and demands for the partners to reciprocate with equal intimacy and positively.

Women are not socialized for self-validated intimacy any more than men are. While it is a common misconception that women need more intimacy than men, research debunks this myth. Guthrie and Snyder (1988) did not find differences between partners' needs for positive emotional behaviors such as touching, nurturing, talking and laughing. Specifically, men did have more trouble with expressing vulnerability and weakness. This difficulty might help explain husbands' conflict avoidance. Maintaining the power balance, and remaining the dominant partner, means not revealing weakness to a subordinate (at work as well as at home).

However, women's dependency on male approval would make them especially sensitive to their partners' responses to them. For a woman, it might be equally threatening to get really close, as she might not get the positive regard her feminine identity needs so acutely. Closeness involves getting criticized as well as getting praised. Also, women's feminine role identity does not prepare them for handling a man's expressions of weakness or vulnerability, and this kind of self-disclosure is crucial for intimacy.

Men intuitively notice that when they express fear or weakness, their wives don't know what to do. This is not due to a lack of nurturing ability (women can be very supportive of other women and children in pain) but to trouble in nurturing an adult male. Women do not know what to do for a male expressing frailty, and do not always know how to recognize the signs that men send out to indicate upset. Nothing may shake a woman's sense of security more than seeing her partner break down and cry. If he is weak, who will take care of her?

The pursuer–distancer mechanism protects both sexes from their own intimacy fears. Men cope with fear of intimacy by escaping to work and extra-marital affairs, while women cope with this fear by obsessively chasing their partners. As the pursuer–distancer dynamic takes over, *overall distance* is conserved. Intimacy is rarely achieved, and the apprehension about it is never mastered.

This dynamic is complicated by the power differential. Many women, feeling inferior in their relationship with men, at least get to feel superior in the ability to express emotions and be close. Their withdrawing partner lets them maintain the illusion that they are better equipped to be intimate. Indeed this is a double-edged sword. Feeling superior is hardly a satisfying substitution for intimacy. To become equals, women need to feel within themselves as equals to men.

Ron, due to his greater relational power, could withdraw from conflict and return to his lover. Monica reluctantly accepted the withdrawal, as it allowed a return to a more comfortable distance for her as well. David asserted his position in the couple's power hierarchy by dictating a withdrawal from therapy. Here again, his avoidance is accepted by Jackie, who fears change in the delicate balance of power they have established. In both cases the wives truly want change, but sense their limited options and fear that challenging their partners' withdrawal behavior could well lead to divorce. The prospects for post-divorce adjustment for the women in these stories is very different than for the men, as we will show next.

How society impacts on the relationship

Powerful social forces are at play influencing couple decisions and roles in daily life. Limited opportunity for obtaining resources in the social environment creates a ceiling for women, limiting the degree of risk they can take, especially when responsible for children. Despite new legislation protecting women's rights, and a more accepting climate, there is no question that sex discrimination in the workplace is rampant.[6] Since marriage is embedded in the social system of inequalities, it reflects these inequalities in areas of decisions around the division of labor and control over money.

Most people prefer to label marital distress as 'love' problems rather than 'power' problems. This obfuscates the direct impact of money on marriage. Women may desire equal sharing but may not carry the 'clout' needed to make this happen in the marriage. The presence of children (and women's limiting their involvement in work outside the home) reduces women's power in their relationships, just at a time in which equality in sharing is most needed (Morris and Sison, 1974). In addition, blatant sex discrimination in the workplace makes it clear that it is the wife who will pay the heavier price if her demands for change lead to a divorce. Her chances to recover economically are very different from his.[7]

This reality becomes known to women through the media and acquaintances with divorced friends. The nightmare of nonpayment by ex-husbands of child support is another frightening image informing women's perception. Sex-role stereotyping means that the aging woman is less 'desirable' as partner for second marriage than the aging man. Awareness of social stereotyping, as well as internalized effects of stereotyping on the aging woman's self-esteem, increase women's fear of marital dissolution.

Monica became increasingly aware of her limited options as a 're-entry' wife attempting to return to work after many years as a homemaker. Her subjective sense of choice decreased; studying and working might be too difficult for a woman of her age and experience.

Jackie was making money and had the power to 'make it on her own'. But Jackie is a woman living in Israel, where her attempts to divorce David would be mediated by a religious court that could even threaten to take her son away. In Israel, unless her husband agrees to divorce her, the wife can find herself embroiled in years of legal struggle for independence that would sap her economic resources and drain her energies. She may never be granted the right to marry again, as long as her husband refuses to grant her the 'get' (religious divorce). In a traditionally family-oriented culture, divorce is stigmatized, especially for women. It means losing her social network of couple friends. It would mean giving up the support in childrearing she enjoyed from David's family, and having to take care of their son alone. Whatever help she got from David seemed better than no help at all.

Denial of abuse

Wives who feel identified with women 'as group' and who subjectively perceive discrimination against women would tend to be disturbed about it.[8] Anger about discrimination would be a logical response, but men do not easily assimilate women's anger. Married women probably need to deny their own oppression in order to maintain marital harmony. In her book *The Second Shift*, Arlie Hochschild (1989) demonstrated how dual-career women developed rationalizations to hide from themselves how exploited they felt by husbands. Social norms function to bolster denial. Messages about the effects of anger on marriage are delivered through the media. Using content analysis, Cancian and Gordon (1988) looked at women's magazines and the degree to which 'emotional expression of anger' was viewed as positive or negative for marriage. Women were found to be held responsible for the well-being of their partners, and the happiness of their marriages. Their anger continues to be viewed as injurious. There is no doubt that many women shut out thoughts about unfairness and suppress their own rage in order to fulfill their roles as wives, to nurture their partners and protect their relationships. They will be more aware of discrimination at the workplace than the everyday unfairness in their families.

Monica had to find a way to reduce her anger at Ron's return to his lover. Denial of her anger is an effective way and serves to maintain both her own and her relationship's equilibrium. Jackie also has to struggle to cope with the anger generated by David's move to stop therapy. Denial of exploitation, abuse and unfairness is a mechanism that helps maintains a woman's sense of well-being, and her connection to her partner.

REASSESSMENT INCLUDING GENDER AND POWER: A MESSAGE FOR THERAPISTS

For the women in our two vignettes, Monica and Jackie, the interaction of individual, interpersonal and societal factors thwarts their ability to sustain their demands for change. For the men, Ron and David, a real desire for a good relationship with their wives is hindered by the threat these changes symbolize to their masculinity and their power position in the relationship.

In a recent unpublished study carried out in Israel by myself and Ofrit Berman, 150 couples were given questionnaires to evaluate the predictors of marital satisfaction for men and for women. For women, equal sharing in decision-making and in household chores and parenting unequivocally predicted increased happiness in their marriages. But for men, the opposite held true. Increases in equal sharing of power as well as sharing of the burdens of family life were predictive of marital tension for them. Thus while both partners in a relationship desire happiness, the pathway towards that goal is very different for men and for women.

This is the social climate in which therapists treat couples today. An important point for therapists to remember is that changes requested by the couple may be more revolutionary than is first perceived. Becoming 'happy' in a relationship may be so different for men and women that very deep-seated changes need to occur on the level of gender roles and power before changes can be negotiated. Couples without this adequate preparation cannot sustain the very changes they themselves desire. By ignoring the confusing current gender–power context in which their relationship exists, therapists are blind to the hidden panic and confusion about tampering with familiar gender roles.

Chapter 2

The egalitarian alternative
What is it? Is it worth the effort?

THE PROBLEM OF DEFINITION: A ROSE IS A ROSE IS A ROSE?

One of the concerns with which couples have to contend today is the creation of a workable, clear and shared definition of equality in marriage. This task may be more central and problematic than first meets the eye. Indeed, it may be 'the issue' for some couples. For example:

Ronit, a 29-year-old therapist, requested therapy for herself due to 'problems in intimacy' with her husband. Having been exhausted and worn out for almost a year after the birth of their first child and full-time work, she didn't enjoy or want sex. She was first referred to a homeopath who helped her overcome her fatigue, but advised either individual or couples counseling, and referred her to me. Ronit wasn't sure whether she should work on her marriage, or her problematic relationship with her cold and rather rejecting mother. Being well versed in psychology, she was sure that her problem with intimacy went back to her childhood. In order to help her decide what to focus on, we met together with her husband Tom, who was very eager to be included.

Tom, a 30-year-old engineer, saw himself as a devoted and concerned father and husband, deeply in love with his wife and wanting very much to succeed in their homelife. Married five years, they both agreed that they had a basically loving relationship, with a lot of warmth and caring. However, they fought almost daily about what Tom thought were the stupid and petty details of married life: who does the dishes, who bathes their daughter, who cleans up, how clean the house needs to be and how much free time each one got. Ronit expressed some guilt about ruining what appeared to be such a wonderful marriage over such relatively (to their overall love) unimportant details. Both presented her as the problem, in her low sexual desire and her attention to petty details.

But she was constantly angry: about picking up after Tom; having to get him and their daughter out in the morning (Tom has a problem with being late which she found herself responsible for solving); and watching him read the paper while she bathed and put their child to bed after a long day at work. Ronit handled this rage by constantly nagging, but eventually giving up and doing everything herself. She was aware that she didn't feel sexy at night after harboring so much anger during the day. When I helped her express her anger directly by saying 'It doesn't seem to be fair', Ronit almost jumped from her chair. 'It really isn't fair – that's just what I have been feeling. I never said it that way, but that's it . . . it's just not fair!'

I turned to Tom and had the following exchange:

Claire: Tom, how do you see all this business about sharing – what do you think about it?

Tom: I think that husbands and wives should share equally. I don't think it's fair either that Ronit winds up with doing everything. But I just don't agree with her about how neat everything has to be, and our daughter seems to want to be taken care of by her more than me. When I do the dishes late at night, Ronit gets nervous that I won't do them at all, and winds up doing them herself after dinner.

Claire: So you believe husbands and wives should share – but how do you see sharing? What does it mean to you?

Tom: Well – it is something I never really gave much thought about. But now that you ask, I know what it is not! I don't want to be Ronit's little helper, doing *her* housework, helping *her* with *her* daughter . . . it's my house and my child too! I am improving and doing more, but Ronit is constantly dissatisfied and angry . . . I feel like I can't win: I can't stand up to her standards and I can't do anything my way. So I guess I have just sort of backed off.

Claire: So let's see if we can get a definition here of what equal sharing is for you ... we know now that it is *not* helping out. But what is it?

Tom: Let's see ... well, I think it's working together as a team, with some flexibility, like one week I may be really busy at work, so Ronit would take care of everything, then maybe later I would take over for a while ... and that our relationship would be at the center of it all, that we would be partners, friends.

Claire: So I guess when Ronit starts to talk about all those details, she seems to be ruining the friendship? Good partners don't have to talk about it all the time, is that it?

Tom: Yes, exactly! I hate getting into that 'accounting' business of who does more, whose turn is it, all that stuff. I think it ruins the atmosphere, it poisons the relationship.

Claire: So, let's look at how you would like to create a partnership that would work for you?

Tom: I want to have some areas that are mine, and that I get to do things my way. I want the flexibility I talked about, but I want to have some authority too. And I want it to come from us, to come from the relationship, not from some rules like fifty–fifty sharing or anything external to us. I don't want us keeping accounts all the time. It should just sort of flow.

I gave the couple an assignment to come up with a joint definition of equal sharing. They were to talk three times that week about their views of equality. They didn't have to do anything about it yet.

I recapitulated my understanding of each partner's convictions about sharing: Tom wanted the relationship to be at the center of their sharing. He resisted having an 'accounting' mentality, but truly wanted to share. He wanted to have areas of authority and responsibility, as well as flexibility between them. Ronit wanted equal sharing, and felt that the current predicament was contributing to her lack of sexual desire. Sharing for her was intricately bound up with the day-to-day sharing of tasks. However, she also wanted things to go her way, and for her to remain in charge at home. I concluded by addressing Ronit:

Claire: You know Ronit, it is really hard for us women to let go of our home territory, to take the risk that our partners will be competent in really sharing. Sometimes it just seems easier to do it ourselves. But the question is, what kind of sharing do you want? Do you want a helper or a real partner?

Ronit: I never thought about it, since I have been so angry and upset. I guess I have been ambivalent. I think that if we went according to Tom's standards, we would be eating on the floor! But maybe I am exaggerating. I usually do things on my own, so I don't really know how it would work out if I really depended on him.

They arrived at the next session having talked extensively. They spontaneously entered into actual problem-solving and made some concrete decisions about sharing. Ronit was shocked that after a year of nagging to no avail, Tom so easily began to share at home. Her trust that he basically wanted an equal partnership was restored, her anger diminished and her desire for sex began to return.

This 'success story' was based on an understanding of the role that definitions of equality play in contemporary marital tension. Tom espoused a rather 'romantic–holistic' view, in which the quality of the relationship is cardinal, and sharing automatically flows from caring and mutual trust into the various areas of family life. He rejected the 'junior partner' role thrust on him, withdrawing from talk about the details which he viewed as interfering with their intimacy.[1]

Ronit unconsciously held to a more 'pragmatic–specific' view, in which the 'nitty gritty' of daily life and its details were central. Ronit did indeed want her standards to be upheld, and was unsure that she could give up authority to him. She could not feel intimate with him until the practical side of life was taken care of.

Having elements of both the 'romantic view' and the 'pragmatic view' can greatly enrich the partnership. The quality of a relationship has an important place in achieving equality, but there is also a need to attend to the specifics of who does what, how much and when. For Tom and Ronit, the absence of a clear and mutual definition was fueling a power struggle. While neglecting to make the conflicting viewpoints explicit, each was attempting to impose a view of reality on the other. They were sabotaging their own goals. Tom wasn't getting his ideal relationship, nor was Ronit getting the help she needed.

Tom came to see that by devaluing the importance of her standards he was in effect harming the relationship. Ronit realized that rigidly insisting on her standards was turning her into a nag and keeping him out of the home territory. They formulated a *joint* definition that included elements of each one's particular view, at the heart of which was the relationship. They both agreed that any kind of equal partnership that didn't further their marital happiness wasn't working. Yet, Tom also had to pay attention to details, a move towards meeting Ronit's standards. These had to be open to negotiation as well.

By first grasping and outlining the two different views of sharing, they independently began a process of joint negotiation based on bridging these differences. Tom took on the evening routine with their daughter, including bathing and storytelling.

Interestingly, their one-year-old daughter immediately seemed to realize the change in family rules and happily let herself be bathed and put to bed by her father. Tom agreed to Ronit's way about dishes, doing them right after dinner. They decided that whoever had worked less that day would be the one to do the dishes. Ronit decided to decrease her nagging, but to rely instead on evening discussions evaluating the partnership that day.

In a sense, they already had been covertly bargaining. Ronit was withholding sex as a way of trying to influence her husband to change, feeling that she didn't want sex. Tom was withholding helping out to get Ronit to be less critical, feeling that he was too tired to assist. Out of awareness, this kind of disguised bargaining is typical of the indirect control strategies used in traditional marriage. Regardless of good intentions, most couples lack models for equality. It is the rare person who comes to marriage from an egalitarian family, having viewed a equal sharing parental marriage. Few people really know how to work cooperatively and equally with someone of the opposite sex. They easily fall back to familiar patterns of control observed at home.

As therapists working with couples, we need to elucidate our own understanding of equality. Do we perceive it as meaning that there are no differences between the sexes? Or that each partner does everything? Does it mean sharing fifty–fifty or just letting things somehow naturally balance out? How do partners know that they have an equal marriage? What is equality in marriage anyway?

DEFINITIONS OF EQUAL PARTNERING

The fact that the proposal of equality in marriage can elicit very different reactions, from 'there is no such thing!' to 'everyone is doing it!', may reflect the fact there are so many different meanings. How we conceive of equality will determine our reactions to the idea, and the behavior used to achieve it. The probability is that the couple coming in for therapy are unsuspecting that they entertain different (and unexplored) views on this subject.

I asked couples what equal partnership meant to them. In talking to self-defined equal partner couples in the USA, in the UK and in Israel, I was impressed with the varied nature of their responses. Equal partners often describe equality using more than one meaning (i.e. 'equality is equal sharing of housework', as well as 'shared responsibility for good communication'). Most couples supplemented each other, so that one partner mentioned one definition (i.e. 'equality means making decisions together'), while the other added on something different (i.e. 'equality is a feeling that things are fair'). Happier partners agreed with each other despite the variations, while the happiest couples had the most diverse and inclusive definitions. Marital happiness seemed associated with having an agreed upon, but diverse, multifaceted, and relatively complex view of equality. Three major themes emerged in their definitions:

Equality as a subjective appraisal

Equal partnership can be seen as having an essential judgment that the relationship is fair. Each person is perceived as both contributing and securing their fair share. People who take this 'subjective' view tend to reject fifty–fifty type sharing, although they will use it occasionally as a means of maintaining fairness. Sharing is more embedded in a system of mutual trust that each partner will do their fair share. They tend to stress the 'romantic–holistic' view of more relationship-oriented equality, based on seeing equality as 'who we are'.

> I don't think it means fifty–fifty in terms of a relationship. Sometimes its forty–sixty and sometimes its sixty–forty. Where egalitarianism comes in it is that you know its gonna come back around ... we have been together for four years and it feels pretty equal.
> Husband (USA)

In the research literature on equal sharing, equity theory best enumerates this view.[2] According to equity theory (Adams, 1965; Homans, 1961) relationship satisfaction is highest when there is a sense that *each partner* gets out of the relationship in proportion to what is invested. A balance of one's own and the other's benefit is needed for the overall perception of fairness. Both partners who think they get more than they give (overbenefited) and partners who think they give more than they get (underbenefited) experience distress, although those who get less are still more distressed.

Equity theorists have also proposed that maintaining the degree of fairness is a complex process, based on the utilization of different 'justice rules' (Brehm, 1985). There are three such rules described in the literature. A relationship can be kept fair, when both contributions and rewards are divided up 'half and half'. For example, a couple might decide to rotate the nights they get up to feed the baby, with each taking alternative nights. This rule guarantees that inputs and outputs are kept equal, at least around the issue of night feedings.

Another way couples can maintain their sense of fairness would be to divide things up *proportionally*; whoever gives more gets more, thus keeping the overall ratio equitable. For example, a couple might decide that whoever worked the hardest gets to rest the most. Or whoever earns the most gets to be more lax about doing household tasks.

A final procedure to insure justice is to divide up resources according to *need*. For example, a couple might agree that the wife is more needy of time away from the family than her husband, and thus she goes out in the evening more than he does. Alternatively, a husband might be the one to read the paper after work, because both believe that he needs time to unwind at home more than she does. Especially for women who stay home with small children, getting out is of high priority, while for working men having time to unwind is crucial. If the couple uses the need rule, they incorporate these differences.

It would seem obvious that those couples who could flexibly use a variety of rules would be the happiest. The same couple might divide up who stays home with sick children by rotation, the one to cook dinner by whoever worked less that day (and got home earlier) and the type of leisure activities by need. It is also apparent that the potential for conflict in marriage around equity rules would be high. Bagarozzi and Wodarsky (1977) found that marital conflict is highest for those couples in which partners use different rules. For example:

Jane and Sam were a couple in their thirties who requested marital treatment due to their violent fighting. Sam worked long hours as a lawyer, and when he got home from work, he felt he deserved to rest. Jane worked part time as a teacher's aid, and was home with the children for half of the day. She also wanted to rest when evening came, and expected that they would share the bathing, feeding and bedtime stories that care of their three young children demanded. Sam believed in sharing, but didn't think he should have to arrive home and 'continue to work'. Jane thought that the evening routine was 'dirty work' no one wanted to do, and should be divided up half and half. Sam thought that since he earned more, worked longer and was more tired, he had earned the privilege of more leisure time. Weekends were the same, as Sam believed that he deserved to play golf, while Jane thought that they should spend Saturdays cleaning the house together, as she wanted to spend weekday evenings folk dancing and couldn't get through all the housework during that time.

Their constant arguments left bitter feelings. Sam felt rejected and hurt, that his contribution to the marriage went unrecognized and that he was being 'punished'. He responded violently to her lack of appreciation. When he saw Jane looking angry after he arrived home from an exhausting day 'contributing to the family' by work, he lashed out with aggressive insults. Jane responded with aggression as well, having the sense that she was unappreciated and her contribution belittled. Their arguments led to physical violence as each tried to no avail to force appreciation from the other.

A subjective sense of unfairness is pronounced in this case, and translated into violence. No doubt that Sam felt his work to be unappreciated, while Jane felt her care for the children unappreciated. Appreciation is itself a 'desired resource': both partners attempt to balance their sense of inequity by getting appreciation from their partner. Neither gave the other appreciation as a result of their power struggle.

However, couples also often believe that it is wrong to keep an 'account book'; openly noting what is given and received is viewed as picayune and ungenerous. Instead, they frame this sense of unfairness in concepts more acceptable to them. In the case of Sam and Jane, a sense of unfairness translated into gender-stereotyped complaints. Sam blamed her for being 'cold' and unloving, while Jane complained of feeling overwhelmed, stressed and exhausted.

Both partners were basically feeling exploited and angry. Listening to the 'music' of their complaints, more than the words, reveals the 'equity' leitmotif of 'I give more than I get'. Both essentially felt the marriage was not a fair bargain, although they might reject the market mentality this seems to imply. Rejecting this mentality, couples are unaware of their equity rules and thus are totally unaware of their differences about these rules.

Sam and Jane were first helped to articulate their underlying sense of unfairness, and received legitimation for the 'self-interest' these calculations involved. Maintaining fairness was redefined as a caring act, rather than a selfish one, as it involved balancing self-interest with relationship interests.

Sam and Jane were then helped to articulate their equity rules. This needs to be accomplished without jargon, using the couple's own language.

Therapist: Sam, you say that when you get home you want to rest. You feel that you deserve this rest? How come?

Sam: Well, it is obvious . . . I have worked all day and she has been home.

Therapist: So you think that whoever works the most hours should get the most rest?

Jane: But wait a minute . . . I work too, and what is it I am doing when I am with the kids . . . isn't that work?

Sam: Well, sure you work . . . but can you compare my work to your taking care of the kids?

Therapist: Let's see if we can clarify this a bit more. Are you saying Sam, that whoever earns the most money should get the rest?

Sam: Sure, I thought it was self-evident, who ever has the biggest burden gets to take time off.

Therapist:	But you are defining burden by how much income, not hours, right?
Sam:	Yea, I know she isn't sitting home with her feet up, but after all, can you compare the stress involved with my work to her sitting here with the kids?
Jane:	That isn't fair ... wait a minute ... sitting here with the kids? I am working pretty hard here.
Therapist:	Jane, do you think that whoever earns more should rest more?
Jane:	I guess so, well ... I don't know. I think that we both work and that it shouldn't matter who makes more money ... after all, taking care of the kids is my contribution. I think we should both get time to rest, regardless of the income. But I guess I am not sure about this, since I do think that money is important to the family, and I know that if he had to take care of the kids all evening he wouldn't be able to work well the next day. But it seems so unfair, somehow!

They both believed that money earned him more free time. Jane had not directly challenged this. However, she also expected each area of married life to have its own rules and the fact that she wasn't earning as much as Sam should not enter into the division of free time. Jane believed that in the home, tasks and rights should be divided equally – the 'equality rule'. She was conflicted about it, and hadn't clarified the contradiction for herself.

They both allowed his view of reality (his rule) to hold sway and went along with a proportional justice rule based on money: whoever earns more money earns more leisure time as well. The fact that both valued monetary resources and saw him as the primary provider gave him the power to impose his rules on their mutual married life. However, Jane did not 'accept' this situation quietly and without rage, making his victory a rather empty one.

Bagarozzi (1990) showed that the development of symptoms in a spouse is a dysfunctional way couples use to achieve a more equitable exchange of contributions and rewards when unfairness prevails. It might be that a continuation of the situation in which Jane's rules are not included, would lead to Jane's development of depression, a common symptom in women. This would temporarily right the balance. As Jane becomes more depressed and less able to function, Sam would be forced to take over the bedtime routine, as well as other areas of household chores and childcare. Her bad mood might result in his having to be with her more, and give up weekend golf. Emotional suffering is typical of the unconscious price women pay to gain a sense of fairness, to the detriment of their own mental or physical health.

The overall sense of unfairness explains the common research finding that women are less satisfied in marriage than men.[3] Women do more of all kinds of family work: emotional work, such as monitoring problems; and bringing up issues for discussion. Even if the husband is sharing household tasks, the wife will have an overall feeling of doing more.

Equality as equal power

Power is a great motivator. The time is 6 pm and both partners have just come home from a long day at work. Who will start dinner? Who will go off and have a bath? Who gets to read the paper? Who plays with the children? The interpersonal power politics of the marriage will determine how couples decide about these daily life events.

It will also inform how they decide larger issues; where they live, how many children they have, who works, who gets to study, and how they spend their money. Power determines who does what, who decides who does what and how decisions about who does what get made. As the underlining process in all decisions, it touches on all aspects of couple life. Power can be viewed as the ability to affect the behavior of others (Brehm, 1985) and is an interpersonal competence needed to feel effective in relationships. As the ability to get the other to change their behavior, it operates in daily life struggles and in major issues.

In one family I interviewed, the husband mentioned that for twenty years they have fought about his helping out, and yet he still watches TV when he gets home while she takes care of cooking, cleaning and children's bedtime. Eventually he helps, but he waits to see how angry she is getting, and when she reaches a certain 'boiling point' he moves in to 'help'. In this way he continues to feel powerful even when doing what his wife wants, having made his own decision about when to give in. She may get a substantial amount of help, but never feels she has any control.

Another husband I interviewed takes on the household chores immediately upon getting home, despite the fact that his wife is a homemaker and spends all day with the children while he is outside in a paying job. Asked about the difficulty in coming home after an eight-hour day and continuing to work, he said that he did not offer much help in the past. His wife demanded that he change and he did. Asked why, he said: 'Do you know how hard it is to stay home with two small children? I think she is working harder then me. She needs the break!'

Power is one of the variables that can account for the difference between these two husbands' responses. Objectively, if we could observe the amount of time devoted to helping, we might find that the first husband does as much as the second. However, the subjective experience is very different. Imagine which wife feels more respected, which wife is happier, which feels more frustrated?

One wife told me how her husband reversed her decision not to allow their son to go on a trip. He simply told the boy that he could go. Her husband replied that he didn't know what her problem was; he helped out each and every day and said she was unappreciative. This same husband also bought a family car without talking first to her. He justified these unilateral decisions by saying that, in general, he left all the decisions about family life to her and intervened only very infrequently.

Another couple, during the interview, displayed the way an equitable decision-making process looks. Their one-year-old child cried for a bottle from the bedroom, while we sat in the living room. Apparently they were weaning him, and each parent had an opinion about whether to give him the bottle or let him cry. For ten minutes, while their son continued to cry, they negotiated with each other about whether to go in to him or not. They did not act until they reached consensus. I worried about the baby, but they were dedicated to making the decision a joint one.

It is not difficult to see that while the decision-making process might be faster and more efficient for the first couple, the wife feels powerless. For the second couple, the process involves far more effort, but the final result included the wife's opinion.

Aida and Falbo (1991) showed that equal partner couples were more satisfied. Underlying power struggles are often at the root of relational distress. The issue of actual sharing takes a back seat (as problems pile up) to the hidden agenda of struggling over who has the power to decide. The outcome of this struggle will determine who retains power and the process will determine the happiness of both partners.

Power indeed played an important role in couples' definitions of equality in my cross-cultural research. Many couples made it a point to note that the wife had power equal to her husband, and that the couple shared all major decisions. Also, the notion of wife power seemed to include the fact that wives could decide alone for themselves issues usually controlled by men:

> It (equality) is not some division of labor as much as it is this decision-making and power . . . I don't remember discussing it in any terms at all other than, 'here are the decisions we need to make, how are we going to make them, and here are things that need to be done and how are we going to do that?'
>
> Wife (USA)

> I think that our marriage is an equal partnership. We are both involved in our occupations, and in our children and all the matters that concern the home, we consult together . . . any problems we might have in the house we discuss those. We reach a decision. In my parents' marriage, my dad made all the decisions. We don't do that.
>
> Husband (USA)

Interviewing in a cross-cultural context underscored the concept relative and subjectively construed nature of power. For the American couples, there was a decided propensity to equate power with money and financial influence:

> The first thought that comes up for me is my determination to lead my life the way I want. That sort of contradicts our generation's marriage (wife is 71 years old). I made up my mind that I was never going to be supported by a man again, so considering how it works in this culture, you're putting yourself in a funny position because our economic system is not egalitarian . . . we are egalitarian in that we have kept our finances separate, our money . . . I think that was essential for me.
>
> Wife (USA)

Other couples in the USA conceded that money is a socially sanctioned source of power, but they rejected its sway on their decisions:

> I feel like I have the right to come home after a long day and put my feet up. If I was working less hours than him, I would think

that maybe I would do a bit more. But if I was working the same hours but earning less, no, I think I would still have the right to put my feet up and rest, just like him. So we have to share.

Wife (USA)

Power was grasped differently in Israel and in the UK. Money was not alluded to as a source of equal power for wives. Rather, power is viewed as having equal ability to convince each other; their 'personal power' in the relationship was at the root of shared decisions and equal power. Wives who could argue their case, could make their point assertively without giving up, were seen as powerful. Here is an Israeli couple discussing their decision to leave the USA and return home to Israel:

> I agreed because Hava convinced me. She said, 'I'll quit my job and it will take me a few months to find another one, and when you'll finish your work it will be the right time for us to go.' I didn't really want to go, but she convinced me by coming up with strong arguments that the time was ripe. And she was right, really!

Husband (Israel)

Couples in the UK also mentioned the importance of wives not giving in, of their ability to assertively make their claims:

> I could never *not* share, because the minute things get out of balance around here, she lets me know. And she is right, she notices when things aren't fair and she lets me know and she kicks up a fuss until I give in.

Husband (UK)

British wives often cited having separate financial accounts, but they do not link money and power. Separate accounts are perceived not so much as a source of power as a source of security for the entire family:

> I have my account which I use to pay for some of the bills. He pays for others from his account. But he is hopeless about money, and he is always running out in his account, so I give him money from my account. He earns more, but he would spend everything on posh stuff, so I keep us on track by making sure the books are balanced. When he gets off track, I make sure we get back on track.

Wife (UK)

The literature on power is equivocal about power in marriage. Although there is little disagreement about husbands' greater power and influence on decision-making than wives, why husbands remain more powerful in marriage remains a controversial research question.[4] Many people think that the greater economic resources of husbands are the source of their greater power, their decision-making authority, and thus less involvement with housework and childcare. This idea is supported by findings that the more the husband earned, the greater his authority in decisions about the home (Blumstein and Schwartz, 1983), and the more the wife earns, the more the husband participates in childcare (Darling-Fisher and Tiedje, 1990).

But this research also suggests that power is far more complex than this. Blumstein and Schwartz (1983) surveyed 12,000 American couples and interviewed 600 married cohabitating lesbian and gay members of couples. They demonstrated that the partner less in love, the partner who felt more independent, the one with more outside options, was the more powerful in the relationship. They found that this person had less fears about the relationship and controlled many important decisions. Subjective feelings and beliefs interact with economic and social conditions to determine power.

Women themselves may be restricting the ability their increased earnings could have to buy them marital power. A study of working wives in England (Stamp, 1985) showed that women whose economic power was significantly greater than their partners reduced this power by ceding authority to their husbands. While women may gain objective power through increased earnings, they may act to reduce this power in order to maintain their gender identity and that of their husbands.

Attitudes can mediate the impact of money. Having monetary resources is related to power, especially when both partners believe in patriarchal norms. Women who reject the idea of the husband as 'primary provider' do not situate power as based in money, and thus reject its potential effects. Kingsbury and Scanzoni found that:

> Wives with nontraditional sex role preferences (egalitarian ideology) were willing to negotiate for their positions and to ultimately affect change or resist change in the process of decision making. In the final analysis, the best interpretation of these

findings about sex role preferences and power lead to the conclusion that it is the *wife's attitude* that has the greatest impact
on decision making. If the wife is more modern than her
husband, she is willing to negotiate for her position, and if she is
traditional she is more willing to accept her husband's position.
(1989:243)

This study points to the woman's sense of entitlement as a central
factor in her ability to increase her power in the relationship. It
places personality as mediating the economic factor in power. Steil
and Weltman (1991) found that while both partners tend to value
the husband's career more, *personal attributes were the most
predictive factor regarding how much say either partner had in the
home*. Equally true for both husbands and wives, the more either
described him or herself as dominant, autonomous, and achievement oriented, the more they reported having a voice at home.
Wives who were reluctant to assert the importance of their own
careers were at a disadvantage in seeking equality.

Women with high self-esteem tend to use more direct power
strategies, such as negotiation and convincing. It is important to
note that women's tendency to link their self-esteem to the quality
of their relationships creates a serious bind. Women perceive
themselves as standing to lose in marital relationship quality if
they assert their power. Hiller and Philliber (1989) found that the
more assertive a wife perceives herself to be, the lower the marital
quality as perceived by her husband. *Women need both personal
power and relationships with men to feel good about themselves,
but often find they have to play a subordinate role to have marital
satisfaction, ultimately paying a high price in reduced self-esteem.*

This case description illustrates how these power dynamics are
reflected in couple interactions.

Richard and Sally, an American couple living in Israel, requested
therapy when Sally threatened to leave the relationship. A couple
in their late twenties with two small daughters, they had lived in
Israel for two years and originally had not planned to stay. They
had come to Israel to represent an American company. Their
agreement was that after earning some money, they would return
home.

However, Richard found that he liked life in Israel and,
changing his mind, decided he wanted to stay. Sally was

adamant she wanted to leave, and was furious that Richard was making no plans for their return to the States. She could not influence him to change his mind.

The couple had worked together establishing the Israeli branch of the company they represented. Their present crisis was triggered when Richard hired a full-time secretary to 'help Sally out'. Sally found herself replaced. She had believed that the business was 'theirs' and was enraged that she had to watch this new worker carry out her own job.

Sally had managed to run the daily functioning of the business, doing all the secretarial and organizational work, leaving Richard free to develop the field operations and contacts. At the same time, she had taken care of their children and home. Since their office was in the home, she had juggled all this in the house, while Richard spent most of his time outside in meetings. He rarely helped out in the house, and returned home late at night. He hired the secretary when Sally became more and more angry at her overwhelming load.

Sally reported that she had wanted to talk to him about the problems, and about her distress at feeling overworked, but that she could never get his undivided attention. When he got home, he made phone calls to the States, gave her instructions for the following day and then collapsed in bed. He said that he was getting fed up with her increasing 'bitchiness' . Hiring the secretary was his attempt to reduce her strain, although he couldn't really understand why she was so exhausted. Compared to the stress he felt in terms of responsibility for the business, he thought Sally had it relatively easy. He was angry that his attempt to help was not only rejected, but made Sally even more angry.

Sally and Richard had met at an American college, and were influenced by feminist ideology. They believed that Sally should be an equal partner, that she should work, and that the business they started belonged to them both.

Sally did not discern that she was never really an equal partner, that their ideology was fraught with contradictions. She was in effect Richard's secretary, although she wanted to think of herself as a partner. Without paying attention, she had been taking orders from the start. Unintentionally, she had accepted her lower status, had given up her own career goals, and had merged her goals with his from a subordinate position. Meanwhile she convinced herself they were a real team. Power differences can be invisible, especially if one partner values their input more than the other. Sally, thinking her contribution was worth as much as Richard's, never realized that he saw his own as connoting higher status.

His unilateral decision to stay in Israel and to hire the secretary revealed the actual power structure of the relationship. Sally had felt in control because she told him what time to be home for dinner, where they were going on vacation, and what kindergarten their child would attend. The discrepancy in status between her perceived equality and her real lack of significant power resulted in explosive anger when important decisions were made by him alone.

Sally was responsible for all childcare, all housework and all contact with extended family. Sally had never questioned her role, was actually proud that she could do so many things at one time and thought herself a 'strong woman'. But she had become overwhelmed and could not influence Richard to take her crisis seriously. Labeling her as 'bitchy' made it seem that she wasn't coping well. Never having stayed home with small children, never having run a home while managing the administration of a business, Richard really didn't understand the stress involved. In addition, Richard thought that a 'real man' took over in times of crisis. He didn't see this as 'paternalistic' but as strong, and was rather astonished that Sally wasn't pleased.

His decision to hire a secretary to relieve her exhaustion reduced her power even more, in effect further limiting her areas of influence. Also, excluding her from the business allowed Richard to avoid conflict with her. Only in therapy did both partners come to perceive the role that unequal power played in their distress. They both believed that Sally should be an equal partner with equal power.

However, this dictated that Sally had to examine the results of her choices; to join him in business rather than pursue her own career goals, to accept a subordinate role as secretary, and to take on all home responsibilities. It was essential she become aware that these were choices, albeit unconscious ones. All had led to an erosion of her power, to a growing frustration, and to severe conflict with Richard.

Sally finally decided to leave the business and apply for a graduate program in the USA in her profession. She demanded that the family leave Israel. Richard did consequently leave with her, but was furious at having to back down, was humiliated by having her dominate, and was resentful at giving up his chosen country. Although I do not know the final outcome, it is highly probable that Richard will attempt to reclaim his authority and make up for the insult to his masculinity.

EMPOWERMENT AS AN ALTERNATIVE TO POWER

Empowerment, or giving power 'to the other', is an alternative concept to power. Whereas power is the ability to 'get someone to do something they don't necessarily want to do', we can see empowerment as 'enabling the other person to expand their range of choices and personal freedom'. Hall has defined empowerment as:

> The individual and collective strengthening of negotiating position in relation to the negotiating position of other people ... the development, growth and maturation of real talents and aptitudes ... and the recognition and responsibility as an equal.
>
> (1992:121)

In this definition, empowerment is an interpersonal process in which personal gain is negotiated within the framework of the collective good of the relationship. Without calling it by name, most egalitarian couples mentioned it. They especially focus on watching out for the other's interest and growth and making sure the partner is happy. They are mindful not to dominate. Empowerment is a prominent element in achieving equality:

> Aliza can express herself very easily and she has a lot of skill about this, so she knows how to make her point. I don't always know how to influence her, like she influences me. I really learned how to talk back from Ellen. She and I have a platonic friendship that is very important to me.
>
> Husband (Israel)

> I think that I really encouraged his friendship with Ellen because it helped him get stronger, and start to deal better with me, and not to give up when we fight. I admit there are many things in which she has helped him when I couldn't. His connection to her helped him kick back, get angry at me, express his

needs. She told me that she had a fight with him, and that he is really getting his anger out. I asked him if he is exercising the law of 'preservation of anger'. It made him laugh, but it was good.

His wife (Israel)

I used to argue with her a lot, she wanted me to pick up, tidy up, hoover, things like that. But then I started the counseling course, and it encouraged me to work on myself, to get more secure and I realized that I am not thick, I am smart and I can learn. I asked her to come into the counseling course, but she wouldn't.

Husband (UK)

I think that he needed his own world, to get strong and be better able to deal with life, with me. I just felt that he needed his own area ... and it is true, that now that he likes himself more, we discuss things properly. He gets the tea ready, sweeps the house and does the washing up. He notices when I am under pressure, and just takes over sort of naturally.

His wife (UK)

These are statements of couples who empower each other. Each clearly feels that the power of the other is for his or her own welfare. Empowering the other is seen as leading to more personal advantage. There is an overall perception that the relationship is substantial enough for two strong leaders.[5]

Thus, rather than using a 'win–lose' model, these are couples who use a 'win–win' cooperative model based on supporting each one's individual growth, similar to the 'non-zero-sum game'. In a situation of mutual empowerment, sharing happens in a spontaneous way.

Equality as sharing household and parenting tasks

I once heard it said that any marital issue, when a problem for the couple, takes up about 80 percent of the relationship, but when it is going well, only about 20 percent. This echoes the attitudes expressed by happy egalitarian couples about household and parenting tasks: No big deal, there is not much to discuss! This reaction is about a matter that has become central in most working couples' lives.[6]

We tend to do the cleaning together, but I don't think we ever really discussed that. We just like to spend time with each other, so while we clean we can talk.

Husband (Israel)

The happiest couples were those who seemed to naturally 'pitch in' without much fuss. Working like a team, they divided up tasks in a strikingly flexible manner. Some chores, referred to by one American husband as 'nasty' tasks, were divided up by equality rules; that is half and half. When no one wanted to clean the bathrooms, then division by rotation kept this onerous duty justly distributed. Other tasks were divided using the proportional rule. Whoever invested more got more privileges back. For example, in the evening, the one who had worked the most hours would rest, while the one who had worked less that day might be with the children.

By far the most frequently used justice rule by happily married equal partners was 'need'. Responsibilities are divided up by perception of need for or desire to do the task. For example:

He does the shopping. He needs to know where the money is going. He actually needs to feel the money go out between his sticky little fingers ... give him a sense of security I guess.

Wife (USA)

These are couples who especially attempt to make the division of labor at home meet individual personal wishes and requirements. They only allocate these chores on the basic of gender when they view gender as expressing individual personality. Even when gender appeared to me to be the most obvious basis for role division, such as the wife doing the cooking and the husband doing the yard work, the couple tended to perceive it as based on temperament.

No, I don't think that I do the repairs because I am a man. I am more like my father that way, good with my hands. I guess it's in the genes, if anything ... but not a macho thing. It is just me.

Husband (UK)

In reality, roles are just as likely to be divided up in a nongendered stereotyped manner, mostly by preference:

He really likes to cook, so he does that. And I like to be out in the world. So he took a job teaching law so that he could be home more with our daughter. I took the full-time corporate fast-track route, cause that is what I like.

Wife (USA)

Roles are *interchangeable*, in that each potentially can take on any task. Thus there is a built-in potential for flexibility, but also areas of expertise based on preferences. This results in clear roles, a willingness to shift those roles, together with a certain respect for the boundaries of the other's territory:

> At first I took care of the bills, paying them, going to the bank, that kind of stuff. Then I got really fed up, so Sara took it for about six months. I could tell she was getting sick of it, when she was shouting at everyone at the end of the month. So I asked her if she felt she had had enough. She said yes, so I took it over again. We both hate doing it, but it has to get done. I guess Sara will probably take it over in a while.

Husband (USA)

CONCLUSION: THE IMPORTANCE OF BEING FAIR

This chapter has shown that there are a variety of ways to define equality in marriage. Problems around defining equality can be viewed as a hidden source of marital distress today. Couples neither articulate nor agree about their definitions, although this disparity is hidden in other complaints.

Three common ways in which couples define equality include:

- a subjective appraisal of the level of fairness in the relationship;
- an equal balance of power and decision-making;
- equal sharing of household and parenting roles.

Definitions are interrelated: couples who achieve congruency between all these elements are highly satisfied with their relationships, and a marked discrepancy between these aspects (they see their relationship as fair but decision-making as unfair) is an origin of tension.

Universally, the happiest couples have a clear appraisal of their marriage as being primarily fair. This subjective sense is a 'world view' of the relationship that allows for the day-to-day imbalances that often occur. This appraisal is held in place by equal power through joint decisions, through the legitimization of direct use of power through negotiation and convincing. Couples actually empower each other. The sense that each partner is looking out for the other's benefit, reinforces the subjective appraisal of fairness.

In this context, actual sharing behaviors in the home become a natural part of preserving the underlying structure of a perception of fairness. As a team, the partners strive to maintain their holistic balance of equity, flexibly using the different justice principles as needed. Where jobs are not desired (the 'nasty tasks'), they tend to be rotated equally. Other tasks are divided up by the amount of effort they entail versus the amount of energy the person has at the moment. Most commonly, couples allocate roles on the basis of preferences, talents and needs. Partners appear able to switch, because they could do everything, but opt to have their own 'territory'. Many of these processes take place out of the awareness of the couple, and their subjective sense is that things just 'balance out' over time.

> She is staying home now, since she is pregnant and burned out from her last job. But we decided that in another five years, I will get to stay home. We are working towards that.
>
> Husband (USA)

A long-term commitment results in more risk-taking. The underlying trust that one's turn will come gives each partner the confidence to dare to compromise without feeling exploited. It helps each partner make sacrifices and compromises, knowing the other will eventually return the investment. Reciprocally, knowing the partner is willing to compromise strengthens commitment.

The entire relationship system functions as a balanced whole over time to insure the preservation of this crucial perception. It appears that a 'quantum leap' needs to be made in which the couple moves to a new belief that their relationship is a fair one. This overall conviction allows them to maintain their trust despite the many events which demand a temporary imbalance.

When this quantum leap has not been made, then the best of intentions may be wrongly interpreted. A husband might make a meal; but in the context of lack of trust, the wife could see this as his manipulating her to get out of a more onerous task. Lack of overall gratitude for sacrifices made can then lead to despair and bitterness. People will give up on attempts to be fair if there is a sense of being victimized. Being fair takes real effort, which is supported by the overall belief that the relationship is a fair and just one. The belief then supports the investment of effort, which supports the belief.

This describes a positive cycle of which equal partnership is the outcome. What are the efforts needed to support the overall subjective appraisal of fairness? No belief can survive in a vacuum. The egalitarian couples have taught us that just sharing household tasks is not enough to create this appraisal. What is? We can now turn to the interview couples to learn how they generated the conditions for equality. Rather than looking at who does what, who earns how much, or any other 'quantitative view' of equality, we will be focusing on the process of making that quantum leap towards a conviction that the entire relationship is fair. These are the same conditions needed by any couple to have a satisfying relationship in a society moving towards equal status for women.

Chapter 3

Friendship
The basic condition of equal partnership

The major goal of this book is to facilitate the incorporation by therapists of the experiences of successful equal partners into work with couples. Rather than attempting to categorize couples into groups (i.e. equal partner or traditional) it is clinically more helpful to assess each couple according to the major themes identified. We can take note of which were happier and those less happy, in order to help understand the process of achieving both equality and happiness in marriage. The material here is translated into therapeutic goals. Where relevant, case information from couples in therapy will also be presented to highlight how these themes are reflected in the problems that couples bring into relationship counseling. Later chapters will then show how actually to incorporate these themes in work towards change.[1]

HELPING COUPLES TO BE FRIENDS

Friendship is an elusive concept, with many different meanings. Rubin (1983) found that most people had an idealized definition of what ingredients go into friendship: trust, honesty, respect, commitment, safety, support, generosity, loyalty, mutuality, constancy, understanding and acceptance. Profound friendship can be seen as an intimate relationship, different from the relationship with acquaintances, neighbors, buddies or pals, close kin, or co-workers. Friendship has been valued throughout the ages as the height of human relations, since it comprises free choice to be in the relationship, altruism, acceptance of differences and a deep connection that promotes each friend's well-being. The qualities of friendship can only survive in an atmosphere of equality, as friendship implies lack of domination, mutual concern and respect.[2]

Given the high idealistic value placed upon friendship, it is significant that the most common phrase used by equal partnership couples in all three countries was: *my partner is my best friend.* This is also noteworthy in light of the lack of friendship in marriage; a recent survey (Associated Press, 1993) indicated that when men and women were asked with whom they would choose to spend a year on an deserted island, most men said their wives. Wives in contrast were not nearly as enthusiastic about spending a year alone with their husbands. Women come into marriage having more experience with intimate friendships than men, who evidence little practice in creating deep friendship. In the happy equal relationships both partners see the other as a true best friend.

How do couples go about creating friendship between the sexes in marriage?

Friendship through shared experience

Intimacy is knowing the other, and an intimate friendship is based on deep empathy for one's friend. Yet, from earliest childhood, the sexes begin to play in separate groups. As a matter of fact, until young adulthood and dating, gender segregation is actually the norm. In marriage the two sexes, so long inhabiting separate worlds, are expected to create the most intimate of relationships. If it weren't such a prevalent and accepted social expectation, it might be viewed as the almost infeasible task it is.

Traditional marriage is a continuation of this gender separation, and as such does not foster friendship. This partly may explain its stability. The traditional expectation was to get emotional support elsewhere; the man in the work world and the woman at home, maintaining the distance between the sexes begun in childhood. Expectations were not so high, and disappointments not so serious.

Equal partners inhabit shared worlds. Since in equal partnerships, both men and women carry the financial burden, are responsible for the home and children and take responsibility for the emotional well-being of the relationship and of the family, both partners know firsthand what the other's experience is like. Both know what it is like to wake in the middle of the night with money worries. They both know the amount of money in their accounts, both know exactly what bills need to be paid. Both notice when a child has a fever; both are willing to stay home with the sick child. Both initiate sex and so know what rejection feels like. Both notice when they have grown distant, which arouses anxiety in both, and both feel responsibility to do something about it.

In these relationships the husband is his wife's best friend. Equal partner husbands have experience with the feminine domain of caretaking, know its stress and understand their wives' dilemmas:

> Rita is in a panic about who will be our babysitter when the baby arrives. I know how she feels, when we had Aliza I went to her mother to ask her to be our sitter. I didn't feel comfortable with anyone we don't know. Her mother can't do it this time, so we are really worried. I tell her it will be alright, but I know the feeling of insecurity until it is all worked out.
>
> Husband (USA)

As opposed to happy couples, distressed equal partner couples tend to retain established gendered spheres. However, unlike traditional couples, they are also highly conflicted about it. Men felt more financial responsibility and worked longer hours, while women tended to be more responsible for the home front and were obstinate about imposing their own standards. Husbands were more likely to be seen as 'helpers', tended to look to the wife for instructions about what needed to be done, and were less likely to initiate doing tasks on their own. Both partners still saw the husband as meeting the primary provider role. Wives were ambivalent about the drift towards traditional roles, and expressed angry emotions. Numerous conflicts revolved around the husband not doing enough at home, as well as not spending enough time there. The men saw their work as more important than their wives' work, demanding that family schedules be juggled around their schedules. Wives were bitter about the lack of contact with their partners and the limitations that the extra burden of home placed on their individual pursuits.

These more unhappy egalitarian couples did not mention that their partners are their friends. Wives talked about feeling lonely, isolated from their partners, and of seeking closeness from women friends. The partners tended to have parallel lives, punctuated by periods of crisis and conflict. These wives expressed a sense of outrage, since their 'marital contract' was to share equally and they felt betrayed:

I wind up doing everything on weekends, even though we have an agreement that Saturday morning he works and the afternoons are mine. But he was supposed to come home around 12, and that seemed to gradually slide to 1 pm, then 2 pm and I finally found that I had no time at all on Saturdays. I have to call him at the office to get him back, and a lot of the times he is away from his desk, so I don't find him. God, it is so frustrating!

Wife (USA)

One wife, a writer working independently from her home, demonstrates her pain when her husband, a high salary executive usually willing to share, suddenly 'pulled rank' on her:

Marvin was very stressed one day and angry that I insisted on his doing a chore he had agreed to do. He suddenly blurted out, 'Who do you think is paying for your writing anyway?' What a nerve – this is my work, it isn't a hobby!

Wife (USA)

Many of these wives attempted to handle their anger by trying to communicate about their problems, often using therapy. However, talking about problems can never substitute for having similar experiences and knowing what those experiences actually feel like.

Tim and Rebecca, an American couple, were living a traditional lifestyle when I interviewed them. Rebecca had just left her career as a buyer, saying that she was totally burnt out. She was home, pregnant with their third child and taking care of the other two. However, prior to the interview, Tim had been a house husband for two years, combining childcare with his work in an independent computer business. He had taken their infant to work meetings and knew all about feedings, changing diapers, sickness and the stress of combining all the above with involvement in running his business. Thus when Rebecca talked to us about her fatigue on days when their two children were fighting, he immediately understood:

The hardest days I used to have were when I was taking care of both of them: Darian and Seth went with me to work. I couldn't believe the amount of competition that a three year old could have with an infant. I constantly had to keep Seth busy with other activities to keep him out of Darian's way – it was really stressful! I was in the middle of an important meeting and suddenly there was Darian, poking a finger in Seth's eye!

The lack of friendship in less successful equal partner couples seems anchored in the constraints of gendered sex roles. While these were couples who firmly believed in egalitarian ideology, husbands continued to play the traditional role of 'strong' partner who didn't want to worry his wife. A doctor held back from his wife that he had gone through a bad spell in his practice; she did not realize that for a while the family was on precarious economic grounds. Another husband did not tell his wife that there had been a robbery in the neighborhood, wanting to spare her the worry. These same husbands also complained that their wives showed little interest in their work. One man said that he could see his wife's eyes start to glaze over when he told her a story about his co-workers. She seemed very bored and he was hurt, but did not see a connection between shutting her out of his worries and her developing an indifferent attitude to his life away from her.

One also wonders if wives were so much bored or unconsciously tuning out due to resentment of their partners' long hours. Amy, an Afro-American wife, complained bitterly that her community leader husband Steve made it obvious that her needs were second to the Black community's needs. Steve responded by saying that it was true, and that the urgent problems of drug addiction, crime and poverty seemed to him far more compelling than Amy's problems with sitters, or the questions about what furniture to buy. Such an attitude sent a signal of disrespect for the 'petty' details of her life. Amy would be likely to retaliate by not showing interest in his work as well. Indeed, Steve later complained that his wife seemed not to want to hear about the kids he worked with. Amy concurred, asserting that the stories were 'grim' and just depressed her. Amy wanted more closeness to her husband, but felt him to be a stranger. Talking to him was like talking to a 'wall'. Having no influence or access to their inner worlds, friendship was impossible for this couple.

For couples where friendship was lacking, sharing of child-rearing or household chores was a source of continual strife. Mostly, the women complained that their husbands promised a lot, but delivered far less. These were women who continually had to remind their partners whose turn it was, what needed to be done, as well as critique their partners' low standards of house-keeping.

It may well be that lack of influence is intricately bound up with inhabiting separate spheres. Partners are more likely to cooperate with requests when they feel empathically connected to each other. Couples who shared their lives developed the essential empathic attachment that underlines friendship: the friend's needs are perceived as influential, as they are felt as compellingly as one's own. This mutual identification results in a willingness to sacrifice for the other's development, and an awareness of the requirements for the other's well-being. This often entails giving the other person space, such as the case of the wife who encouraged her husband to take a year off and live alone in the mountains, because this is what they both knew he needed. It may entail giving the other's goals first priority, as in the case of the husband who took a less attractive job so that his wife could be nearer to her university. These are aspects of friendship that women have traditionally offered to their partners, but have rarely received themselves in return. These wives' influence on their husbands, leading to a willingness to balance the wives' needs with their own needs, seemed anchored in solid friendship.

An example of lack of shared worlds and its impact on relationship distress can be seen in this young Israeli couple. The wife requested marital counseling:

Tami, a 28-year-old intern, married six years with two small children, came in alone saying that she was in the midst of a marital crisis. Her husband Ami, a successful 35-year-old doctor, was not willing at first to come to treatment, saying that he couldn't understand her problem with him. However, he agreed to one session alone with me to 'help his wife' by telling his side of the story. After this individual session he agreed to come together with her for several sessions.

Tami was attempting to complete a difficult internship in pediatric medicine, while also feeling that the primary responsibility of the home was on her. Her major complaint was that he didn't listen to her expressing all the stress she felt, was patronizing, and she didn't feel any sexual desire. She thought more and more about divorce, feeling that she could make it on her own as a doctor and that she wasn't really getting much out of the relationship. Ami had been her teacher in medical school, and was also a mentor to her. He wanted her to succeed, and was instrumental in arranging her prestigious internship.

This was a couple who shared the medical world and could talk about their work. However, Tami complained that Ami wasn't interested much in their two sons, was bored when she talked about the stress of rushing to work and to home, and dismissed her need for emotional support from him by saying 'I don't know what your problem is – you have a live-in au pair.'

However, in later sessions Ami revealed that he also felt detached and lonely in the relationship. He worried a lot about money, and Tami seemed to feel indifferent about his providing her with the good life. Tami did not at first see any discrepancy between her need to have him as her friend, listening to her difficulty being a dual-career mother, and her lack of interest in 'his' money problems. She said that her family had emphasized getting rich and she developed an allergy to this ambition. However, she admitted that the au pair allowed them both to have their careers, and that she enjoyed the many vacations they were able to afford.

Their therapy progressed quickly when they began to define friendship as their primary mutual goal. Ami wanted her to become far more involved in finances, to know the state of their account and to be willing to talk with him about spending. She agreed to try to overcome her distaste for the subject and was able to express her gratitude that Ami's earnings bought her the ability to combine career and motherhood. Her increased appreciation of him resulted in his increasing willingness to listen to her. It soon became obvious that he was very aware of the home front, was basically family oriented and caring. He had been unconsciously retaliating for her lack of equality and the expectation that he would be the sole provider, by tuning her out. When he felt respect from her for the contribution he made to the family, and a willingness to share the midnight anxiety attacks he had about meeting the bills, he was more than willing to listen to her feelings of guilt at leaving the children and her fears that she wasn't going to make the grade in her work. With this willingness came a willingness to learn the skills of listening. Ami had been used to being Tami's teacher and tended to interrupt often and lecture her. However, he quickly learned to listen in the context of feeling that she was now listening to his problems.

This was the friendship she had missed. And Ami learned that he needed friendship as much as Tami did. The couple successfully completed therapy after six sessions.

Women find it hard to give up the comfort of the strong male provider role, since it gives them the support to go out into the world and cope with the discriminatory salaries and lack of respect they often find there. These are compelling reasons to want both the excitement of a career and the support of a provider husband. Many men sense the implicit unfairness in the new expectation that they should now share household chores and childrearing and yet continue to carry the worry of the provider role. An American husband plaintively beseeched: 'Doesn't my earning all that money buy me *any* rights here?'

The traditional role-playing may be more concealed when the woman earns well. She contributes to the economic base of the family by putting her salary into the joint account, while still playing the traditional feminine role of not knowing what the financial circumstances really are. The husband is thus left with the emotional responsibility of the traditional role, without the benefits of getting out of doing household tasks.

As we will see in later chapters, many 'liberated' husbands do not feel that they have the right to complain. They tend to reject the macho role and repudiate dominating. Yet they have a harder time rejecting the provider role. They have yet to develop alternative ways of voicing their discontent. Many are terrified that if they let themselves get angry, they might get aggressive. Men retaliate by not giving their wives the listening, affection and support that is demanded, and using their penchant to avoid conflict to tune out their wives' demands.

Because so many couples share these dilemmas, making friendship an articulated and primary treatment goal entails considerable change. Men have to get in touch with a type of intimate friendship they have denied themselves. They need to learn nurturing behaviors that care for relationships, including listening well and responding empathically to emotional distress. Therapists have to locate the individual gender-related prejudices which curtail shared experiences. For some, the wife resists sharing her husband's fears about work or money. In others, the husband is fearful about his own competency in childrearing, emotional expression, and giving support. Some wives do not allow the husband equally to share childrearing, and some husbands won't tolerate wives initiating sex. All these confine the degree to which the couple share experiences and thus the quality of their friendship.

Gender restrictions can be so pervasive as to preclude friendship at all. Status and power differences result in traditional men keeping counsel only with themselves, sharing little of their internal debate about any problem. Women will not share their successes, fearing that to do so would threaten their partners' sense of security or arouse competitive feelings. Thus women may find it easier to reveal weakness or areas of confusion rather than their successes, joys or pride in coping well. Often this gendered role-playing has the husband acting 'all knowing' while the wife shows all the helplessness or pain.

One couple in treatment included partners both of whom had affairs, painfully hurting each other. However, it was only the wife who expressed jealousy and pain, repeatedly asking for emotional support from her husband. He behaved as if he was well over his liaison and all the feelings caused by her. In actuality, he was still hurting badly. He could not listen to her tears, as they brought his pain to the surface and he was bent on hiding his experience from her. He needed her support no less than she needed him, and in the end, neither got the friendship from the other so important in rebuilding trust. Stereotyped gender roles limit the sharing of both weaknesses and strengths, while friendship means sharing the whole person and being able to be a whole person in the relationship.

Therapists can locate gendered restrictions to shared worlds in the stories partners tell about their conflicts. For example, this Israeli couple in marital counseling related an incident that had caused them a painful fight:

Dan, a 35-year-old engineer and Rachel, his 45-year-old physical therapist wife, had been married for eight years. A second marriage for Rachel and a first marriage for Dan, they had overcome considerable family opposition to their marriage due to their age differences. They requested marital counseling as they fought about Dan's tendency towards lateness and what Rachel called his 'irresponsibility'. Dan admitted that he often lost track of time, but felt that he was committed to the family and rejected her label.

In a therapy session early in treatment, Rachel arrived crying. She related through her tears that he had come back at 12 am from a farewell party for a colleague at work, after calling at 10 pm to say he would be home in half an hour. She was furious also that he had gone off to the party exactly when she was in the middle of a session with one of her private clients. According to Rachel, he left their young son sitting in front of the television, rather than putting him to bed. She had refused to talk to him since he returned. She said that this was a good example of his tendency towards irresponsibility.

In analyzing this incident during the session it emerged that throughout the week Dan had been solving the problem of the party on his own. He had first invited Rachel and then heard that only workers were going to be there. Knowing she wanted to go, and worried about disappointing her, he had not said anything. Rather he had waited until the evening of the party to tell her and said he would only go for one hour. He figured to himself that if she was working, that might be the best hour for him to go. He also determined that she would probably finish her work within a short time, and that she would then put their son to bed. His call to her was his attempt to be responsible, but he was also continuing his solitary problem-solving. At the party it turned out that his boss wanted to talk with him. He knew this would take a while, and also did not know how long. Concluding that he could not call Rachel every half an hour, he solved this predicament in assuming that he would explain when he got home.

Dan saw autonomy in a male stereotyped way. For him, a self-reliant man does not consult on problems and presents a decisive front, exposing his solutions only after they are formulated. Sharing uncertainties with a women was childish to him, and a man should not reveal his musings to anyone. He had learned that sharing any lack of security left him open to attack, and a 'real man' did not let anyone see him insecure. However, he was utterly unaware that he was programmed this way, that he even made these assumptions or that he acted on them. Seeing how he had tried to 'go it alone' was an eye-opener for him. Dan essentially wanted to be Rachel's friend, so he was quickly able to see how he had shut her out. This short segment from the therapy session shows continued work on this theme:

Claire: Dan, you say that you wish you had shared more with her and that you really want above all to be Rachel's friend and equal partner. So how would you write the script of this week over again, knowing what you now know?

Dan: Well ... let's see. I would first of all tell Rachel right away that partners weren't invited and that I am going alone. Then I guess I would have put Roi to bed by the time I had to leave. I probably would have called Rachel from the party when my boss asked to talk to me and would tell her that I am going to be late. That is about it.

Claire: I think that is an improvement ... but let's see if what you just said would help you two to feel more like friends and equal partners. Rachel ... does this new scenario change things for you? Does it help you feel that Dan is your friend?

Rachel: No, not really, although I can see him trying and I agree that he should have put our son to bed. I don't know why, but I don't think I would feel much better really.

Claire: Let's see if this helps you think about your needs. If you two were functioning here as good friends, what would he have done differently?

Rachel: I think he would have shared his thinking with me. His new scenario is still him solving everything on his own. He might ask me if I had any ideas about what to do ... like maybe he could talk to his co-workers about bringing me, for example. And now that I think about it ... his new idea was for him to put Roi to bed. But here again, he is solving it himself. If we had thought it through as a team, I would have been glad to put Roi to bed myself before I saw my client. I would rather he feed Roi dinner, which would have made the evening go much smoother for me. And now that I think of it, maybe I would have thought of a way to meet him after the party. We might have been able to go out with some of the people there. . . . A friend would want my involvement too.

Dan: Rachel, I had no idea I was doing this. I do it at work too, come to think of it. I didn't realize how much I try to solve every problem by myself.

Developing friendship leads to the formation of teamwork and cooperation, basic ingredients in equal partnership.

Friendship through personal autonomy

What is it that makes equal partners so able to trust each other? They are not worried about giving too much or getting too little, not afraid of being exploited or used in any way. This provides them with a secure base to give freely, confident that individual interests eventually will be considered equally.

The previous discussion of shared worlds suggested that joint experiences generate a sort of deep empathy, paving the way for partners sincerely to yearn to help each other out. This interpretation stresses the 'collective' dimension of partnership. To the extent that couples genuinely comprehend each other, they feel so attached as to naturally want to further each other's best interests.

The cross-cultural study indicates that it is the balancing of this collective side with an emphasis on the individual that completes the picture of attaining friendship in marriage. Equal partner couples are able to rely on the partner's personal integrity, each secure that the other will be responsible in refusing to allow unfairness to develop. *Each partner actually monitors the self for personal contribution, rather than monitoring the other partner for how much is provided.* A homemaker wife in the USA relates how she puts herself on an eight-hour schedule:

> I know that Rick will come home from his studies at the university and do whatever I didn't get to that day – and all that in addition to putting the girls to bed, doing the dishes ... that kind of stuff. I realized that if I didn't make sure to watch the clock, to really put in a full day of work, it would be so easy to sit on the couch and read a book during the afternoon. I mean, who's to know? I have to watch out for myself that I do enough.
>
> Wife (USA)

Less satisfied partners tend to monitor each other, rather than themselves, so that each is concerned with how much the other is doing:

I have to stay on top of what is going on here. He would never do anything if I didn't check up and point out things to him. He is basically a lazy guy, and if I don't get upset about things he would let them go.

Wife (Israel)

Equal partners check in with the other about the level of fairness, initiating discussions as to whether the partner is satisfied:

I usually ask Jane how things are going, if she feels that she is doing too much around the house. When I kind of notice if she is looking upset about something, I ask if it has to do with us, is she feeling put upon? She does so much. I don't want to abuse that.

Husband (USA)

Husbands in less satisfying relationships may feel they are getting away with doing less, and thus prefer not to talk about sharing. They avoid conversations that might bring up their wives' demands. The happier couples demonstrate a high level of ethical awareness and requests for feedback; each partner seems personally concerned with how moral their own behavior is and they expect their partner to help them stay responsible.

To be this responsible without losing track of one's own needs, each person in the relationship has to have a high level of personal autonomy. Equal partners, along with their stress on togetherness, are also intensely individualistic. They balance their intense stress on relationship quality with a focus on the self.

There are many examples from the interviews of individualism and self-responsibility for growth.

I know that I have to be a strong person on my own right to be in this relationship and to succeed as husband. I went into therapy and have been in therapy for the last five years. I am always working on my self-security.

Husband (UK)

I think he has improved considerably. I am thinking that we can now work together more at the church because he isn't threatened any more by me, or anyone for that matter.

His wife (UK)

Doron is a very secure person. He just knows who he is. That is a tremendous comfort to me. He isn't out to prove anything to anyone.

Wife (Israel)

I am who I am . . . Doron, that's me. I have this sense of who I am – I always have been that way.

Her husband (Israel)

This degree of self-security leads to the ability to be nonconformist about gender roles and thus to share more. The same husband continues:

I have always been different from others, as long as I know myself. I went against the crowd. I knew this about myself from childhood. So it doesn't really bother me when people laugh at how I clean the house, iron, all that. I don't hide it, I couldn't care less. I am who I am.

An English wife noted that she had to buck the reactions of her family to their 'weird' lifestyle:

When my Mum comes to visit us, she is amazed at how much Paul helps out and kind of thinks we are very strange. She thinks I am not much of a wife, letting my husband work so much at home. I should be doing my job better – making him comfortable, like she did for Dad. But I have come to the conclusion, in general, that it really isn't important what other people think . . . it is important what I think.

Individual autonomy and self-reliance only seem to further equal sharing when tempered by combination with a focus on the relationship and shared experiences. Otherwise, autonomy results in separate lives, with self-interest threatening couple identity. An Israeli wife mentions this angle of individualism:

Amiad thinks mostly about himself and puts his needs first. He is very involved with himself. Now his new interest is photography, so he goes off on long weekends with a club he joined to photograph nature. I am left home with the kids. He says he cannot live without his interests . . . but what about us?

This statement contrasts dramatically with the statement of this satisfied American wife:

The first year we were married, John was kind of freaked out by all the responsibility of setting up a home. I suggested that he go off for several months to live in the mountains. He had always dreamed about his having a cabin in the woods. I figured that this was a good time to get it out of his system ... later on there would be kids and he would never get to it. So off he went, and I think it did him a world of good.

When does independence further the relationship and when is it a problem?

The interviews reveal the context in which the first wife is resentful and the context in which the second promoted her partner's getting his independence needs met. The first couple share few joint experiences; the husband studies most of the time and sees his wife's need for time together as a burden, limiting his own time to pursue his hobbies. The second husband is far more attentive to the relationship. Forsaking a lucrative building business to work at home as a carpenter (so that the couple would have more time together), this is a man who disconnects the phone all day Sunday so that no one will disturb the family.

This husband demonstrates how his own sense of autonomy supports his furthering his wife's interests:

It is hard for me when she is out of the house in the evenings. I guess it is true that I would rather she be with me. But I also know that for her to be happy, she needs that art class, and even if she goes three times a week, I make do. I trained myself to manage on my own, and lately I cope by reading more than I used to. I think Sari was holding herself back, so I was the one to go to the community center and find that class for her. I told her to do it.

Compare the autonomous husband who is independent enough to tolerate and foster his wife's personal development, with the dependent role taken here:

Jan went for a visit to Paris ... I managed, but she found the house a madhouse when she got back. I guess she got the message that it really wasn't such a good idea; she hasn't tried that again! May be someday, when the children are bigger. But right now we need her here with us.

In equal partnerships, couples empower each other so that both take equal responsibility for getting their own needs met as well as meeting their partners' needs. Neither plays the role of victim or exploiter. Couples in distress often come to therapy with polarized roles; one is the exploiter and one is the victim. Neither is happy. The following therapy case shows how gender and power interact to create an imbalance in the meeting of individual needs. The unequal power structure resulted in exploitation, making friendship impossible. Gender-stereotyped attitudes support the inequality and maintain the abusive behaviors:

Danny is an Israeli lawyer in his early fifties, married twenty-five years to Talia, who is 45. They have three teenagers. Talia works sporadically in Danny's business, is obese and has been in and out of therapy for many years for depression. Many attempts to involve Danny in marital therapy failed, and Talia related that the last therapist called him hopeless, suggesting that she find herself another man.

Talia has never given up trying to get Danny to pay more attention to her, be nicer to her and make love to her more. Danny makes a great deal of money, is verbally skilled and intelligent. He has had numerous affairs, and is open about this. Talia has only as much money as he gives her, is far less facile with words, and feels too fat to attract other men. Her world revolves around him; his coming home in the evening is a source of anticipation for her, as well as of anger when he is late. Talia makes sure he gets to work every day with a freshly ironed shirt and she goes on during the day to make appointments for him, get to the bank, and meet the accountant.

Talia had tried to find meaning in life through furthering his welfare. However, she was constantly aware that she wasn't getting anywhere, that she was empty inside and that meeting his needs did not really fulfill her. When she thought about taking a course at the university, Danny convinced her that it would be too hard for her to compete with all those young kids. He told her tales about the traffic in the morning and the hard time finding parking around the university. He also came up with tasks at work that suddenly needed to be done. Talia felt that he needed her too much for her to take her course. She had never faced the fact that she was scared herself about competing in the world.

Power is clearly in the hands of one of the partners. Power is exploited so that one partner is getting his or her needs met far more than the other. One plays the role of independent one, the other the dependent one. In actuality, the overtly stronger member is not really autonomous. There is a dependency on the assistance the other supplies, and underlying terror that the other might abdicate their subservient role. The dependent partner has given up personal autonomy in a constant struggle to obtain the other's regard. This kind of neediness only serves to increase the more powerful partner's rejection. There is no autonomy because each partner (no matter what place in the hierarchy) is hooked on 'getting something' from the other.

Personal unhappiness is a result of inhabiting such an oppressive relationship. Danny employs fear to keep Talia out of the university. The submissive partner makes the stronger partner's life miserable: it really is no pleasure to be the center of someone else's universe. It probably comes as no surprise that the power imbalance is mirrored by inequity in the home; the less powerful member does an unfair share of housework and childcare, gets little help and has very little time for personal pursuits. It may be that the powerful partner, feeling trapped in a non-nurturing relationship, tries to extract whatever can be obtained in concrete services.

Equal partners do not allow these kinds of imbalance to transpire. These relationships develop a 'joint couple identity' whereby the self and the relationship are intricately bound up as one. Exploiting the other is like exploiting the self. To promote one's partner's advantage becomes synonymous with promoting one's own interest. Reciprocally, individual growth is the cornerstone for empowering partner growth, and vice versa. Actual sharing in the home is a natural offshoot of an ensuing high level of relationship friendship.

Friendship by overcoming 'gender ambivalence'

Outspoken ambivalence about changing gender roles was typical for most couples. Anyone aspiring to equal partnership quickly encounters the many barriers to change discussed so far: intrapsychic insecurities about gender roles; couple conflicts that maintain the status quo; and societal resistance to equality between the sexes. These are all given in our contemporary transitional environment. How do couples cope with the fact that while change might be ideologically desired, it is complicated to achieve? The 'good old ways' lurk in the background, a seductive solution to the complexity of change. Since we really have no direct experience of a totally liberated society, how do we know it is worth the effort?

We don't. The quite substantial degree of doubt divulged in this study confirms this. Typically, wives reported: guilt about giving up sole responsibility for the parental role; fear of decline in their standards for cleanliness, nutrition and upkeep of social and familial contacts; confusion about how much help to ask from husbands, or how much to limit husbands' work involvement; and reluctance to allow themselves the pleasures of the traditional feminine role, such as staying home with infants.

Husbands mentioned: fear of harming career advancement and social disapproval; anxieties about competency in caring for young children; worries about not earning enough compared to their wives; fears of being thought to be not masculine enough for letting wives provide financially; guilt in enjoying the financial benefits of wives working; and confusion about their own desire to stay home more.

It is impossible to cite all the permutations of gender ambivalence; they were sometimes quite idiosyncratic. Some were humorous. For example, one husband with a homemaker wife said that he did the ironing, but told people at work that she did his shirts, so not to embarrass her. Many wives had their pet terms for their husband's way of doing the wash: 'it turns out a blob' or 'all our clothes are gray' are just two examples.

Some were poignant, demonstrating the heroic attempts of these couples to fashion and create their own gender scripts. A young wife broke down and cried when she related the stress of her first year as both medical intern and new mother. Not willing to take time off from her career, she worked the typical frenzied hours of the intern, while her husband brought the infant to her in the hospital for breast-feeding. She not only ardently missed her new baby, but was the butt of ridicule by colleagues.

Stories showed the apprehension people feel in trusting the opposite sex in typical gendered domains. A wife recounted how her husband had allowed their young son to fall down two flights of stairs when he was home alone with two small children; her husband looked extremely pained during the interview, protesting that it had happened only once. His wife replied that obviously it happened once; she had never left them alone with him again.

An unanticipated difference between happy and unhappy couples attempting to be equal partners is in their management of ambivalence around gender roles. Heightened tension results from ambivalence, and when this is handled poorly, these conflicts reduce the quality of friendship. Friendship was fortified to the extent to which couples helped each other out. Many people voiced their gratitude for a kind of mentoring role their partners took on. A wife was coached by her husband in dealing with an aggressive boss at work, another was taught to fix the car, and another to balance the checkbook. Husbands whose wives let them have their own standards in the kitchen, with the children, and in cleaning, were both most involved with the home and were the happiest.

These men had wives who deliberately moved aside; one wife described intentional outings on the days he is in charge of the children, specifically to allow him to 'bond' with them alone. The wives of these husbands were rewarded by the initiative their husbands took. One husband notices when the bathroom needs cleaning, and does it. This ability to initiate, so coveted by wives, is mostly dependent on the husband having his wife's permission to have his own say in traditionally women's territory. Where husbands were more hesitant, there were signs of wives' subtle devaluation or lack of confidence. One wife mocked her husband's inability to cook without spilling on the floor and leaving spots. Another pointed out that when meals are left to her doctor husband, they eat only frozen foods. (Her husband protested to me: 'What is wrong with frozen fish?' I didn't have an answer to that!)

Husbands inevitably looked abashed at these comments, weakly defending their abilities. An Israeli family therapist husband related this rather sad outcome:

> When we had our first child, I was eager to do everything. I had taken care of my own brothers and sisters and felt I knew what it took. But Ruth deliberately kept me out of it. She insisted on having her way with feedings, like when to introduce solid foods. Slowly, slowly over the years I stopped helping. Today I am totally uninvolved. She is unhappy about it, and we have discussed this openly. She is sorry about what she did.

But I am still very resentful. Anyway, my private practice has grown so that even if I wanted to become more involved now I couldn't. And Ruth wants us to move to a bigger house; that means more money and that means more work. But I feel a sense of loss – I never got to feel I was a real father, the way I wanted to be.

Tension was especially pronounced when partners sent confusing messages to each other, transforming internal turmoil into couple conflict. For example, Jenny, a 70-year-old feminist community organizer, longed for her husband Sam to both provide well for the family, but also to share a great deal of time with her. She never let up in voicing her dissatisfaction that he was such a poor provider, and after fifteen years of marriage, divorced him in order to prod him into taking more financial responsibility. They continued to live together, with the divorce as a deliberate attempt on her part to turn him into a more achievement-oriented man. Sam liked to putter around on his boat, was good with his hands, and liked staying home. Jenny did not appear aware that there was a contradiction in her desire for both a 'new' type of man who spends most of his time with his wife, and a fast-track man who is out in the world. Married previously to a successful doctor, Jenny wanted it all; she could not respect him without the money, but needed the intimacy as well. Instead of working her ambivalence out herself, she projected it back into the relationship.

For his part, Sam was ambivalent about his role. On the one hand, he rejected the traditional male provider role. On the other, he had not mastered the emotional expressiveness of a more androgynous role. He therefore avoided conflict fervently; whenever Jenny's demands got on his nerves, he went out to farm for weeks at a time.

The degree of personal autonomy, discussed previously, supports the ability to work out ambivalence within the individual, and not in the relationship. Paradoxically, the most satisfied people also mentioned the most ambivalence. However, they claimed their doubts as their own. Their happiness seems related to viewing their ambivalence as personal dilemmas, not feelings caused by the partner. The most happy people were able express the most self-doubt about gender issues:

I really wonder sometimes if I am being a sucker – after all, I see the way other men here live, how they get to put their feet up when they get home, and I know that what I want, what we need, is for me to be involved. It is hard, especially when friends joke about me being a sucker ... it is hard.

Husband (Israel)

A firm sense of personal autonomy permits these people to endure ambivalent feelings; not being sure of being 'enough of a man', or 'enough of a woman', is very scary. These are people who are daring to create their own gender scripts, without models, often without support from extended family or from colleagues at work. They need to be personally autonomous to perceive their lifestyles as a result of their own choice. When not an expression of such empowerment, ambivalence about change in gender roles is a major force in creating relationship conflict. These examples, taken from transcripts of the more distressed couples, illustrate how internal anxieties about change get translated into couple tension:

I do like the perks of Lana's working – we got to go to Hawaii last year. But it bugs me that she isn't here when I get home. And quite frankly, I do make life hard for her. I don't feel very good about myself since her salary is higher than mine ... I wasn't prepared for that. I find that I am in a bad mood a lot of the time, and I get irritated at her more than I used to.

Husband (USA)

Women especially seem to feel bad about themselves in these situations, as they are well aware that they are increasing couple distress, and feel they are also failing in their roles as family peacekeeper. Many of these more unhappy women used self-derogatory language, calling themselves: 'selfish', 'bitchy', 'a pain'. One English wife called herself 'a medusa'. Often these were 'superwomen' wives who felt they had little choice but to fulfill both traditional and more modern female roles. They expressed a great deal of stress and rarely felt entitled to time for themselves.

The uncompromising demands of these women were evident in all three countries. However, the form it took was culturally determined. An Israeli psychotherapist wife was seeing forty clients a week, supervising students and teaching. She also felt that she had to make hot meals for her children every day, and invite her relatives to dinner on the weekends. To her, it was obvious that she had to cook for these family dinners as well, showing her relatives that she was keeping up with all the other 'Jewish Mamas' in the neighborhood. An American university lecturer wife was full time at the university, but felt that she had to drive her children to their numerous after-school activities, so that they would not feel different from all the other suburban children. An English high school science teacher worked full time, accompanied her husband to all his football matches, went to watch him race cars, volunteered in their church, and personally arranged and carried out weekly visits to both his and her parents.

Compare these examples to Sonia, an American mother who stayed home with her one child and also took in foster children of mothers on crack. She considered this work a calling, and devoted many hours to it. However she was careful to nurture herself:

I always make sure to get to see at least three friends a week, and I make it a point to hike alone in the mountains often. I have numerous activities, but sometimes I just decide it is enough, I need a rest. So I take off a week. I don't feel bad about it, on the contrary. I know that I am entitled to it and that everyone will be a lot better off if I feel good. Some weeks I have to work round the clock because these crack babies cry all night – they are in a state of withdrawal. So after care for a particularly harrowing one, I will take off for a while, not accept a new one from protective services. When I feel emotionally and physically ready, I call them. The social workers know me by now, they don't pressure me.

This assertive woman used the term 'entitlement' in describing her ability to care for herself. This is a sense that happiest women had about their lives, and it is supported by the friendship they received from their husbands to pursue life their way. The combination of a high level of personal autonomy and friendship allowed these women to work out their own lifestyles, to navigate the turbulent waters of gender changes, devising their own course. One American homemaker mother said:

My mother is a biologist and that is what she wanted from me. She pushed me from day one to have a career, preferably in biology, but certainly in science. I love her dearly and want to make her happy. But what can I do, it just isn't me. I am happiest staying home with the children. I feel it is a privilege and I am grateful to Jon for helping me do it. My Mom doesn't really understand it, but she sees how content I am, so she has learned to accept it.

One of the most startling revelations for me was seeing how equal partnership women seemed to have created the context to live in ease with their being women. They find their own unique balance of motherhood, work, leisure activities and social relationships. They take responsibility for their choices, and have the friendly support of their partners, who made sure that these women had conditions to actualize their choices. Often these husbands were envious of their wives:

> I wish I had the freedom that Janet has. I am too dedicated to my job, and she seems to feel the freedom to follow her heart. I could if I had the guts, I know she would support me. But I am not as adventurous as she is, I care too much what people think!
>
> Husband (USA)

Truly, it seems that women in the happy equal relationships have managed to find a lifestyle that allows them to combine the feminine and the masculine traits in a unique combination suitable to their personalities. Their partners often cited being happy primarily because their wives were happy:

> Sure it is hard to stay home with the children when they are sick, especially since the other teachers feel like I am slacking off, they are resentful and I understand it ... since they have to substitute for me. None of them stay home with their children. I probably won't get promoted this year, even though I deserve a better position, for that reason. But it is worth it ... just knowing how Sarah is blossoming these days ... it makes up for it all.
>
> Husband (UK)

An important part of therapy, targeting and working on gender ambivalence, is described briefly in this example:

Yael, a 33-year-old public relations executive, came to therapy saying that she and Gabi, her husband of five years, were living parallel lives and were sullenly angry at each other all the time. Yael worked a 60-hour week, despite having a 13-month-old son at home with an au pair. Gabi was angry that no one took responsibility for the home, and expressed it this way: 'It feels like there are two men in our marriage.' No one wanted to be 'the wife', so the au pair had the responsibility. Both Gabi and Yael agreed that this was not a realistic solution, since the au pair could not decide what needed to be done. Yael was nervous and stressed and blamed Gabi for blaming her. She did not see the home as any more her responsibility than his and was furious at his lack of participation. Gabi, also a busy executive in an engineering firm, was interested in being an equal partner and wanted to be her friend, but Yael didn't believe that.

Sessions alone with Yael revealed the extent of her own ambivalence about work versus home. Her parents had been overly critical of her, saying she would not amount to much. Her father, a career officer, was especially important to her and his lack of encouragement was deeply hurtful. Yael took it upon herself to prove her parent wrong, although she had internalized their negative opinion in her low self-esteem. On the fast track, no amount of accomplishment gave her satisfaction – she could not assuage the gnawing feeling that she was not okay. She adored her young child, but rarely saw him and when she did she was exhausted. At work, she was exploited by her two male co-partners as she attempted to show that she was worthy of their decision to make her a partner. She had never explored any of these issues; Yael was unfamiliar with the language of emotions and was rushing about too fast to slow down and reflect. Seeing men as authorities and more knowing than her, she believed that Gabi was omnipotent. The fact that he didn't comprehend what to do made her feel he did not want to help; it was inconceivable to her that he did not have the solution to their problems.

Individual sessions with Yael shifted her focus to herself, and allowed her to start to articulate her ambivalence: she began to speak of not having friends, of wishing to be able to relax and not having any hobbies of her own. She also began to see that she did not know how to be a friend, and therefore could not give Gabi adequate support. Focus on herself paved the way for couples sessions that enhanced their communication, allowing Gabi to start to talk about his emotional needs. Yael began to see him as another human being, and not the mythical 'Man' who had all the answers. Her emerging ability to support him, and her securing the support from him that she needed, resulted in increased sharing at home. Yael also felt that Gabi was her friend, and his more attentive listening facilitated focusing even more on herself. Eventually she quit her company and spent six months at home, re-evaluating her work goals. She eventually obtained a partnership in an organization that genuinely appreciated her; a new reflection of her developing self-appreciation.

Chapter 4

Shared power

The road to mutual empowerment

Shared power is the cornerstone of shared partnership. Empowerment in intimate relationships is the concept that best sums up shared power; empowered partners both feel powerful, have maximized choice and autonomy, but share decisions and a focus on the relationship. There is a distinct balance between individual and couple concerns, fostering the reciprocal growth of both partners and development of the relationship.

Empowerment of both partners is a process of mutual growth created over time. Rarely do partners begin a marriage with the ability to empower each other. It appears that for most empowerment is accomplished by changes and developments occurring throughout the couple's history together.

THE TRANSFORMATION

At some point in the interview, I took out a piece of paper and asked if the couple would agree to do an experiential exercise.[1] Each partner had to obtain the paper, representing a cherished issue or item for each. They could not jointly hold the paper (this would have been one half the solutions) nor could they tear it in half (this would have been the other half). Rather, the couple had to figure out which individual should get the paper. Despite differences in what the paper signified and in the process of negotiation, for every case but one, in the end the wife got the paper. In the one case in which the husband held the paper, it was because they both decided that it was safer with him; he was seen as the practical one. What do the results of this exercise in negotiation mean?

For partners to empower each other, wives specifically have to quit their submissive and self-effacing role with regard to men.

Compared to traditional marriage equal partnership vests women with an unusual degree of power and control. Perhaps equal partnership allows each gender to experience the unexperienced: women get to assert themselves, while men in happy equal partnerships seem delighted to lean on someone else, rather than be in charge. Many of these men appear attracted to strength in women, often noting their admiration for the wives' intelligence, guts and strong character.

To reach this state, women need to perceive themselves and be perceived as unusually strong, and this has to be alright with both of them. The process of getting stronger for wives emerges as a crucial turning point in many equal partner relationships. It was often the wife who initiated the change in power dynamics by becoming stronger. This was true even when her strength was obtained through her partner's efforts on her behalf:

Judy and Leonard, an American couple, had been best friends since high school. Judy, coming from an abusive home in which her father was an alcoholic and her mother a battered wife, suffered from anxieties and low self-esteem. A confirmed feminist, Leonard encouraged and coached her since she was 16, helping her make friends, get a job and go to the university. By the time she was 25, she was strong enough to demand that he treat her less as a child, and more as an equal. She said she started to feel he was patronizing her; for example, he told her how to take care of the house and their child. Leonard was delighted, even though it meant giving up the familiar protector role he liked. He said, 'Even though Judy was angry during that period, I knew it would end up alright – I even had the thought that I had really succeeded with her if she was confident enough to take me on! I did feel for a while as if I was out of a job, but then I began to get more involved in my own career and I think it was really good. I knew it was important to Judy that I stop patronizing her ... I did not always have all the answers and it was a relief to be able to rely on her for a change.'

The motif of female strength was typical of all the couples, whether the outcome was advantageous to the relationship or not.

For second marriages, often the wife went through the transformation in her first marriage or alone after her divorce. These were women who wanted never again to be dominated, and remarried resolving 'not to take it anymore'. Other wives were assertive with their partners early on at the start of the marriage, setting the rules and making it clear that they were not going to be like other women:

Yuval and Miriam, an Israeli couple in their forties and married twenty-five years described many years of sharing and happiness. Miriam related that when they first married, Yuval tried to tell her not to wear so much make-up. Coming from Hungary, make-up was a sign for him of her being 'cheap'. Miriam, a native-born Israeli said: 'I made it clear that he better forget trying to tell me how to dress, behave or think about anything. I had no intention of being like my mother, who was terrified of my father's tyranny. I was going to have a relationship in which I was my own person. Yuval was taken aback by how determined I was, but he accepted it. He tried once more to tell me I should not go to folk dancing, since I might meet someone. I told him off again, and that was that. That kind of thing hasn't happened again in many years.'

For the majority of first marriages, the transformation initiated a period of transition for the marriage. Generally wives wanted more emotional contact, more concrete help or wanted their husbands to participate more in the decision-making around family issues. There were numerous stories of how the transformation was initiated. Triggers included: wives joining a group such as Overeaters Anonymous; going into therapy; having to be the sole provider and seeing she could do it; getting fed up with husband's insulting behavior such as interrupting her conversation at parties; the husband's breakdown as when alcoholism became severe; leaving a familiar part of the country, friends or family and finding herself alone; going through a major illness such as cancer; getting fed up with one aspect of the traditional role such as responsibility for the couple's social contacts; having a series of accidents such as almost burning down the house, losing a parent, or having a child. This is only a partial list! The individual

stories are just that, personal stories but all resulted in wives
starting to expect more for themselves and push for change in the
power balance of the relationship.

The transformation theme was cross-cultural. A British couple
told of the wife taking on the traditional stay-at-home role without
enough reflection; then of her having a breakdown, feeling that
this taken-for-granted role did not fit her needs. She decided to
work full time outside the home. An American wife told of
attempting to be superwoman both at work and at home, doing
it all, and getting burned out and quitting her job. An Israeli
woman transformed her life when she went into therapy, discovering that she had automatically rejected feminine roles, did not
know where the kitchen was, and wanted to become more home
oriented.

The theme remains the same: at some point the woman feels
the need for change in her lifestyle; the transformation was a
search for the true self, for a more firm identity and usually
involved an integration of the feminine and the masculine traits.

Men did not report this phenomenon to nearly the same extent,
although some men also changed careers or reduced their workload. Women's stories always connected their own personal
growth to their demands for change in their marriages. One typical
aspect of the transformation was the woman's increasing willingness to leave the marriage. Although only a few actually did, an
'emotional divorce' was common. The transformation was thus
distinguished by the woman being dead sure of her right to
demand change, and her resolve not to back down, no matter
what.

The period of change is uncomfortable. Some women used
dominating tactics, such as refusing to have sex or refusing to talk.
Others stopped being affected by their partners' previously effective dominating strategies. One woman used to get very hurt by
her husband's silences; after entering the university, she let him
stew. Another woman knew that it was very important to her
husband that she attend therapy with him; she refused to go unless
he start helping at home. Women became indifferent to their
husbands' needs. One American woman described how her
husband entered their marriage with a physical problem, causing
him to sleep an inordinate number of hours and naturally limiting
his participation in childrearing. After the wife joined a support
group, she lost patience with him. Despite his ailment, she stopped

getting up early to get their son off to school, insisting he do it. He got over his problem by going into individual therapy and working on the underlying emotional cause.

The vicissitudes of the outcome were determined by the degree of the wives' stubborn resolve and by the manner in which the husbands responded. Happy relationships are characterized by the husbands' acceptance of the transformation as a positive transition. Husbands may not have enjoyed the tension, but they basically realized that wives' requests needed to be taken seriously. These were men who were willing to make considerable changes for the sake of their wives' happiness. The wives' transition often led to husbands' change as well; some husbands entered therapy, some took less demanding jobs, some changed their behavior at home. All made some changes that were in the direction of more equality.

In more unhappy marriages, the men did not view their own interests as ultimately served by their wives' changes. Rather, they were put off and threatened by the increasing demands. More traditional men felt put down by taking orders from a woman: while they might have believed in equality, their pride was hurt that she was the one demanding the change. In resisting, men either entered into an open power struggle with their wives or withdrew, leaving the relationship distant and cold.

At the time of the interview, many of the unhappy couples appeared stuck in this transitional stage; the husbands stubbornly refused to budge, the wives were often depressed, the marriage quality very poor. In two cases, the wives had serious symptoms; one was severely agoraphobic and the other clinically depressed, needing occasional hospitalizations.

For example, an Israeli couple were open about their impasse:

Reuvan and Dorit are a young Israeli couple in their late twenties with three small children; a son of three, and twin girls of a year and a half. Reuvan had never ever changed a diaper. His equal partnership existed solely on the attitude level. He believed in equality for women, but not in the home. His egalitarian ideology was expressed in the idea that Dorit should work outside the home. This was an advancement from his own upbringing, as his mother stayed home to raise the children.

Dorit was from a poor Moroccan family and was used to the

idea that women serve men. She had been very happy to marry Reuven, who came from a higher status wealthy family. After the birth of their first child, Dorit gladly took on all the care of the baby, never questioning that this was solely her responsibility. She continued to work as a secretary and managed also to take care of the children. She always believed in equality and was content to have it expressed in her going out in the evenings to a class. She always made sure to get a babysitter, so that Reuvan would not have to care for their child. Compared to her own mother, going out alone in the evening was a daring and unconventional thing to do. After the birth of the twins, Dorit simply could not manage. She was unable to care for all three children and continue to work. She was severely depressed for a while, as Reuvan said he had no intention of helping out.

Dorit had become obese, and joined Overeaters Anonymous. The women there were very supportive and encouraged her to become more assertive. She began to demand that Reuvan take on more responsibility. He made it clear that if she expected to stay with him, he would not do this. After a great deal of marital turmoil, she prevailed and he did take on some care of the twins, but no more. Dorit was left with few options; she wanted Reuvan and also did not see a way to raise three small children on her own. She was bitter, but resigned. Dorit had asked to be interviewed as part of her continuing battle to try to bring up the topics she wanted to address. The couple rarely talked, but when they did it was to fight about Reuvan's not helping enough.

Reuvan began the interview by stating defiantly: 'Equality – there is no such thing in marriage!' He used the interview to make sure Dorit got the message: he was doing about all he ever planned to do – she should expect no more.

An intriguing variant of the transformation going awry was an American couple, both medical doctors. The balance of power in this couple was deceptively traditional, although they might not agree about this.

Here, it was the husband John who wanted children, wanting to stay home with the babies himself, and limiting his career advancement to do this. The wife, Alice was more committed to her career, wanted to limit the number of children and was interested in putting off starting a family until their careers were more firmly established. John insisted, and she felt she would lose him if she did not give in. Obviously she was the one to become pregnant, while he took the 'paternal leave'. She was miserable since the pregnancies were difficult and she would return to work two weeks after birth. She had to give up her dream of work on an Indian reservation and her commitment to their social cause; they could not take small infants to a reservation. However, she also felt she could not complain; all her friends and family thought she was so lucky to have a husband who wanted to be so involved in the home!

Not having the social support for her complaints (he not only helped, he ran the home), Alice could not identify the power imbalance that was making her so unhappy. The transformation was swamped. Is this a new type of male domination to be seen more in the future – 'new' men who want to fulfill their own personal longings to nurture children, but who bulldoze their way into this lifestyle without fairly negotiating with their wives? The therapist could be caught up in enthusiasm for the 'new man', without realizing he is the old man in new clothes.

The transformation discussed here is a microcosm, in the home, of the transformation in women's status in society in general. Women are becoming stronger. Will they persist, despite the backlash? And will men eventually accept the changes they demand?

WOMEN'S ANGER: LEARNING TO EMBRACE BITCHINESS

How the husband handled the wife's anger emerged as a common concern for many couples. Related to wives' transformation is the degree of wives' anger which the male partner is able to absorb. As women become aware of varying degrees of unfairness in their relationships, they feel the anger they might long have denied. Traditionally, men have been threatened by anger in women, whether because it shakes the power hierarchy, or because it demands competency in dealing with intense emotions. Anger from an intimate partner is uniformly hard for men to handle.

Women also find male anger threatening; fear of violence, domination, and previous traumas from male aggression all make intimate partners' anger scary for wives. However, women are openly fearful and tend to back down when their partners are angry. While underlying fear may be playing an important role for men, their partners' anger makes them angry; they retaliate. They may withdraw, disconnecting the intimacy so needed by wives, or may become aggressive and preoccupied with 'winning'. While research shows that verbal and physical aggression is equally expressed at the pre-marriage and newly wed stage, by the first year of marriage, wives are expressing far less anger than their husbands, a decline that continues throughout the marriage (Tavris, 1989). Obviously this is not because the wives are becoming increasingly happy, research is clear that the opposite is true. However, the results of getting angry are far more dangerous for women than for men; women learn to curb their anger, often turning it into depression, overeating, or other self-destructive behaviors.

Many women in this study mentioned being angry with other men, such as their fathers, brothers, bosses, or previous husbands due to injustice, discriminatory, or abusive conduct. This was especially true for ethnic minority women from traditional cultures, such as this American woman born in Mexico:

> My family was the typically patriarchal family in Mexico; my father's word was law, and I was expected to accept my brothers as my authorities. They could even come over to my school and make sure I was behaving myself. I had to serve them all dinner, together with my mother and sisters. I remember from a very early age hating it, feeling it was wrong, but not being able to do anything. My sisters did not understand my anger – today they are all married to macho Mexican-Americans and they still don't understand me. I refused to marry Ricardo, although I am happy to live with him, because I just don't trust men.

What was special about the happily married husbands was the sensitive and accepting way they handled their wives' anger, regardless of the source. These men do not appear threatened by anger; some even appear to enjoy it. Often they married the particular woman because she seemed gutsy and strong, or they thought that with help she could become strong. One American man related this incident:

> Sandy had been bitching for ages about my not helping out enough. I was kind of enjoying ignoring her. It made her so pissed off. So one day, when we had a whole bunch of people over for dinner, she comes in with the laundry and dumps the whole thing on my head. I thought she was great actually! She was right, I deserved it. I knew she meant business.

Husbands in happy equal partnerships tended to be sensitive to signs that their wives were angry or fed up about something. One husband understood his wife's chronic problem with her knee as an expression of rage at her father and at him, initiating talks that changed the balance of power between them. Some men helped their wives get over their fear of expressing anger; such was the case of Peter, who helped his American wife June work through the trauma of her first marriage to a traditional American-Indian man. An African-American man told of staying home with his wife when he noticed she was depressed; despite his busy career, he said that he knew she was nursing rage at her former husband and needed his support. This same man taught his wife to express anger directly. Telling of an ugly racist incident with their middle-class neighbor, this husband coached his wife to fight back.

One of the most common findings in all three cultures was the expression of gratitude on the part of wives for their husbands' willingness to listen to their anger attentively without reciprocating. It seemed that for many women, this was so important that when they had it, they were willing to overlook many other limitations:

> I don't need him to talk much. It is really OK with me that he is kind of quiet. What is important is that he lets me get my anger out, I don't have to sit with it. I know he wants to know what is upsetting me.
>
> Wife (UK)

It seems that by encouraging wives to express their anger openly, husbands are rather unconsciously helping them become equal. In a marriage in which the husband felt less powerful (there were a few like this), it was the wife who coached the husband to stand up to her, so that it was the husband who underwent a transformation. In this situation, it was also the husband who had to learn to get angry, and the wife who had to listen to his anger. It appears that helping the less powerful partner become more powerful is an expression of these couples' commitment to mutual growth. Empowerment means that each helps the other actualize their potential and thus strengthen whatever is lacking.

Many therapy couples evidence the husband's underlying difficulty with his wife's push for change and her concomitant anger at him. For example:

Hannah and Rami are a young Israeli couple with a baby daughter. In the course of their seven years together (three before marriage) they were very close and loving. A rather unconventional couple, both saw him as the sensitive one, and themselves as very lucky to have found each other. She devoted herself to his emotional well-being, finding this very satisfying. It meant many long conversations (mostly about him), a great deal of emotional sharing and togetherness. They said they shared equally at home.

Thus it was a total shock for Rami to come home and find Hannah in bed with one of her high school pupils. It did not make any sense to either of them, and Hannah, who usually behaved in a rational manner, was afraid that she was going crazy in her infatuation for her young student. In therapy it quickly emerged that Hannah had repressed all her anger and never allowed Rami to see her upset. She was essentially tired of his being the one getting all the attention in the relationship and discovered that she was repeating a pattern started in childhood. Her father, a charismatic figure, used her to listen to his stories and troubles, which she gladly did since it made her feel important. With Rami, Hannah also felt that she had this important role, but was increasingly angry about neglecting her own needs. She never thought that she could rage at him; he was too sensitive, and anyway, she was so lucky to have such a devoted sharing husband.

This couple was able to utilize therapy quickly and effectively once the underlying dynamic was uncovered. Having a firm commitment to friendship and sharing, they were able to adjust the relationship to create more space for her. It did mean changes in his dependency on her attention, but he was willing to make them. She realized that protecting him from her anger was risking her marriage, and resolved to be open to him (and to herself) whenever she felt irritated. Rami later called to say that he felt that the affair was actually for the best. He learned to be more emotionally independent and this helped him grow as well.

CONVINCING

In learning to handle their anger, many of the equal partnership couples moved towards helping the wives negotiate with their husbands. One theme that emerged in the interviews is that of wives learning to convince their husbands. Wives had to learn to be more logical to reach their husbands, to take their place along-side them as equal partners. Being competent to argue one's point, using facts and options in a rational manner and refusing to give in are all excluded from the feminine role. In this study, there were women lawyers who mentioned that they were easily able to be equal partners because they entered marriage knowing how to develop a logical argument, were not afraid of conflict, and thrived in the give and take of verbal sparring.

Most women, however, are intimidated when their husbands begin to chop away at their ideas. Women tend to take this behavior personally and see it as aggressive, whereas their male partner views pulling an opinion apart as the natural thing to do. However, men can be unaware that they tend to impose their view of reality on their female partners. Feeling rather entitled to being the authority in a male–female relationship, the imposition is invisible to men. Neither partner may be aware of just how handicapped the wife may be in getting her view of reality across to her husband.

One American wife in this study took a course in bookkeeping just to be better able to convince her husband in their talks about money. Women are required to overcome several deeply held convictions to become good negotiators: that their view of reality is less objective than their male partners; that a logical argument is more significant than an emotional one; that to stick to your opinion is inconsiderate and stubborn; that to be 'nice' you need to accept the other's point of view. Obviously, this means ditching the subordinate female role. The feminine role is so intimately tied into making the other person feel comfortable, that it conflicts with being convincing. For many women, to win a point is somehow to lose (the relationship). Consider the statement of this American wife:

I have been fighting with him for years to be more involved with our sons. But especially since I am working, I don't know if I really have the right to ask this from him ... he is so tired and I earn so much less than he. So I back down, but I still want his help.

Compare this to the attitude of this American wife:

I wanted us to have children, and he didn't. So I spent about five years convincing him. I never gave up. I tried to find all the arguments I could. The funny thing is that the most obvious one is the one that worked. I talked to him about his denying me one of the more important experiences a woman can have. He sat on this one for a while and then said ... 'that's it, you are right!'

Of course, he may have given in because he did not have the strength to resist after five years. But other couples demonstrated that being convincing is a crucial principle, and where the husband is cooperative, convincing works:

She is usually right, so it isn't that hard to convince me. Living with her I have learned that she is more intuitive than me, and she has lots of experiences I have not had. So once she really wants something, and she doesn't give in quickly but explains her side, I usually go along with her ... she is usually right.

Husband (USA)

Power struggles in marriage develop when wives who cannot convince their partners on important issues try obsessively to get their way on smaller issues. A wife in the study called it 'settling for small victories'. Many cases in therapy reflect this dynamic:

Irina, a housewife, came to therapy because of depression. In meeting with her husband Saul, it was obvious that Irina was angry at him, but fearful of expressing her anger directly. He was forceful and dominating, and always had an answer for everything. Irina had realized early on in their thirty-year marriage that if she wanted to get along with him, she had better go along with him. She took on the traditional stay-at-home feminine role that was imposed on her. Although she wanted to be a nurse, he was against her working nights and being out of the home. She knew he was limiting her, but could not see how she could defy him. Consequently, their marriage was dominated by frequent fights on daily life issues: who promised what, who was supposed to do what, who didn't, who was late, who said what. At first therapy seemed like a myriad of issues, and as soon as one was successfully tackled, another appeared. There seemed to be no escape, until Irina's overall lack of control and helplessness became the treatment focus. She was terrified to articulate her major complaint: her inability to chose her lifestyle. Irina needed a lot of support from the therapist to face Saul about this. In the therapy sessions, all the daily life issues seemed to dry up as the underlying power structure came into view.

Every relationship counselor has had the experience of feeling out of control; therapy can be a free-for-all of accusations, counter-accusations and blame. These frustrating sessions lack focus, and everyone present knows the real issues are being eluded. The problem of focus reflects couples' resistance; often both partners are afraid to face an unpleasant fact – that the entire relationship has become exploitative. Both the victim and the exploiter are loath to confront this directly, although there is relief after the initial discomfort.

HONORING THE FEMININE

One of the central forces behind equal partners' ability to accept and nurture wives' empowerment is their acceptance of femininity as equal to yet different from masculinity. In the Jungian sense (Canarton, 1992) femininity includes an emphasis on: feelings, merging, cooperation, passive acceptance, a process orientation, intuition, and 'being'. According to this view, masculinity includes: rationality, striving, competition, action, an outcome orientation, logical, and 'doing'. Seen this way, both sexes require having both, each being the 'shadow' of the other. Neither is better.

Western society is built on the elevation of masculine values, such as achievement, and on derogation of the feminine values, such as passive acceptance. Far Eastern cultures have reversed this preference, making them attractive to many in the West who are searching for a way out of the straitjacket of competitive striving.

It is the masculine values that stress the dichotomy of 'more than' or 'better than', which itself negates the potential for both masculine and feminine being mutually interdependent and both necessary.

Reflecting these values, the feminine tasks include caring for others, interest in beauty, and involvement in daily life maintenance tasks. It appears that happier equal partner husbands are more in touch with their own 'feminine processes', and are thus more able to accept the feminine tasks of homelife as worthy; they are seen as equal in value to those tasks more valued by society, tasks that earn money. For example, the happiest husbands in the study allowed their own intuition more freedom. One American husband decided to become a nurse, moving from the fast track of corporate life to the feminine world of caring for patients. His explanation·

> It felt like the right time to do it . . . I guess it really isn't logical, since I am now making a third of what I made before. I tried not to think about it too much, because I would have backed out. Jill encouraged me to go with my gut feeling, although it meant that she had to take on a full-time job while I was studying. We now earn $30,000 each, a lot less than before. But this is much more who I am.

This is a radical shift for both men and women, who from early childhood learn to view the masculine as better. It is a deviation that gives power to women, who become the family 'experts' on femininity; women are teachers in nurturing, emotionality, beauty. Men in this study voiced their urge and willingness to learn from their wives:

> She had to invest a lot in teaching me to open up. I am like my Dad – a closed book. She has a lot of patience and I don't envy her, being with me. All that I know about expressing myself comes from her investment in me. She is like my teacher.
>
> Husband (Israel)

> We came to realize that issues like who does the dishes are not the real problem. We got to be aware that what we really wanted was emotional closeness, but if we weren't getting that, then we started a fight about the dishes. But the problem was, that I did not have the ability to be as open as Julie. I went to therapy and that lasted five years. She was very supportive, and

was like a second therapist. It is getting a lot better but I don't know if I ever will get to be as open as she is.

Husband (UK)

A phrase that became key in identifying happy equal partner men was 'I still have a long way to go to catch up to her'.

For couples where the husband evidenced less power, their transformation entailed their wives coming to value femininity as well. In all these cases, the husband was responsible for the home while the wife rarely went into the kitchen:

For years I ran by the kitchen – I didn't want Ari to think I was going to stop off there! After our crisis, and after Ari got stronger, I went into the supermarket for the first time in ten years. I was so scared of being like my mother that I rejected all the female things. Now we are more balanced – I never will be much good at that stuff, but I think it is important work and needs to be shared.

Wife (Israel)

Problems honoring the feminine exist in one or both partners in the less happy group. For example, an American wife expressed sorrow that she was never home with her son, now aged 13. She looks back at her decision to work full time in law as a mistake and envies her lawyer husband, who took a teaching job to be home more. She clearly was not able to allow expression of her feminine side and valued outside work more than childcare. A more satisfied American wife reported how she moved between full-time involvement in her career and periods of staying home, depending on her felt needs. This woman said:

But even during those periods when I stay home, I am earning just as much in my own way. I am part of the 'Miser Club'; we have our own magazine, save coupons, I cook all the meals, grow all the vegetables, and we share cooperatively between us to cut down costs.

Her husband appears to share her respect for the housewife role. This in sharp contrast to this American husband:

I told her that she really should be out there making some money, like many of the other wives. It doesn't look good that she is afraid to go out . . . we don't really need the money, but hey, she hasn't got much of a life, right?

Often satisfied husbands had stayed home for some substantial period to care for children. They usually enjoyed this period of their lives and it reinforced their appreciation for the feminine role. Also, many spoke with fondness of their mothers, seen as strong role models, worthy of imitating. Many appeared to identify more with their mothers than their fathers, saying that they did not know their father enough and could never be themselves around them.[2]

The distressed couples seen in therapy often both unconsciously derogate femininity, mirroring society's elevation of masculine values. The at-home wife is viewed as working less, even though her day probably involves less rest than his; she concurs as well, blaming herself for her fatigue and stress. They may both view him as the stronger, more rational partner, her the 'hysterical one' who has emotional fits, needing him to steady her. Rather than viewing her emotionality as a resource for the couple, they see it as a liability to be defeated. This supports women's self-devaluation, hinders their chance to overcome their own ambivalence, erodes their sense of entitlement, and ultimately undercuts their capability to be equal partners.

Chapter 5

Towards an integrative model of treatment goals for couples

The foundation of equal partnership appears grounded in the creation of a deep friendship, supported by shared power and mutual empowerment of both partners. Two further themes were located that together can comprise an integrated model of equal partnership and form treatment goals for couples. The egalitarian couples interviewed had to overcome gender differences in communication in order to create a relationship system based on friendship. In addition, they had to create a coherent ideology of values concerning their relationship, their family and their community. These two themes will be described next. A discussion of the way that these themes interact and the manner in which they form treatment goals will pave the way for the next chapters on the treatment methods.

OVERCOMING THE GENDER GAP IN COMMUNICATION

Communication is the central pathway of contact between intimate partners, be it verbal or nonverbal. Communication comprises all those micro-interactions that make up a relationship: who says what to whom and how; who does not, and why not, as well as those messages embedded in actions. It is through the profusion of significant interactions that couples communicate their respect and sense of fairness, or mutual derogation and sense of injustice.

In an early but seminal text on communication, Watzlawick *et al.* (1967) set out the basic pragmatics of human communication, introducing the notion of 'metacommunication'. Any communication implies a commitment to the relationship, defines what relationship the participants have, both conveys information and at the same time imposes behavior (Bateson *et al.*,1956).

Power issues are primarily encoded in metacommunication. The more powerful partner chooses the topic for discussion, interrupts more, changes the topic, ends the conversation, or chooses the time and place of conversation. Having the freedom to comment about the metacommunication rules is also governed by rules related to power. In equal relationships, both partners can initiate topics, interrupt each other equally, disclose intimate information equally, end the conversation, etc. They can also 'metacommunicate' about the communication: both can freely analyze their communication, and both partners can comment on dissatisfactions about the communication.

There were many examples in the interviews of equal partner couples 'metacommunicating' freely about their dialogue with the interviewer. An American couple interrupted with this:

> When you were just talking now about our fights I had the feeling you were angry about something right now . . . is that true? What is going on? You don't think I explained it right?
>
> Husband (USA)

Power inequality makes this type of disclosure impossible; by its very nature, power can not be freely commented on. In a distressed couple this kind of comment might be met with: 'Me? Upset? What are you talking about?' Distressed couples have rigid power structures not allowing for an open dialogue. It is on the level of metacommunication that intimacy is most damaged through inequality; it is through the ability to comment about the communication that people get to feel the closest. Strangers on a train can share their deepest secrets (content), but would be very hesitant about commenting on their own conversation (metacommunication). In effect, to metacommunicate freely is to be able to say anything. And to say anything is to feel intimate. In the section on therapy methods, we will see how the therapist can foster equality by using metacommunication discussions with the partners.

The common gender differences found in the research on marriage can best be understood as reflecting the interaction between gender and power (see Thompson and Walker, 1989, for a review of this literature). While these are gender differences, they could be expected to be found in the relationship between employers and their subordinates as well:

1 Men discuss facts and women discuss emotions, so that men have a narrower range of feeling talk, disclose less about themselves, and are less understood by their partners than vice versa. If they discuss a negative emotion, it most likely will be anger.
2 Women are aware of more problems than men, are more anxious about the relationship, monitor relationship problems more.
3 Men end conversations more by withdrawing from conflict.
4 Women offer more compromise solutions and more supportive statements than do their partners.
5 Women become increasingly more negative and critical in talk with intimate partners during conflict situations, and their partners become more increasingly intellectual and withdrawn.

Tannen (1990) proposed that men's communication revolves around 'report' while women's revolves around 'rapport'. Men reaffirm the power hierarchy and make commands; women maintain and nurture their connections through communication. Since their goals are different, many misunderstandings are created. Many of these 'misunderstandings' occur when the male partner attends to the power dimension of metacommunication, while his wife attends to the meaning the communication has about the state of their connection. For example, a couple are lost during a trip; the wife, wanting to help, suggests that they ask a passerby for directions. The husband, concerned with his self-reliant image, feels put down: 'I can find it myself with this map'. He is angry, she feels hurt and misunderstood.

This interaction actually reflects the problem of lack of shared consensus about hierarchy, a central problem in intimate relationships. If the man were traveling with his subordinate, the worker would not think to make the comment, knowing full well that it is the employer who can ask for help; it is not offered by a subordinate since that might connote that the boss is not competent enough. The wife is behaving 'as if' they had the equal relationship of peers; each one can freely offer help to the other. She is attending to their connection and, locating a 'need', is trying to meet it. The husband unconsciously does not share that view; he feels put down by a subordinate (a woman) having the nerve to suggest he needs help. However, if he traveled with his (equal) business partner the same suggestion could have been made with impunity. Women unfortunately tend to ignore the power issue in relationships and feel 'hurt' when their partner doesn't.

Men tend to ignore the state of the relationship, and leave most of that work to the female partner. Looking at intimate communication as the 'emotional work' of marriage, it is easily apparent that men's greater power gets them out of doing this rather difficult job. Men know that their wives cannot stand the home to be messy and will do the washing up themselves. Similarly many men know that wives cannot stand too much alienation in the relationship and will initiate the emotional work of communicating. The emotional and the instrumental tasks of maintaining the quality of the relationship are often carried out by the least powerful member. In a relationship where the man is the less powerful partner, he tracks the relationship and brings up the problems, talking more about emotions than the wife.

These communication points are crucial in comprehending the way equality functions in marriage. The most equal partnership couples mentioned their communication in the first moments of the interview: 'We communicate very well – we can say anything to each other ... we communicate like a team ... he listens to me ... she is free to say what she feels'; these are all comments that couples offered in their very definition of the partnership. On a superficial level, they are saying the obvious, 'We have a good relationship – we have good communication'.

However, they are also making a metacommunication about equality: by placing communication first, many couples locate it at the heart of sharing. These are couples who have established an equal power structure in communication. They both attend to the relationship aspects of the communication, the task traditionally left up to the woman. Both are free to comment on the level of the metacommunication, and both do it. We can conceptualize metacommunicating about the communication as doing the 'housework' of the emotional relationship! Both partners have the responsibility to keep the communication clear, congruent and functional. This is no different from both partners having the responsibility to keep the house clean.

It is in the arena of communication that the core respect, or lack of respect, for partners' equal rights is revealed. Subsequently, it is also in this arena that therapists can have a major impact. By learning how to intervene in communication from the perspective of equality, therapists have the opportunity to get as close as possible to real change. We can best learn the key elements of intervention from the happy equal partner couples.

Reducing men's avoidance of conflict

Equal partners often cited conquering what one couple called 'The Problem'. True for Americans, British and Israelis, 'The Problem' to be overcome was male lack of expression of feelings through avoiding intimate conversations. Even the most verbal of men had difficulty being verbal about their emotions. Specifically problematic was lack of self-disclosure of their problems: fears, weaknesses and insecurities were not easily revealed by men. As one wife said, 'It is like pulling teeth!' However, wives of the happily married ones were insistent that their husbands learn how to do it and their husbands cooperated and were agreeable to try.

Men's training to hide their weakness from others is part of their training in power; powerful people do not talk about their problems to less powerful people. Thus equal partner men were especially eager to do it, apparently sensing that their wives' need for this kind of sharing was important to meet. This comment from an American husband seems to sum up the general feeling of many men:

> Rhonda needs me to express my feelings for her to feel close to me. I do not need it much – I would be perfectly content sitting next to her, reading a book, or watching television together with her. I feel intimate like that, but she doesn't. So I try to give her what she wants, although it is slow going, I am getting there more than ever. When she is happy, I am happy.

In the first sentence of an interview with an Afro-American couple, the husband said:

> Equality ... let's see ... I guess I would say it is my learning to talk to Silvia. The more I learn to talk, the more we can negotiate and change things and the better the relationship. But for us to talk, I have to learn to open up.

Wives of these husbands were sensitive to their partners' difficulty, without giving up their own needs for verbal expression. Wives tended to be very encouraging, reinforcing every attempt of their husbands to express feelings. Upon the conclusion of an interview with a couple in the USA, in which the wife did all the talking, she parted from us at the door saying: 'Wasn't Tim talking a lot tonight? He is really making such an effort!' One wife said that she wanted to do the interview in order to give her husband a chance to talk.

Some wives were content to have their husbands mostly listen to them; just the fact that the wife could speak openly about vulnerable feelings without being interrupted was seen as helping him talk as well, through her. The happiest wives were not content with this, going for more self-revelation. They were, however, acutely attuned to their partners' limitations on this topic, showing considerable empathy about their difficulty.

> John comes from a family of introverts, while I come from extroverted people. We had to work out this difference somehow, compromise. He knows my need to talk and be with people, and I know his need to be alone and we try to be sensitive to these differences. But I need to talk to be close, and he knows it. He tries. But I know it is hard for him . . . he is basically shy, and it is hard for him to gather his thoughts about his own feelings . . . I sometimes think he really does not know what he feels. Sometimes he discovers it only in talks with me . . . and later he will say . . . 'I did not even know I felt that!' He needs a lot of support to get to what is really going on in there.
>
> Wife (UK)

Equal power seems to rest in the bridging of this central gap. Wives are willing to invest, not criticize, to help their partners. And their male partners are willing to learn from a woman, a shift in the power hierarchy itself. Equal power makes men more willing to try to change and women more assertive about their requests.

Partners who experienced more difficulty in achieving equality were preoccupied with the lack of emotional sharing:

> Saul saves all his thoughts for his friends at the workshops he attends. I am the last one to know what he feels about anything. We fight about it constantly.
>
> Wife (Israel)

> Why should I talk openly with you, you are always unhappy about something. I wish you would stop interviewing me about my feelings all the time.
>
> Her husband (Israel)

Some of the men felt shame while others were defiant. But most central was the question of whether they withdrew from interaction or not. Happy husbands did not allow themselves the luxury of avoiding conflict:

> I just force myself to either stay in there, or come back and talk right away. It is the responsible thing to do. You have to learn to swallow your pride.
>
> Husband (UK)

Unhappy couples were most characterized by withdrawal of the husband from conflict situations. The withdrawal can take many forms, not only by physically leaving the room:

> He is a wall. You cannot get to him. I stand there, while he is watching television and he knows I want to talk, or need help and that I am waiting for him. But he just goes on watching, he is so self-absorbed and ignores me.
>
> Wife (USA)

The happy couples also mention the husbands' propensity for withdrawal; there were many statements about husbands' need for more space, time alone or privacy. But both partners view it as an accepted difference that still needs to be bridged. An American husband mentioned that he caught himself resenting being told to make dinner, and withdrew emotionally in response. He corrected this on his own, telling himself it would damage the relationship.

Couples in therapy almost uniformly exhibit this problem on some level. Early on in the session, the therapist can observe the husband's eyes turn away when his wife shows emotional distress. He may interrupt, a form of stopping the interaction, when the subject gets too emotional (for him). Therapists who catch these micro-behaviors as they are played out in the session have a glimpse of the couples' metacommunication around power: the husband terminates the interaction when it gets hot, the wife may acquiesce to this move. Or the couple may be embroiled in a power struggle; as he withdraws from her emotionality, she gets all the more negative. These subtle shifts in the interaction, reflecting the overall power structure, will be revealed in more global interactions and give the therapist concrete access to power and gender issues. Interactions on the level of communication can modify the entire relationship.

Celebrating gender differences

Couples often mentioned how different they were: he is introverted, she extroverted; he is good with his hands, she is good with children; he is addicted to his work, she loves being with her friends. Very often these differences were gendered. However, gender was not viewed as the source of their differences. Invariably, they attributed these differences to personality and family history. Yet, the happy couples were not threatened by differences, tending to picture their differences as complementary and a source of strength:

> I think that we are very different people. That is what makes us so good together. We complement each other, each one brings in their unique gifts, and cach has their own place, their own contribution. I have this ability to relate to people, so I keep us connected to the world. But John, he is good at keeping us more serious . . . he is the one who gets us out alone in the woods, who makes sure we take time for ourselves. I have learned how to do that from him; he knows how to give to himself and I have learned how to give to myself.
>
> Wife (UK)

Unhappy couples fought about their differences, viewing them as the source of problems:

> Ron likes to be by himself. I cannot stand it, and I have become quite a nudge about it. But if I did not remind him to be with the family, he would stay by his computer all night. I like to be with our family and I think he should be more like me.
>
> Wife (Israel)

The ability to celebrate differences maximized the potential of the marital team as a unit. Each makes his or her unique contribution, as well as helping the other incorporate an aspect of their personality that is underdeveloped. The couple that fights differences behaves like an undifferentiated organization with only one type of worker, missing the variety that differences provide.

One of the interesting differences mentioned in the interviews was the ability of women to gossip. This was cited as a resource for teaching men about relationships:

> We sit down to talk at the end of every day, over a cup of coffee. We like to tell each other everything that happens –

every detail about everyone. I call her at work as well, and we sometimes tell stories on the phone if there is time. Through these stories I know every one of the people she works with, some of whom I never met, but they are real to me.

Husband (Israel)

Learning to gossip can be seen as sharing experiences and honoring the feminine; learning to gossip can only occur when the man is willing to adopt a typically feminine behavior and results in friendship through shared worlds. However, 'gossiping' is a channel of communication that allows for all their differences to be expressed. In delving into the details of their lives, couples also reveal who they are; these are actually very intimate conversations, allowing each to take a real peek at how the other functions.

Happy equal partnership couples spend a great deal of time invested in keeping the other abreast of the events of daily life. The most astonishing example was an American couple who claimed that they talked four hours a day. Keeping up their ongoing dialogue was their major form of entertainment; they had no television, and after putting the children to bed, they put on music and talked. An English couple made a point to do this each evening with wine, feeling this ritual was cardinal to their happiness.

Equal partner couples foster mutual dependency on knowing what is happening to the other; they create the need to be constantly 'in touch'. This is what girlfriends do for each other, as well as extended kin. Men, seeing gossip as an unmanly interest in the trivial, have not traditionally been partners for this kind of connection. But they can develop the need for it.

Increased sharing of daily life information reveals the differences that exist between the partners. Each learns who the other is, how each one behaves and also what is unique about the partner. Differences in styles, attitudes, beliefs and behaviors are exposed. Conflict is a natural outgrowth of disclosing differences and areas of lack of agreement. Happy couples accepted conflict, although there were marked differences about the way they went about their fights. Some were rather avoidant of conflict, tending to settle disagreements through rational problem solving and compromising. Others seemed to enjoy conflict:

We rarely fight, since we talk every day and pretty much take care of everything as it comes up. I cannot remember our last

real fight and I got over being angry a long time ago. We solve
our problems all the time. Most of our problems are not
between us, but because of all the many things we do, and all
the many demands made on us.

Wife (Israel)

We say the worst things to each other when we fight. I told
him last time that he was a fag – and he slammed out of the
house, and came back a few minutes later roaring. I don't think
that our fights are good for our daughter, but they sure are
good for us. The sex afterwards is wonderful ... and we get
all our hostility out. We show each other our worst sides, we
are disgusting. And then ... there we are, in bed.

Wife (USA)

I think that we are constantly testing our love – if it can survive
that degree of wallowing in the mud, I guess it can survive
anything.

Her husband (USA)

What these couples have in common is their attitude to disagreement; not whether they have major battles or minor squabbles.
The couple that is accepting of their differences recognizes that
disagreement is an acceptable part of their relationship.

Conflict is expected in equal relationships because there are
essentially two leaders. When both partners have the right of
expression, there are multiple opinions, everything is open to
negotiation, and many trivial matters need to go through the negotiation process to be resolved. How much more efficient (in the
short run) to have one person decide! Some of the happiest
couples in the study really seem to enjoy conflict:

We look for areas of disagreement – we just love debating
with each other. In the car, at meals, in bed ... we just
love to disagree and never let go of any issue till we run it
to the ground. Politics, movies ... you name it, we will discuss
it!

Wife (USA)

Couples in therapy often begin with the assumption that differences are the problem, and not their attitude about differences.
Many presenting complaints are framed as differences: he doesn't
like X and she does; he hates Y and she doesn't. For example:

Sharon and Tom were a couple described earlier. Sharon had discovered that Tom was having affairs throughout their marriage. Tom was the husband who wanted to put off our session for three weeks due to his work.

In getting to know the couple, their differences quickly emerged. Tom was a self-taught philosopher. He spent all his free time reading Socrates, Plato, and Kant. He was an expert on the Cabala. His wife raised their five children and spent most of her time planning meals, driving children around and doing all the hundreds of tasks involved in running a home. Tom's double life developed as a result of his perception that he and Sharon were incompatible sexually. He concluded this by noting their differences; she wanted sex less frequently than he did, and she was less adventuresome than he. He also noted that she was not developing outside interests and hobbies as he did, and concluded that she was not interested in self-development as he was.

Sharon had always wanted Tom to tell her more about his life, but her requests to share his world were met with rejection. He was exhausted when he returned home from work, and found talking about problems upsetting, wanting only to hit the books. During therapy it became clear that Tom had automatically equated 'different' with 'irreconcilable'. He had sought out women similar to him.

In therapy he came to see that he had taken for granted how much he benefitted from their differences. Sharon provided Tom with stability. Tom found a new role, teaching Sharon both philosophy and enhanced sexuality. It emerged that she had a lot to teach him as well. She found talking about problems quite easy; talking helped her feel better. She began to teach Tom how to deal with emotions, how to share them without hurting so much and how to use the support of another to feel better. They each had something of value and each learned to appreciate these contributions.

FOSTERING A SHARED IDEOLOGY

A surprisingly small number of the couples mentioned feminism as a reason for equal sharing. However, most couples did have ideological reasons, often anchored firmly in deeply humanistic values, coupled with a pragmatic understanding that equal sharing works best. They both 'believed' in equality and also adopted it because it insures good relationships. It was evident that these beliefs found expression in diverse practices. Many were deeply religious people of all orientations: Bahai, Jewish, Mennonite, Baptist, Anglican. Others were involved in the Black Pride movement, looking for spiritual sustenance in their roots. Some were committed politically to leftist progressive movements, others to sects such as the Salvation Army. There was a marvelous assortment and diversity, making the interviews a stimulating learning process for me. Groups I never knew existed gave sustenance to people's lives.

What these couples do share is the firm commitment values that guide their lives and which stress respect for all people:

> We belong to a group that supports family unity and cohesiveness. It means having weekly family meetings, where we discuss everyone's concerns. It also means that everyone at home has their tasks and chores. The 12 year old takes out the trash, and even the 5 year old is responsible for vacuuming the stairs. We have a globe on the wall and talk a lot to the kids about children in other countries. We take them to meetings of other families so they will feel part of something bigger than themselves.
>
> Husband (USA)

It is this commitment to all people that seems to help couples keep their focus on equal rights for one another in the marriage. They firmly believe in equality as a value, and they trust that the partner is also committed to this value. Compare this to the statement made by this American husband:

> I started being a feminist in college. It was just the only way to get girls in those days. No self-respecting woman would go out with me if I wasn't a feminist.

This was the same man who stated later on in the interview that he watched his wife to see how angry she was about his not helping, and only when she got really upset did he move in to help. And his wife had fought with him for years to help more, never trusting that he really wanted to share. Clearly his equality ideology was not internalized, but a response to social pressure.

This point is further illustrated in differences between two religious Israeli couples. For one, their ideology was a source of strength. For the other, it was a source of restriction. One was a happy equal partnership and the other very conflictual. The first defied several religious tendencies which appeared to contradict their own beliefs, such as not supporting the Jewish religious sector's desire to maintain the Occupied Territories as the Jewish homeland. This clearly alienated them and their closest friends came from outside the religious community. The other couple appeared constricted by their religion; the wife said that she wished to work more but that this would be frowned upon by the community.

Truly equal couples are nonconformists. Highly autonomous, individualistic people, they tend toward what they deem right, with their values offering the backing to buck the system. One couple gave the children the wife's last name, feeling that this contributed to the children's awareness of sexism.

They describe always having been different from the crowd and resisting the social order. Several recall standing up for the weak schoolmate on the playground or complaining about unfair practices at school. Many cited breaking from their families' expectations. One English couple included an upper-middle-class husband whose father was a judge married to a wife whose father was an unemployed miner. His mother refused to speak to the wife, but family disapproval did not deter or interfere with their marriage. Because of their family values, they made sure that his mother came to visit and felt welcome, even through she totally disregarded the wife during these visits. The wife was not happy with this situation, but shrugged it off, saying, 'his mother has a right to her opinion.' The wife had assimilated this rejection into her support of individual rights. Happy couples seemed to absorb disapproval from the community in this way.

Feeling different fostered an empathy for others who are different, and a deep sympathy for the underdog. Several interracial couples mentioned having to get used to social rejection, and how it sensitized them to rejection in general. One mentioned speaking up in a restaurant when they saw a Black customer not getting adequate service, even though neither of them was Afro-American and calling attention to themselves had been painful.

The happier couples' equality is rooted in an integrated and holistic way of life: partners can no more oppress each other than oppress anyone else, and they cannot accept oppression around them. Supporting their ideology, husbands especially were clear that equality simply worked better. It may be that the combination of clear values combined with an appreciation of the overall benefit keeps sharing firmly in place:

> If I want to be happy with her, she has to be happy and that means me doing my share. There is no way around that ... it is the right thing to do and the only thing that works for us.
>
> Husband (UK)

Relationship quality as an encompassing shared value

All the couples in this study mentioned having a strong family focus. They placed their children's welfare as high in their priorities and were concerned about providing their children with both maternal and paternal caretaking. If there was one area that united all equal partners, regardless of couple happiness, it was in the high degree of fathers' involvement with their children. For some, this was almost the only characteristic that might allow them to be called equal partners.

What did distinguish the happier couples was the mutually high value given to the couple relationship. These were couples who perceived keeping the relationship satisfying as part of their contribution to their children. Some couples institutionalized this by having a regular night out, while others took frequent vacations. For others, the daily sharing of ongoing homelife was seen as a way of maintaining the relationship. But while beliefs might foster both a focus on marriage and on children, there was an ongoing strain concerning time allocation. For some this entailed considerable tension and loss:

> I am constantly aware that Carol and I do not get to be alone together enough. We feel that we have to sacrifice a lot of our time together and know that it will be years until we have enough of each other. We can wait, knowing that it will come around, but it has a big price. We hardly have any sex, we are too tired in the evenings.
>
> Husband (USA)

These are parents who are not instinctively authoritarian with their children; some couples had the children present during the interview, running freely around and interrupting at will. For many it seemed that they were committed to having their children feel unconstrained and unfettered, impairing their capability to impose limits. This intensifies the conflict between couple and family time, and left many young couples drained. Since so many of these couples firmly live by their principles, everyday acts were held up to moral scrutiny. They did not shout, did not punish their children, and agonized about their childrearing practices. Some did not allow themselves the time out that television would give them from parenting; they did not believe in having a television in the house. But even if they did, they tried to spend 'quality' time with their children, further reducing time alone. Many of their conversations were about their children.

Therapy with couples making the transition to equality, needs to be sensitive to this built-in conflict. Often couples need permission to place limits with children, to behave in a more authoritarian manner and to put themselves first. Not by coincidence, the happiest equal partner couples saw rule-making with children as part of their egalitarian ideology:

> Sarah has some serious rules about toys; they have to be all stored in separate containers, according to a system of labels she has. She believes that this is educational, and I must admit that I find it a royal pain. But I think she knows what she is doing, so I do try to support it, get on to the kids about putting things away. You see, this is her way of teaching responsibility; she wants the children to realize that we all live in a mutual system and that if the place is a pigsty then we all suffer. I think they have to learn that ... so do I, as a matter of fact!
>
> Husband (UK)

Community involvement

An outstanding characteristic of happy equal partners was their high commitment to community involvement. An Israeli husband volunteered in an organization for the prevention of traffic accidents. Another Israeli husband organized the neighborhood council for housing improvement. An American couple lived with another couple to be part of a community. An English couple devoted all their free time to running their local church. The list goes on and on, but the principle remains the same: *the sense of equality appears anchored in a commitment to people in general, a sense of being part of a larger world community.*

The less happy couples seemed to suffer from a sense of isolation from the community, especially true of the American couples. These couples felt they inhabited separate and alienated worlds. Often the husband worked long hours in a highly competitive field, with all the competing demands on his time and energy. The couple also felt separate from others. Some rejected social invitations because they felt uncomfortable with the dominating behavior of other husbands. However, they had not found an alternative source of support:

> We are really different than everyone else here in this town (a small village on the East coast of England). We came down here from London, and left all our friends. We have not made any new ones in the eleven years we have been here. We are not like the others and yet have not many people like us.
>
> Wife (UK)

The happier couples, while mostly relying on each other as the predominant source of friendship, also sought out social support through their commitment to the community and through their activities.

Therapists working with couples moving towards equality need to remember the built-in strains of this lifestyle. People who cast off traditional roles are different; they will not find much support in the work place. If the couple is still attempting to obtain the respectable lifestyle that money can buy, they will find themselves pulled in many directions, with no guidelines about values. They want to be together, they want to devote time to their children and they also want to provide a high standard of community life. Trying to have all three can be highly stressful and perhaps ultimately disappointing.

CONCLUSION

The egalitarian couples have helped to locate four major themes in the attainment of an equal partnership, which form the basis for therapeutic goals and interventions: helping couples be friends, empowerment, overcoming the gender gap in communication, and fostering a shared ideology. Each theme forms part of an interlocking and interconnected system.

The ability of the couple to be friends is determined by their communication, which then fosters their sharing of experiences and their friendship. A coherent ideology placing the relationship as central supports the investment needed to deal with conflict and overcome gender differences in communication. Overcoming gender differences allows for the sharing of power as well, which further supports friendship.

Couples differ in their attainment of equality, and specifically in the way they handle these themes. The interview couples who reported conflict are similar to couples who seek therapy today. Many profess to having egalitarian values, but have a hard time translating these values into reality. Seeking out the problems conflicted couples have with becoming friends, empowering each other, overcoming the gender gap in communication or in establishing a coherent ideology, can help us understand why they are stuck. When relationships are stuck conflict may be avoided by leading parallel lives, or open crisis is experienced and the threat of marital dissolution may be high. Yet most couples today would like to reach the sense that their relationship is a fair one. Couples in therapy today are stuck in their ability to achieve real equity, which is the basis of marital happiness in contemporary relationships.

The therapy model to be presented next is grounded in these treatment goals. Work on different themes aimed to bring about more equal sharing of power which would result in more equal sharing of housework and parenting tasks. Within this model, the ultimate goal is for *both* partners to reassess their relationship in totality, and holistically, as a fair one. Maintaining this subjective appraisal becomes the motivation for maintaining equal power and equal sharing of tasks.

Figure 5.1 sums up the treatment goals derived from themes of equal partnership.

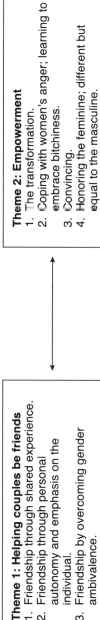

Theme 2: Empowerment
1. The transformation.
2. Coping with women's anger; learning to embrace bitchiness.
3. Convincing.
4. Honoring the feminine; different but equal to the masculine.

Theme 4: Fostering a shared ideology
1. Relationship as an encompassing value.
2. Community involvement.

Equality as a subjective appraisal of the relationship

Equality as equal power

Equality as sharing of household and parenting tasks

Theme 1: Helping couples be friends
1. Friendship through shared experience.
2. Friendship through personal autonomy and emphasis on the individual.
3. Friendship by overcoming gender ambivalence.

Theme 3: Overcoming the gender gap in communication
1. Stopping men's avoidance of intimate communication.
2. Celebrating differences.

Figure 5.1 Equal partnership treatment goals

Chapter 6

Assessment

Each couple in treatment can be viewed as a microcosm of the wider social change with all its inconsistencies and challenges. Assessment mandates fleshing out how this couple is assimilating the social transition in its relationship. Is there an adequate couple friendship based on fairness that copes positively with the exigencies of social change? If not, why not? Which conditions are lacking and what needs to be done to help this specific couple make the transition towards greater equality? For example, the research shows that husbands in equal partnership constructively handle their wives' anger. A couple in treatment may demonstrate problems with this; the husband may withdraw from his wife when she is angry, or may retaliate in a way that makes her hesitant to express herself. Each and every theme located in the research forms the basis for assessment, and eventually for intervention.

There may indeed be many relationships where traditional roles are consensually accepted and the current societal change is rejected. However, these are not the couples that usually seek out help. When the traditional couple requests relationship therapy, it is because something about their traditionalism is not working. Their presenting symptoms may be varied; loss of sexual desire, frequent fighting, avoidance and alienation; over-involvement of another family member, affairs, depression. These form only a partial list of the couple complaints brought to the relationship therapist. Common to these traditional couples is that the initial stirring of the wife's transformation has unbalanced a traditional relationship system, or that the male partner wants more equality than the wife can tolerate.

In looking at the common reactions of couples to our shifting social context, we need not lose sight of individual personality differences or family-of-origin histories. On the contrary, we need to tie these into our central concerns: how is this particular couple, with its unique personality composition, history and couple narrative, coping with the social exigencies of gender role change? We therefore do not have a standard treatment program in which all couples are pulled through a predesignated 'conveyor belt' of treatment modules. We need to know what goals we have and what tools exist to reach them, develop the ability to think creatively about how to utilize the tools with the particular couple in treatment.

Presenting problems and symptoms often reflect an underlying power imbalance in the relationship system. Developing a symptom can be the only way a subordinate partner has to experience some degree of control in the relationship. Depression, for example, can result from a lack of relational power (for both sexes) in addition to resulting from emotional and physical causes. However, depression also fosters power and control when the depressed partner becomes more central due to the symptom.

A couple in treatment reported how the wife's moods determined their social life; if she felt good they could go out, and if not, they stayed home. Asked whether she would be able to influence their coming and going without this problem, they both acknowledged that it is the husband who would be the one to decide. Similarly, agoraphobia can result in the household being organized around the symptomatic member (most often the wife) who then commands the power to be driven places, have the partner stay home, and getting out of chores that involve leaving the home. Husbands' alcohol or drug abuse can reflect the difficulty men have with the increasing power of the wife.[1] These problems constitute a high price to pay for control.

AREAS OF COUPLE ASSESSMENT

No couple is either entirely stuck nor has entirely completed the transition to equal partnership. Each day brings new challenges to confront, and each period in the lifecycle upsets the previous equilibrium. Illness, unemployment, changes at work, war, economic changes all disturb the patterns of couple sharing and demand new solutions to questions such as who does what around the home or how a couple makes decisions. To the extent that the couple has progressed to a solid friendship, these fluctuations are assimilated within the context of their expectation of fairness, and the overall relationship happiness is maintained. Couples who do not view their relationship as fair are less adaptable and less able flexibly to incorporate the inevitable changes occurring over time.

Aside from assessing whether the couple perceives the relationship as fair, areas of importance need to be pinpointed to help decision-making around interventions. This guide to couple assessment sums up some of the themes derived from the research study, posing them as questions therapists can use to sharpen their thinking about these issues. These areas are explored over time as therapy progresses, joining is established and couples begin to reveal their underlying relationship structure. These questions are not by any means an interview protocol, but a therapist guide for conceptually organizing the wealth of information gleaned throughout therapy sessions.

Assessment questions

1 *In what way do the presenting symptoms reflect gender–power issues?*

a Are sex roles stereotyped and rigid, or androgynous and flexible?

b Does the presenting problem reflect the gender tensions line, the ceiling to change in gender roles?

c Does the pursuer–distancer dynamic function in maintaining symptoms?

d Are partners' options impeded by societal limits around gender and in what ways does this influence power in the relationship?

2 *How does each partner define equality and to what extent are the partners in agreement about these definitions?*

a To what extent do partners base their allocation of resources and tasks on need, proportional input or on rotation and turn taking?

b How interchangeable are the partners in actual sharing tasks at home?

3 *To what extent does each partner perceive the other as a real friend?*

a To what extent does each partner know what it is like to be in the other's shoes?
b To what extent does each partner monitor the self and the relationship for the level of fairness?
c To what extent does each partner recognize and take personal responsibility for ambivalence about changing gender roles?

4 *To what extent does the relationship empower both partners?*

a How does the couple make decisions and do they have equal input on the final result of the decision-making process?
b What is the history of the less powerful partner's attempts to transform the relationship towards more equality?
c How does the couple handle the less powerful member's expression of anger?
d Do both partners honor the feminine regardless of the money tasks based on these traits bring into the marriage?

5 *To what extent is the communication work of the relationship equally shared?*

a Can and does the male partner express feelings without withdrawing from emotional contact?
b Do partners recognize and celebrate their differences?

6 *Have the couple developed a shared ideology fostering?*

a Does the couple value their relationship so that it takes priority above competing values?
b Does the couple balance their emphasis on their relationship with a real investment in their community?

ASSESSMENT OF COUPLE INTERACTION

Power and gender themes are reflected in couple interaction during therapy sessions. From the moment the couple enters the therapist's office, metacommunication messages translate couple rules about power and gender norms into patterns of communication. Some of these key patterns are revealed by attention to:

• who sits where;

- who opens the conversation;
- who chooses the topic;
- who interrupts whom;
- who talks more;
- who changes the topic;
- who looks away more;
- whose schedule the couple takes into account in setting up the next session;
- who pays for the session;
- who decides if there will be a next session.

The list of potential microbehaviors that reflect the rules of couples' relationships is endless and impossible entirely to catalogue. However, sensitivity to this level of interaction, juxtaposed with attention to the content level of communication, completes the picture of gendered power politics in intimate relationships. In-session behaviors 'leak' the power structure of the relationship:

A husband declares: 'I think my wife is an equal partner – we believe in equality and I think she should work and invest in herself.' He may well mean what he says. However, in interaction with his wife, this same husband interrupts her train of thought, changes the topic or does not relate to the topic she has brought up, argues with every point she tries to make in a derogatory manner, or looks away when she talks. His wife sits with her body facing him, while his is at a 90-degree angle, legs away from her. She searches out eye contact; he avoids eye contact. She relates to topics he brings up, follows and tracks his conversation, building and commenting on his thoughts. He leads the dialogue, she follows.

The therapist can look to the symbolic meaning of different behaviors as reflecting the way the couple is organized at home around power and gender. Power–gender rules of the relationship translate into in-session behaviors in many ways:

Unequal access to or control over finances

Does one partner have primary control or responsibility over money? Financial issues evident in the therapy include who makes the financial arrangement or pays for the therapy, who decides whether therapy can be afforded, and who enters into discussions about payment for therapy.

Unequal sharing of household chores and parenting demands

Does one partner carry an unfair burden of the 'dirty work' of family life? In therapy, men often do not assume responsibility for the arrangements around therapy, leaving these 'trivial' tasks to their wives. These might include: setting up appointments; keeping track of homework assignments; arranging babysitting for children; taking initiative in giving the therapist feedback about progress of therapy; any nurturing behaviors to the therapist, such as giving a present, sending holiday cards, complimenting the therapist, asking how vacations went.

Unequal influence on decision-making

Does one partner impose his/her will on the other by dominating the decision-making process? Who decides to begin therapy (not the one who first suggests it!); who decides which problems are to be worked on; who decides to stop coming to therapy; who decides if therapy is achieving couple goals or not (whose view of the therapy process is the accepted couple reality?)

Unfair burden of emotional work in communication

Does one partner do all the opening up, all the self-disclosure of weakness or vulnerabilities while the other expresses all the anger. Who withdraws from conflict more? Who asserts their wishes more clearly? Who offers more empathy for the partner's feelings and more support for the partner? Who shows more caring behaviors, such as remembering topics of concern to the other and bringing them up? Who discusses emotions more and who stays on the intellectual, logical level of analysis?

A brief example of this level of assessment can be viewed in work with Emi and Joe, an American wife married to an Israeli husband.[2]

Emi and Joe requested marital therapy after discovering that Emi was pregnant. The couple already had three children and were in complete disagreement about continuing this pregnancy. Emi wanted the child, whereas Joe was adamant about terminating the pregnancy. Joe insisted that the marriage was so poor that there was almost no point in going on. While Emi agreed about the relationship she did not want an abortion.

In sessions, when Emi started to cry, demand or complain, Joe would avoid her by either criticizing her to the therapist, looking away or making sarcastic, humorous remarks, such as 'there we go again – poor, poor Emi'. Emi would then talk in a rambling, incompetent way, not getting to the point or clarifying what she wanted to say. These long monologues were punctuated by Joe's sarcastic statements about her intelligence, by avoidance of eye contact, looking at his watch or glancing towards the therapist with a look of contempt for his wife.

During the first session the following gendered behavior was evident:

Joe: Avoidance of confrontation and conflict, use of aggressive attacks on Emi as a means of gaining control, avoidance of emotion and moving the conversation from the emotional level to the rational level whenever he was the focus of the conversation.

Emi: Avoidance of her own anger through confused speech, incompetence, nagging and blaming. Instead of direct confrontation, becoming scattered and confused, allowing her to avoid conflict. Immediately moving to self-blame whenever Joe became aggressive.

These interactional patterns restricted Emi's ability to influence Joe as power imbalances are revealed in the conversation. Power imbalances are reciprocally created through the conversational process. Emi's rambling and Joe's aggressiveness reduce Emi's influence, and her power is continually being eroded. Changing Emi's rambling and confused avoidance of confrontation or Joe's aggressive 'put-downs' would change the power structure.

In effect, therapists have a great deal of leverage in changing these microbehaviors, and thus having an impact on the overall power structure. If Joe would start a dialogue with Emi, in which he actually listened to her, he would be handing over some of his power. Concomitantly, if Emi would focus on one topic, and become a more forceful speaker, she would increase her power in the relationship. Methods for changing these interactional sequences will be presented in the section on therapy techniques.

Partners' behaviors with the therapist often mirror gender and power patterns as well. Partners used to being in control of the couple interaction often attempt to gain control of the therapy interaction: this is accomplished by interrupting the therapist, changing the topic, becoming aggressive, ignoring therapist statements, or avoiding eye contact. The more submissive partner, used to attempting to please or placate, will be more collaborative: will pay more attention to therapist statements, show agreement (head nodding, eye contact, verbal comments); defer to the therapist (stop talking immediately when the therapist talks, allow the therapist to change the topic); look to the therapist for leadership, or give the therapist support and encouragement ('What you said was so right; how did you know that?').

A risk in relationship therapy is giving in to the temptation to work more with the subordinate partner. This danger can be revealed in the therapist turning more often to this partner, asking this partner more questions, having more interactions and being more expressive with this partner. This dynamic often results in overfocusing on the female partner, as well as asking more change from her. As the more powerful partner is bypassed and ignored, a power struggle may ensue, affecting couple interaction. The therapist is unbalancing the system prematurely, impairing the objectivity needed for assessment and for joining with each of them. A female partner related to me that in two previous therapy attempts, both therapists continually addressed her, paid more attention to her attempts to change, as well as supporting her more. This client reported: 'I started to feel pressured and blamed, although I don't think that was the intention ... I realized that both these therapists expected more from me than from my husband, and that isn't fair! That is what he (her husband) expects, that I will do all the work. The problem is, I realized it too late!'

Therapists zooming in on in-session behaviors are looking for *interactional configurations:* a one-time behavior does not constitute a pattern, and does not indicate unfair sharing. Behaviors need to be repeated often and consistently to reflect structural patterns. These in-session behaviors need to be supplemented by careful analysis of the couple's story as well. Together with the other types of assessment, the therapist creates a picture of the underlying structure related to fairness in the relationship.

THE PROCESS OF ASSESSMENT

Assessment is an integral and continuing part of the therapy; emerging understanding of gender and power informs the treatment, which results in increasing comprehension, which in turn informs the treatment process. The following case example illustrates the movement from observing couple interaction in the session, and using probes focused on a hypothesis, to firming up a conceptualization which takes gender and power into account. This process also helped to move the couple from viewing the problem as lack of sexual desire towards a new understanding related to equality.

A GENDER–POWER ANALYSIS OF LOW SEXUAL DESIRE

Susan and Bill, a religious American couple living in Israel, requested treatment for a severe sexual problem: Susan could not have intercourse and experienced no sexual arousal whatsoever. The couple had three children, the number of times in their ten-year marriage they had had sex. Susan experienced intense pain at penetration, and a high level of anxiety about any sexual contact, even nonsexual hugging and touching. While in the USA, they had undergone two unsuccessful sex therapy attempts in major medical centers; treatment focused on her vaginismus, lack of desire, their lack of sensuality, their fights and other interventions of a behavioral–marital treatment program. Each treatment course spanned two years, to no avail. Although seriously discouraged (over half their married life had been spent in treatments), they were willing to try once more before divorce. They loved each other and reported few other problems in their relationship. However, tension about sex ruined the atmosphere most of the time.

Both partners defined Susan as having the problem, which started on their wedding night; both virgins, the event was a fiasco. Susan described it in terms recalling rape. She had tightened up, while Bill continued attempting penetration. Instead of pausing, their continued attempts created a serious trauma for Susan, who suffered throughout the experience. She had endured, not wanting to hurt Bill's feelings. Later attempts were increasingly painful, leading to her phobic avoidance of anything sexual. By the time they came for treatment, watching a movie sex scene caused her anxiety.

They were often tense and withdrawn, with Susan feeling guilty and Bill feeling angry and fed up. They fought a lot about this problem. Susan usually ended up crying desperately, and Bill withdrew from the conflict in disgust. He felt she wasn't trying hard enough and was losing faith that she wanted a sex life at all. His fear that maybe she was content to live in abstinence fueled his anxiety and his pressure on her, which in turn increased her phobic avoidance of anything sexual.

Susan, a lawyer, worked in an American firm in Israel specializes in corporate law. All her colleagues were male, all were willing to work the extra hours the firm routinely demanded. Susan had a special deal in which she could go home at 5 pm; for which she felt indebted and guilty, constantly needing to establish to her bosses that she could hold her own. When she returned home, she took over all childcare, since Bill was starting an import–export business and came home around 8 pm. Influenced by the feminist movement, the couple firmly believe in equal partnering. Bill wanted Susan to fulfill her career goals. When he got home at night, they shared equally. At the same time, they both also believed him to be the primary provider and devised the family's scheduling around his work needs. She was predominantly responsible for the children. Both agreed that she had a better rapport with them and that biologically she was better equipped to parent. Moreover, he had to take many trips abroad for his business and was therefore out of the home at least one week every month.

According to the couple, their previous sex therapy treatments had bogged down because of their pronounced tendency to

renege on homework. They could not account for their avoidance of the assignments and both felt guilty about it. Because
they felt responsible for treatment failures, they were willing to
give therapy one more try.

During the first session, I noticed that whenever Bill got angry
and argumentative, Susan got quiet and withdrawn, often looking
at the floor. She expressed no anger, only pain and grief about
'her problem'. It appeared that they both perceived the therapy
for her, with his presence necessary to help her out.

I wondered how they were dealing with having such a severe
problem. Could they be friends about this, or were they essentially functioning in a win–lose model?

To probe the area of *friendship,* I asked them if they felt they
were being good friends about the problem:

Susan: I never thought about it like that, because we really are
          good friends about everything else. No, I don't think we
          are friends about it.
Bill: What do you mean by friends about the problem?
Claire: Well, do you think that you are both 'on the same side
          of the fence'; are you cooperating to lick this thing? It is
          a pretty stubborn problem, and I imagine that you need
          to team up to do anything about it.
Susan: Not at all! (first expression of anger seen in Susan) Bill
          thinks it is all my problem ... maybe it is.
Claire: Perhaps, but let's say it is your problem ... are you being
          friends about finding a solution? Even if you have the
          problem you still need Bill as a friend to overcome it,
          don't you?
Bill: If you put it that way, no. I do not feel we are friends. I
          don't feel that Susan cares enough about it to solve it. I
          feel all alone in this. If I didn't push her, she would be
          happy to forget all about sex.
Claire: Bill, it does sound lonely to feel that you have to cope
          with this yourself. Susan, do you feel lonely as well?
Susan: No, I feel angry, I am really angry about it. I am at fault
          maybe, but I am tired of being blamed. What kind of
          friend blames all the time?

Claire: Susan, do you know how it feels to feel so alone with this thing? Is there any problem you have that you feel alone about?

Susan: Yes, I keep trying to get Bill to help me about my problems about work. I have been thinking that I might be in the wrong field. I have no time with my children, I am stressed and tired. I try to talk to him and he just listens, but has no solutions at all. I feel very much alone.

Claire: So you know how Bill feels about the sexual problem, because that is how you feel about your work issue. Bill, is there any area of your marriage that you feel blamed for?

Bill: Not that I can think of.

Claire: So Susan, you do know how it feels to feel so alone with a problem, while you, Bill, don't really know what blame feels like from the inside?

Bill: Well not blamed, but you know, I am responsible for the finances around here. Susan's salary is peanuts ... it's a joke, looking at all those hours she puts in. I have been really worried about whether my business will take off. I don't get the feeling that Susan is concerned about that either. And if I tell her that our account is in overdraft, she gets mad! She starts blaming me that I am not careful, why did I buy this or that ... yes, I feel blamed ... but I don't tell her anything, so I don't get blamed often!

It is easy to see that the couple were not functioning 'on the same side of the fence'; they were not a cooperative team. Their friendship was limited due to the restrictions of gendered role segregation. Susan refused to participate in the male experience of financial worries; it made her too anxious and she became critical instead of supportive. Bill could not experience her female world of sexual anxiety; never allowing himself to feel vulnerable or incompetent, and staying within his male comfort zone of expressing anger.

Their gendered roles kept them on opposite sides of the fence. Susan expected Bill to come up with a solution to her work problem, reinforcing a gendered stereotype of male superior knowledge. Bill had a hard time coping with Susan's emotions about finances, and avoided telling her information that might arouse her anxieties. While the couple had initially described their

relationship as a good one, it decidedly lacked real companionship or goodwill.

Susan

Individual sessions with Susan generated the following
hypotheses: Susan expects Bill to have a solution for her work
ambivalence, blaming him for being as helpless as she. She has
turned her ambivalence about sex roles (staying home with her
children versus competing in her fast-track career) into underlying frustration with him. This unempowered position keeps her
a 'girl child', never taking responsibility for any major problem,
including both the sexual and the work difficulties. She was too
angry and disappointed in him to make love, or to commit herself
in trying to be intimate with him.

Accepting him as the strong one meant she accepted his power
to define reality. Her definition of sharing entails a belief that
because he earns more and is the 'primary provider', he also gets
to be right. While she knows that he is also responsible for their
sex problem, she has accepted his view that she is to blame, meanwhile sabotaging any attempts to improve the situation. A
common problem for women, she blamed herself as the cause of
the problem, but saw him (the powerful partner) as having the
solution. Her role of victim made it hard to take charge of her
own life.

Susan generally sees men as having more *power*. A further
probe of this reveals that she sees her father as all-powerful and
her bosses as stronger than she. Being a feminist and a professional woman, she is furious about this. But she is ambivalent as
well since her self-esteem is low. As a professional woman within
a religious community, she is very different from the other wives,
most of whom either stay home or work part time. She continually
experiences doubts about her femininity. Maintaining Bill in the
role of the strong one allows her to feel more feminine, a strategy
not helpful in solving their sexual problem. But at the same time,
she is furious that he isn't living up to her expectations as a man.
From the start, she was secretly disappointed that he was a poor
lover, that he has continued to be helpless and that instead of
being the one to solve the problem, he blames her. A real man
would have worked it out independently long ago.

Susan cannot reveal anger to powerful male figures. Instead she unconsciously uses her very stubborn symptom to right the power balance. She was the one who avoided the homework assignments, not telling the (powerful) therapists that she was resisting doing them. With therapists, she played the role of compliant 'good girl' and only expressed her opposition at home. Just as she experienced her low sexual desire as out of her control, she experienced her noncompliance in therapy.

A metaphor for her overall lack of empowerment, the sexual symptom gave her the opportunity indirectly to express her rage without owning it. Susan really wants to scream at Bill: 'You are a lousy lover – if you had known what to do, we never would have been in this situation!' She was too nice, and needed him as the strong one, to challenge him so directly.

In probing this hypothesis, she revealed her extreme passivity in sex:

Claire: So what did you really expect to happen during your wedding night ... when both of you were continuing to try to make love and you were hurting so much?

Susan: I wasn't aware of thinking. But now that you ask, I guess I thought that he should know to stop ... or to do something differently.

Claire: What gave you the idea that he knew more about sex than you? You both were virgins, and neither of you had much sexual experience ...

Susan: I never thought about it ... it just seems obvious that he knows more. I don't know where I got that idea, but I just had it ... maybe I still do. I somehow think that Bill knows what to do, and he just isn't doing it!

Claire: Out of stubbornness, perversity?

Susan: Well, maybe he doesn't know much, but that is pretty sad! I mean, what am I supposed to do, teach him about sex?

Claire: Why not? Teach him what you like, what might turn you on, what doesn't. Why not teach him?

Susan: I don't know – it seems so pushy, or dominating or something.

Claire: Maybe it just seems too masculine a thing for a woman to do?

Susan: Yea, I guess I just wouldn't feel very feminine acting like I was the one who knew about sex and he wasn't. I think it would be insulting to Bill.

Of course, Susan had never hinted at any of this; undermining the male ego about sex would contact her gender-tension line. She could not feel adequately feminine if she had a male partner who was not adequately male (according to her definition of male). As long she felt insecure as a woman in a male-dominated profession, constantly failing to keep up with the boys, Susan maintained her doubts about her femininity and her self-esteem. The fact that none of her co-workers had to run home at 5 pm did not occur to her as a reason she was having a hard time. Instead she blamed herself, feeling something was lacking and needing all the more to lean on a strong husband.

Bill

In individual sessions with Bill the following hypotheses emerged: Bill assumed himself to be responsible for sexuality and consequently felt that Susan was undermining his competence by not letting him be the man he could be. By blaming her, he circumvented the vulnerable feelings prohibited in his sex-role stereotyped male role: feelings of weakness, incompetence, helplessness, insecurity, or fear. He never had to put his competence to a test, as they never had sex, protecting his fragile masculine self-image. This dynamic was revealed in the couple's in-session interaction; whenever Susan began to talk about what she might like sexually, Bill started to blame her, taking the focus away from him and back to her. He continuously used blame when the focus moved to him, effectively keeping the spotlight on her.

Bill also felt responsible for the financial situation and for solving all of Susan's problems, although he at first denied this:

Claire: You say that you think Susan should work out her own issues about her job.
Bill: Yes, I don't know what she wants from me. I listen to her, but it isn't enough.
Claire: O.K., let me see if I can understand what you mean by listening. Let's say I am now Susan and I am trying to

	talk with you about my dilemma. I say, 'Bill I just am sick of it . . . I cannot go on with this double load.'
Bill:	I usually say something like: 'You should just quit . . . I told you a million times, I can make it once the business takes off, and you can be at home . . . '
Claire:	So when you listen, you also seem to feel you have to solve the problem for her?
Bill:	Yes, but I can't solve it for her . . . what can I do . . . I think she should stop complaining and just quit. Well, I guess telling her to quit is telling her what to do . . . she says that I do that. But I really am just trying to help.
Claire:	I know that you are, and it must be so frustrating you cannot help her. Why do you think that you have to come up with a solution . . . is that your role as husband?
Bill:	Isn't it? I always felt that I had to be on top of everything. I do get so frustrated with her . . . she won't listen to me. She asks for my opinion, but she does not do what I say. So why is she asking?

This is a typical example of male 'help' for the helpless female. He is valiantly trying to help her by telling her what to do; her not doing what he says makes him feel incompetent and as if she is not respecting his authority. In a relationship context of inequality, help becomes patronizing and is resisted. There is no real friendship, as the one 'helped' struggles to maintain autonomy. But at the same time, Susan also expects him magically to come up with the solution, and sends him confusing messages: 'help/save me', and 'don't tell me what to do'. These unconscious assumptions are revealed in their gendered communication.

This is essentially a traditional couple in transition to a more egalitarian lifestyle. The underlying inconsistencies cause severe tension, communicated in a symptom that rights the balance of power in a dysfunctional way. Instead of continuing to target their sexual problem, treatment aimed at increasing equality would focus on:

1 How their friendship is faring, and the gendered limitations that interfere.
2 The gendered communication patterns they need to overcome to become friends.

3 The development of more personal autonomy around gender
   ambivalence.
4 The development of a relationship focus that makes their egalitarian ideology more anchored in reality.

All this may seem like quite a detour. It did involve relabeling
the problem and bringing to the surface unconscious assumptions
and beliefs. With this couple, individual and joint work took over
a year. After realigning the power structure of their marriage,
they jointly tackled her work problem and his financial worries
as friends. Their sexual problem was completely alleviated as they
utilized the sex therapy exercises they had been assigned in
previous therapies. This time around, without underlying power
struggles, the exercises were not resisted and proved helpful.

Chapter 7

Types of couples seeking therapy

Couples today are all facing issues related to the sharing of power and the degree of flexibility of gender roles. We can situate relationships on a continuum in relation to their degree of progress towards equality between the partners. Understanding the unique dynamics related to the degree of change the couple is experiencing can be helpful in matching treatment to the relationship. These are not rigid categories or fixed couple types; couples move on a continuum, shifting from more or less equal power as their life situation changes. However, it does appear that once the couple becomes egalitarian in its definition, in sharing power equally and in actual sharing of communication and household/parenting tasks, they have made an irreversible quantum leap to equality.

THE TRADITIONAL COUPLE

In traditional relationships, the wife has clearly taken on the subordinate role, deferring major life decisions to her husband, while often taking on the burden of most of the daily life problems on herself. Both partners assume husband responsibility in earning, in solving problems logically, and in initiating sex, with wife responsibility in running the home, taking care of the children, keeping up social and family contacts and in handling emotional issues.

In their acceptance of sex-role stereotype their unique personalities are distorted: men are uniformly viewed as the more solitary, stubborn and rational partner; women as the more social, adaptable, and emotional partner. These are attributions held regardless of inconsistencies and lack of fit. These support the traditional gender roles and are used to explain the division of labor. She spends time looking for babysitters because she is the 'more adaptable' personality and is expected to be more flexible about her time. He has to solve family emergencies because he is the 'more rational' partner, and is expected to excel in problem solving. The anchoring of power and roles in personality attributes creates substantial resistance to change.

However, a handle for change is the discomfort individuals feel when whole parts of themselves are suppressed. It is exhausting continually to play any role. In traditional relationships, the pressure for change is usually germinating in the wife. Both partners are oppressed by their rigid roles, but there is also a built-in unfairness: the man gets to feel better about himself, as he has all the socially desirable traits, while the wife is more racked by self-doubt, playing the role associated with less valued traits. The man will only see the benefits of change when he comes to realize that what benefits the wife also benefits him. These couples do not entertain an egalitarian ideology, and change in the husband is contingent upon his perception that he stands to gain from the results.

Couples who refer for marital problems with relatively traditional relationship structure present the three characteristics below.

Wives' anger

The wife is angry, but is often hiding it in some symptom, like depression, sexual inhibition, obesity, agoraphobia, panic attacks, or apathy. Her denial can be relatively superficial, and thus disappear at the first accurate empathic therapist response. Usually these are women who have begun the transformation towards increased power and have already consciously felt anger at home.

Anger may be massively denied, and take far more therapeutic intervention to emerge. Where denial is more substantial, it does more damage to the relationship and to the woman herself; symptoms are more extreme and indirect expression of anger more pernicious. One very obese wife could never get herself to lose weight; when her husband stayed late at work, she ate obsessively. Another was hospitalized for depression when her husband became totally unavailable through overwork.

Lack of personal autonomy

The wife tends to be overinvolved with her husband, compulsively monitoring his attention to her, pursuing him and arguing with him about not getting enough warmth and care from him. These women tend to bring up their husband in conversations alone with the therapist, so that the husband seems more present in the session than the woman herself. Clearly getting his love is the focus of her life. Often the woman does not work and builds her life around his coming and going, or when she works, she retains all the functions of the traditional wife.

Power imbalance

The husband in this situation tends to abuse power. The exploitation may be mild, and include having more rights to leisure time or going out at will without consulting the wife. One husband who worked with his wife at home had his own table, while she had to work in the kitchen. Another disappeared for hours on weekends without telling her where he was. Or the abuse of power may be far more serious, such as making degrading statements, shouting at her in front of the children, keeping secrets about money and affairs, or using physical violence and intimidation. Some of these men are 'Don Juans', humiliating their wives publicly with their adultery. The abusive nature of these relationships appears to include sadistic and masochistic interactions which are deeply embedded in sex role stereotyping.

In the most extreme cases, the couple may come into treatment because the wife can no longer tolerate the abusive situation and is on the verge of a breakdown. A woman requested individual therapy because of severe panic attacks, which were increasingly limiting her ability to function both at home and at work. She in no way saw a connection between these attacks, nor the deterioration in her condition, to the fact that her husband had increasingly violent rages, in which he threatened to strike her whenever she displeased him. She saw the anxiety as a reaction to a situation in her extended family. Countering her denial about her husband and his effect on her was a painful and prolonged process, resulting in the release of explosive rage on her part and the alleviation of her panic attacks.

The wife may be acting out her anger indirectly, reflecting a power balance on the way to change. The husband may initiate the therapy because he no longer gets what he used to from his wife. This English couple is an example of this type of traditional couple, experiencing the beginning of change in gender and power:[1]

Audrey and Mark, in their mid-thirties, are referred to the marital clinic due to Mark's depression. The local family doctor reports that Mark is not getting enough attention at home and is sickly too much of the time. The couple have three teenage children who are doing well. Mark, a car salesman, works many long hours to make overtime pay. Audrey, a former kindergarten teacher, has been home since the children were born. Now she is thinking of getting back to work for the first time in eighteen years. Audrey did not want to come to the consultation, but Mark resolutely insisted. She right away reported that she had a great deal of housework left undone. Mark's complaint was that Audrey cares more about the washing up, the ironing and planting their garden than she does about him. She is sullen and not talkative; he wants her to listen to his stories about sales and she is very bored.

During the session it emerged that Audrey had always made the family her major focus. Now that she was contemplating going back to work, she was preoccupied. Mark wanted more attention, but was unwilling to listen to her ruminations about work issues. He wanted to talk about himself, as he always had. In response, Audrey got busier with the garden and home. Mark tried to get more time with her by making himself very busy as well when he got home, hoping that if he got all his chores out of the way, they would have time in the evening. But he did not consult her about his 'solution'. Audrey was unable to articulate that she did not want more time with him, she wanted some attention for herself, perhaps for the first time in their marriage. More time with him only meant more pressure from him to listen to him. So evening time found her asleep in front of the telly, exhausted from all the housework.

This wife had previously been content to be her husband's helpmate, finding her own satisfaction in this role. Her changing needs demanded a new balance in which the emotional work of the relationship would be divided up more equally. However, never feeling entitled to having her needs met, Audrey had no idea how to ask for what she wanted. Her traditional sex-role feminine identity demanded that she wait for Mark to figure out what she needed; when he did not, she felt bitter. Since nice English women do not directly express rage, she expressed indirect anger by obsessively doing housework, in effect shoving the 'benefits' of the role down his throat. With too much of a good thing, Mark found himself getting depressed.

THE TRANSITIONAL COUPLE

Relationships in transition evidence more wife power than in traditional relationships and show the tensions inherent in this passage. Without the other concomitant aspects of equal partnership, an increase in wife's power greatly increases the potential for marital conflict. Some couples find themselves stuck in a kind of role reversal, in which the wife dominates. Men withdraw from the conflict resulting from wife dominance. Other couples exhibit more open conflict, which while painful for the partners also promises potential movement towards equality and marital satisfaction in therapy.

PARALLEL LIVES TRANSITIONAL COUPLES

These are relationships in which the wife has developed her own personal autonomy, often with a fulfilling career, but where the couple has avoided the conflict inherent in having two strong leaders. The wife has power at work, brings in money, openly asserts her opinions and feels entitled to free time, personal pursuits and self-advancement. Often the husband rejects the traditional male 'macho' role and attempts to be less domineering and aggressive in his personal life than his father or other men. However, he is ill equipped to deal equally with a strong woman, having no model of equality in mind. He may withdraw from her altogether.

Alternatively, the wife fears being dominated by a man and can not envision intimacy with the opposite sex that does not compromise her independence. Closeness is scary for him because of the conflict it entails (arousing his aggression) and for her because of the intimacy it involves (arousing her dependency). Each partner rejects traditional gender roles but has not reintegrated the rejected masculine or feminine characteristics into their lives.

These couples present a typical scenario. For example:

Aviva (aged 29) and Ezra (aged 39) are an Israeli couple with two small children, married seven years. Aviva requested therapy because she was having an affair with her boss, was madly in love and was compromising her ability to work as the company's accountant. She was terrified her husband would find out. Ezra, a career army officer, had been married before and was very happy to settle down and have the children his first wife had not wanted. He took all responsibility for the children; got them up in the morning, bathed them at night, and cooked all the meals. He was late to work as he had to do the shopping for dinner as well. The couple rarely went out together, and all family excursions consisted of Ezra taking the two children to the country to give Aviva, who hated nature, a chance to rest.

In her sessions alone, Aviva wanted to talk about her lover, whom she viewed as exciting and masculine. He often forgot to call, ended the affair, and then renewed it. Aviva's moods fluctuated with his attention; when he found time for her, she was in heaven. If not, or he had initiated one of his separations, she was severely depressed and stopped eating. It was this last symptom that alerted her husband's suspicions and Aviva's panic that he would find out.

In sessions alone with Ezra he criticized Aviva's maternal abilities, and said that he was content to be solely responsible for the children and home. He pulled out a list of complaints, saying that overall he was satisfied with the marriage, and I should not think that this list was really important. There were ten items on the list, all relating to her total lack of attention to him, lack of caring and self-involvement. He made sure to say, upon finishing reading the list, that the things he got from Aviva far outweighed the things he did not get. When asked about those things, he could think of one only, that she was very beautiful.

The couple never talked about problems, mostly because Ezra saw himself as having a bad temper. He believed that his temper had caused his divorce. Aviva, who had seen him explode a few times, avoided talking to him for the same reason. She also said that while she had nothing to say to him, he was an excellent husband and she was very lucky. She blamed herself for needing her lover and could not understand why she was cheating on the husband that her family considered 'a real find'. He was the only husband she knew who took over household care the way he did and she was grateful.

Typical of these transitional parallel lives couples is: power imbalance and gendered communication patterns.

Power imbalance

The imbalance results in exploitative behavior on the part of the wife. Reversing the traditional roles, it is now the husband doing an unfair share. There are real similarities with traditional couples, with one partner feeling unable to assert needs, while the other feels entitled to getting needs met.

In the previous example, Ezra found it difficult to ask for anything for himself, afraid to complain lest his masculine aggression surface. Although he earned more money than Aviva, she had more power. Her power was not grounded in money, but in her forceful personality, her youth and beauty, and mostly in Ezra's panic about failing again in marriage. Ezra also felt more needy of children and homelife. Like husbands in traditional marriage, Aviva was out of touch with her dependency on her partner. She felt she could do without him, giving her more power than Ezra who was aware of his needs.

Gendered communication patterns

The possibility of conflict negotiation is limited by both partners' fear of male aggression. Whereas for traditional couples the husband often uses his aggression (or threat of aggression) to dominate, avoidance becomes the motif of these parallel couples. They therefore have very separate lives with little intimacy.

These transitional wives may have affairs to meet their emotional needs. Affairs allow them to feel more feminine without the ongoing emotional intimacy in marriage which carries the threat of male domination. While the woman may be caught up emotionally in the affair, as was Aviva, the nature of affairs creates boundaries that actually protect the woman.

In the traditional relationship, the wife is striving to get her emotional needs met in the relationship, often pursuing the husband. In the transitional relationship, distance is maintained by the wife, who is terrified of being sucked into the traditional female role. It pays to remember that these women's concerns about male dominating tendencies are not totally unfounded. In all the parallel transitional couples there is evidence of underlying attempts by the husbands to dominate. This is not surprising, given that men have so little experience in equality with women. Therapists who work towards couple intimacy for the transitional couple may actually be undermining the wife's new-found independence. This is a serious danger as male dominance in the transitional couple can take subtle forms. These are not men who batter, impose their wills openly, or force themselves on their wives. Their tendency to dominate is usually couched in rational arguments that attempt to define reality for the couple and impose his standards on their lifestyle.

For example, Ezra's criticism of Aviva's mothering effectively kept her of out of parenting by defining what constitutes good mothering for them both. Aviva actually longed for more closeness with the children, but bought into Ezra's view that she was less competent and for the children's sake should keep her distance. In therapy she gained respect for her own style of mothering; it might not be the traditional 'chicken soup mamma' style he preferred but she discovered that she had a lot to offer the children in her own way.

Gender ambivalence

Worked out between the couple instead of within each person, gender ambivalence limits individual growth.

Aviva has seemingly rejected the traditional female role and has little to do with the home. But she is actually split off from her femininity. She plays the traditional female with her boss, waiting for him to make the moves and is devastated when he hints at abandoning her. With her husband she is assertive and masculine. Aviva has bought into the culture stereotypes of female/male roles; females are weak and males are strong, and the strong exploit the weak. In her imagination, she has to be exploitative at home to make sure not to be left doing everything.

She winds up exploiting Ezra, who is so afraid of his destructive temper that he prefers the exploitation to explosion.

Ezra has divided up his masculine and feminine sides: at work he plays a powerful army officer role, in charge of many soldiers. At home he is the 'new man' who nurtures his children. He keeps all his aggression (and vitality) for work. He has bought into the same role-playing as has Aviva, but he brings his 'weak' sides to the home and leaves his strength for the office. The relationship loses out in this kind of gendered segregation. Aviva is bored with him as he has left his vibrant masculine energy at his office; he is frustrated emotionally as she has left her nurturing feminine side at her office.

Lacking in these transitional couples is a vision of cooperation that goes beyond gendered roles, does not allow for exploitation of either sex, and allows each partner to maximize their personal growth. They need to redefine sex roles. It is possible that Aviva does not feel attracted to a man who does not play the traditional macho role. Ezra may not know how to share the home front, feeling that having her 'help' him would mean he is not doing an adequate job. Thus both partners are probably far more motivated by sex-role stereotyping than is apparent at first glance.

OPEN CONFLICT TRANSITIONAL COUPLES

Further on in the continuum of change are couples who allow the conflict around gender roles to emerge. They may seem more distressed due to their open fighting, but actually respond well to a therapy that articulates the nature of their conflict. These couples directly experience the pain of the transition to equality, the lack of models and uncertainty that results. They are openly engaging each other in the conflict, so they either divorce or improve, but are not stuck. Therapeutic intervention is especially crucial for them as their active crisis leaves them open to change.

Characteristic of these couples is the relatively high power of the wife, the willingness of both to experience the conflict her increasing power brings, their refusal to avoid each other, and the overriding value they place on the relationship. Sometimes these are the younger couples who have rid themselves more of gendered expectations and have not accumulated the backlog anger of years of exploitation and inequality. They are committed to their relationship and to making it work. Sometimes these couples come to therapy after the wife has actually left the home and are actively questioning whether to continue the marriage. Most often these couples are stuck in one or both of two areas of the model.

Gendered communication

Despite good will, the husband does not actively deal with conflict and avoids eye contact, cannot express feelings, does not listen well, and gives patronizing advice.

The wife may not know how to help him open up, and may be impatient with his progress. Having considerable resources of her own, she is not about to wait the years her more traditional sisters wait, hoping her husband will eventually come around. She thus may not realize how far along her partner actually has come, may not appreciate what she does get from him and demands change immediately.

Sometimes the change in the husband has already occurred due to the wife's increasing power to influence, but she is so angry about past hurts that she does not see this. She may also be suspicious about the changes the husband promises. In two cases I recently consulted on, one in the UK and one in Germany, the wife had moved out and was convinced that the changes her husband promised were a type of manipulation to get her back. Both women were frightened that by returning home they would lose their leverage for getting him to change. If the changes the husband promised, increased sharing or more emotional expression, were based solely on fear of losing his partner, then these wives are probably right. However, continued investment in increasing equality can turn the changes triggered through dominating tactics to changes which are internalized as part of real friendship.

The German husband posed what seemed to him a bewildering question: how could he show his wife that he respected her right to decide for herself whether to continue the marriage, and at the same time show her he wanted her. He was worried that his being too passive would signal to her that he was not really that interested in her. This is a question grounded in sex-role restrictions. He could not imagine demonstrating his love in a passive fashion. I said, 'It probably is hard for you to believe that it is exactly *by doing nothing* you will be demonstrating your love.' He was taken aback – but his wife was delighted.

Definition of sharing

Acceptance of proportional equity instead of need equity results in overvaluing financial input. The couple attempt to live a more egalitarian lifestyle but have not really learned to appreciate feminine values.

Both may think that money should buy more than the unpaid nurturing done by wives, or both may refuse to fulfill the nurturing role. When no one nurtures, not only the children suffer. The marriage suffers as well as both partners are competitive, achievement oriented, and unwilling to put in the necessary effort to care for the other.

The following couple was actively in crisis, with open conflict as a consequence of the emergence of an equal partnership lifestyle.

Jennifer and Rob, an American couple, had a traditional lifestyle for ten years until Jennifer underwent psychotherapy and began to change. She started her own gift store with a friend. To her surprise the store 'took off' and they were offered to make it part of a chain. Within two years, Jennifer found herself going from being the stay-at-home wife of a successful businessman to being a high-paid executive for her chain of stores. Rob was very proud of her, and had mentored her all the way. He was the one who had brought the investors who wanted to create a chain. He helped her work out a new contract with her friend partner. Then their marriage suddenly seemed to come apart. Rob became so depressed he could not get up in the morning. He started hanging out with male friends, all of whom had affairs. He took to traveling more for his business, and when at home spent time mostly on the phone. When they came into therapy, they were serious about divorce and had already contacted a lawyer.

In individual sessions with each the following information emerged. Rob was sure that there was no such thing as an equal partnership. None of his friends had it, and he had never seen it. He was convinced that as Jennifer got more successful, she would eventually leave. His crisis was triggered when she talked about going on a month-long buying trip without consulting him. He found out about it from her partner. Since they had plenty of help with their children from a live-in nanny, she did not think that she had to talk about it first with him.

Jennifer no longer wanted to consult with him about everything, nor see him as her mentor in business. She saw no way of continuing to be close to him and still feel she was in charge of her life. Whenever they talked he offered helpful advice, but was hurt when she did not automatically take it. She did not feel free in their discussions, preferring to make her own mistakes than to feel dominated.

In joint sessions, they persisted in their gendered styles of communicating. All the soft emotions were expressed by Jennifer and all the anger by Rob. She had the convincing skills needed to make her points but used them in business only. In talking with Rob, she let him interrupt her, dominate the conversation and determine the topic. She looked angry, but mostly cried. They could not negotiate any topic, as she wound up feeling hurt and he got so angry that he withdrew.

For this couple relationship, a rapid unbalancing of power resulted in marital crisis. The wife's power increased suddenly due to her larger income and success outside the home. So long as the husband could feel in charge, as a mentor knowing more about business, they could maintain the illusion of equal power based on both pulling in high incomes, while also allowing him more power due to his expertise.

This was an ephemeral equilibrium based on Jennifer feeling rather incompetent. Rob was so anxious about Jennifer's increasing power that in a self-fulfilling prophecy he began overreacting to her being 'too independent'. Jennifer really did not want to be a 'junior partner'; she wanted equality, but did really not believe it possible. She sent mixed messages. In fear of being dominated and to protect Rob's 'masculine pride', she stopped consulting with him, cutting him off from the one real avenue he had to her world of work. He retaliated by creating his own separate male world that she had no access to, further curtailing their friendship.

Their gendered communication meant Jennifer could not use her considerable convincing skills. If she had, she would not have needed to withdraw, and could have felt freer to disagree. His anxieties about losing her got expressed in anger, instead of as raw vulnerability. Thus she could not reach out to help him.

An underlying issue in both types of transitional relationship is in the wife's power to avoid conflict, previously the sole prerogative of the traditional man. In the transitional marriage both partners have the ability to avoid; it is easy to slide into parallel lives or, when open conflict erupts, into divorce.

THE EQUAL PARTNER COUPLE

Equal partner couples use therapy in the same way they visit the family doctor. They tend to come to therapy early on in their conflicts, use therapy on a short-term basis, and will also keep in touch with the therapist to prevent problems from escalating. These are couples who place a primary value on their relationships and are anxious to nurture them in any way possible. Therapy is usually only one avenue these couples use, with groups, classes, workshops, travel alone and other outlets of growth having equal value to them.

It is important to recognize the equal relationship as having unique therapy needs. These couples are distinguishable by the characteristics below.

Friendship

These couples are very close, will sit together in the therapy room and talk immediately with each other in the presence of the therapist.

Equal partnership couples tend to leave the therapist out of their conversations and the therapist can only gradually be included in a consultative role, without playing the role of authority. The couple is empowered and will let the therapist know what to do.

Individual growth

Couples are introspective and growth oriented. Their interest in therapy is a reflection of their interest in personal growth, so that in addition to using 'I' language, they search for personal meaning for each one via therapeutic interventions. Interventions are filtered back by each partner into the relationship system, and they are intensely aware of the other's reaction to everything that happens. They will often challenge the therapist when an idea appears not to fit, and will look to each other for feedback about how interventions affect the other.

Androgynous communication

The man often speaks openly of his feelings, cries easily and listens intently to his wife. The wife is often the dominant speaker, and asserts her ideas freely and easily. They talk easily about differences between them, even seeking out these differences to analyze and reinforce.

The paradox here is that while they talk about differences, they are actually quite androgynous. It is equally likely that either partner will be emotional, or either will be forceful.

Clear values that guide their lives

The couple is involved with many different and competing activities, often out of the home a great deal and stressed by giving to many different causes.

These relationships can need help when the partners' intense involvement with relationships is out of balance with their equally strong need for individual growth. These couples give so much, to each other and to others, that they are at risk for stress, over-involvement in others and loss of focus on the individual and on the couple. They go off course in any of the possible directions: the demands of community activities, their extended family, colleagues at work and individual pursuits all compete with their need to be with each other.

These couples need assistance in reaffirming their basic commitment to the couple relationship, in realigning their various activities and energies and in allowing adequate space for individual pursuits. For example:

Gabi and Michael are a couple in their mid-twenties. They have been together for five years and have a ten-month-old son. They are still passionately in love, have a deep friendship and commitment to their relationship and their child. They tend to talk daily, keep in touch during the day and go to sleep holding each other. They share all decisions, housework and childcare equally. They came to therapy on the initiative of Michael, who noticed that Gabi was sadder and more withdrawn after the birth of their child. He tried to figure out together with her what was wrong, and when neither could come up with answers, they came to therapy.

When they arrived at the first session, they were holding hands and sat next to each other on the couch. They looked intently at each other during the conversation, and checked with each other through eye contact whenever the therapist talked. It was hard not to feel like an intruder.

However, they were in intense pain, seemingly out of proportion to their rather vague complaint. Their open communication allowed Michael to check with Gabi if she was feeling that she wanted an affair. She stated clearly that this was not the problem. But their difficulty in creating and maintaining boundaries emerged. Intense commitment to each other was in conflict with individual autonomy needs: Gabi recently felt a desire for more time alone and more privacy than formerly. She was concerned that Michael might feel abandoned and hurt when she became more self-centered. However, she was not willing to give up on these unfolding needs, and became more quiet and withdrawn. Michael read the signals correctly at the start, and gave her more space. He did not feel hurt, thinking it natural that after birth a woman might need to be more alone.

Gabi began to feel guilty and initiated unwanted closeness. Her resultant confusion led to her feeling depressed, which paradoxically made Michael more attentive and vigilant in his anxiety about what was happening. They increased their conversations, which made her feel more crowded and consequently worse off. Now she became worried about the relationship, as previously their talking only made her feel better. She wondered if she was doing enough to make the conversations productive, and knowing she secretly just wanted to be left alone, she felt she wasn't doing her share.

Equal partner relationships can be like a finely tuned violin, where the smallest change in the tension of the strings is immediately picked up in changes in the sounds. This problem is also a strength. Fine tuning can occur in brief interventions. One session alone with Gabi reassured her that she had nothing to be guilty about, that the relationship was in fine shape and that she could enjoy her time alone without remorse. Their relationship 'instrument' tuned, the couple renewed their sense of balance.

Chapter 8

Creating an egalitarian therapeutic system

Since a major goal is to further equality within the couple relationship, therapists must be willing to address issues of equality within the therapeutic system as well. Behaviors speak louder than words; relationship therapists must be able to demonstrate that equality can work in a situation in which one member of the system provides more expertise than the others. Many times professional knowledge is translated by clients and therapists into professional power; to define reality, to make pronouncements about who is right or wrong, or magically find solutions. This process is the same one that allows the husband more power because he makes more money, is more educated, or older. As the couple need to equalize power within the context of status differences, so do the clients and therapist have to solve this dilemma constructively. They do so by pooling resources: the therapist is the expert on relationships, the clients on themselves.

Therapists who wish to increase couples' level of equality need to be working towards more equality in their own lives. This certainly does not mean that therapists need to have a perfect equal partnership in their intimate relationships. Rather that there is an awareness of what the struggles involved in trying to achieve equal partnership feels like. This furthers the development of the empathy and compassion needed in the therapeutic endeavor. Having these experiences leads to more easy identification of themes related to gender and power, and the ability to use self-disclosure about one's own personal struggles to enhance the sense that we are all 'in the same boat'. Mutual identification with the process of working towards more equality promotes the notion of being part of a current universal struggle, which can be quite relieving for couples in crisis.

Creating an equal partnership in the therapy means consciously paying attention to clients' deference behaviors and rectifying them. We can do this by taking a stance of mutual investigation and curiosity, offering our ideas in a tentative language, as hypotheses for the partners' consideration. We also help by clarifying and demystifying our own views. By making transparent what we think, we attempt to be real people and not a professional role. This means that we are less of a target for projections around authority issues.

Therapists take responsibility for mistakes or negative reactions to an intervention. By openly contemplating our own work, we invite an egalitarian attitude that does not include a mystified perfectionistic omnipotence. Statements of reflection, such as 'perhaps I was not clear here ... ' or 'I wonder if maybe that idea was not really on target?' can help foster a self-reflective attitude and more openness to honest feedback. When the partners are comfortable challenging our authority, they become more comfortable challenging each other's authority.

Therapists can also reflect about the alliances in therapy by asking openly if a partner feels that the therapist is siding with the other. Processing the 'power politics' of the therapeutic system can be used as feedback towards the end of a session; the therapist invites comment about how the session was perceived. Did any partner feel left out? Was someone feeling overly focused on? Was there any tension with a move by the therapist? These questions induce the creation of an egalitarian therapeutic system in which each person's opinion is honored.

Often it is with the more dominant partner, especially when that partner is the man, that this therapist behavior signals real strength. Therapists who are comfortable in reflecting on their own interventions, clarifying their views and inviting feedback, also indicate their lack of defensiveness. We are comfortable enough with our own authority to be open to criticism and comment.

Our goal is to make empowerment an essential part of the therapy process, by collaborating and fostering client choice and personal autonomy. Therapists who take the time to contemplate different therapeutic options, reveal to the partners the reasoning behind the methods and offer them a choice of alternatives, are continuously empowering them. We can include clients in our deliberations, and work towards creating deliberations for this type of teamwork. Here is one such example:

Claire: We have been meeting together the last few weeks and I am considering how to continue. It appears the couple sessions have given you both a handle on communication; you have started negotiating more at home. Is this true?

Nahum: Yes, we have . . . we are using the skills. Rachel is especially more forceful about expressing her opinions these days. It sometimes seems like a blessing, sometimes a curse!

Claire: Rachel, what is your take on this?

Rachel: I think it is true, and I have been noticing that Nahum is a bit tense about it. On the one hand he seems to like my speaking up, on the other he gets sort of quiet and withdrawn.

Claire: Here is what I have been thinking and I would like your feedback about it. I think that the couple sessions are offering you the chance to try out some new behaviors you might be hesitant to try out at home. So there would be some benefit in continuing this, making sure that you both feel more secure about Rachel's new forcefulness and maybe giving Nahum a chance to get used to it, deal with her more constructively while I am present. On the other hand, if you Nahum meet with me a few times individually, we might get more depth about what is uncomfortable for you and perhaps think together how to help you work through this transition. Then we could try the couple sessions again if necessary . . . which they might not even be, we would see. What do you think?

Rachel: I would love Nahum to meet alone with you . . . I think that he has some real blocks about getting close to me, and I feel these confusing messages, like 'be yourself, speak up' . . . but also, 'don't say anything I cannot handle'.

Claire: I think that for you, Rachel, my meeting with Nahum may take off some pressure and help you by knowing that Nahum is working more on his own. But I am not sure that you Nahum feel like being the focus of treatment right now. I have a feeling that you do need a forum to voice your doubts about what is happening, but I don't know if it should be alone with me or together with her.

Nahum:　I think it might be a good idea for us to meet alone a
couple of times ... I have been getting rather tense the
last few weeks, but I did not connect it to what is
happening with Rachel. I have not been sleeping well.
I assumed it was all the tension at work. Now I am not
sure. I would like to meet alone.

The therapist equalizes power by demystifying therapy and openly
clarifying the model used. Sharing our thinking offers the client
a chance to accept or reject ideas, assimilate them when they fit,
modify them when they don't. We attempt to make the clients
our partners, showing that empowerment can work to strengthen
autonomous thinking and personal responsibility. As in the couple
relationship, this process is an investment in negotiation and
problem solving; it takes added time and patience and can result
in increased conflict. While it might be simpler to give an assignment without this consultation, the moments spent in deliberating
pay off in activating the partners. Gradually the couple gives up
the fantasy of therapist omnipotence.

Much of the work related to relationship equality involves
universalizing couple complaints within the context of the social
transition to gender equality. However, this is not a *carte blanche*
to begin lecturing couples about feminism. Couples need to be
introduced to these matters in a gradual, simple and nonthreat-
ening manner. Collaboration is increased when the therapist keeps
in mind how emotionally sensitive these topics are. Gender roles
are experienced as the natural order of things; tampering with
them feels scary. Sensitivity requires not flooding couples with too
much change by matching the rate of introducing these issues to
the ability of the couple to assimilate them, and by carefully monitoring the couple's reactions.

It is also important to individualize discussions around gender
and power content. Even when generalizing about men and
women in society, the therapist needs to remember that this kind
of talk tends to turn people off. The natural response to statements such as 'most men ... ' or 'most women ... ' is to feel
'well maybe – but not me!' These types of generalizations have
their place, but need to be undertaken in a empathic and person-
alized style that reassures the couple that the therapist is not
imposing preconceived political ideas. Rather they are presented
as information about norms, and as questions about whether they

fit the experience of the partners. For example, in talking with a couple about power:

Claire: You have said Shira, that Ram makes all the major decisions, but that somehow you get stuck with the daily decisions and all the responsibilities at home. You want him to be more involved in helping you decide, and you want to be more consulted about his decisions, right? You want to share decision-making more?

Ram: I let Shira decide a lot of important issues ... I don't know what she is talking about.

Claire: Ram, you know that your 'letting her' may be part of the problem ... in the end, do you kind of get the final say? Could you veto her decisions?

Ram: I guess so ... yes, I think that is true.

Claire: You are both dealing here with an issue that almost all couples have to deal with today. You both mention that you come from families where your father had the final word and yet, you both don't want your relationship to be like that. It is so hard however to imagine anything else – we all get confused about these issues. Do you think that is true for you?

The therapist is empathic, knowing full well that ambivalence is healthy; we want to legitimize and encourage the questioning stance. No one has all the answers about equality between the sexes in marriage, and we also know that the happiest couples are more open about their doubts. These are the provocative questions which form the core issues in the treatment model. Answers evolve as the therapist gains information, looks carefully and asks probing questions. Building and maintaining an equal partnership with the couple in relationship counseling is a crucial and ongoing task.

ANALYZING THERAPIST–COUPLE INTERACTIONS AS AN ASSESSMENT TOOL

In building an egalitarian relationship, the therapist can use the ability of each partner to establish a partnership in the therapeutic relationship as part of the assessment. Couples who are well along towards being capable of teamwork with the therapist are cooperative and use therapeutic expertise as a resource. Partners who tend towards hierarchal relationships may expect the therapist to solve their problems, or conversely challenge the therapist's authority. In the traditional power structure, partners waver between controlling the therapy session through dominating the talk time, and abdicating responsibility by sitting back expecting the therapist to perform magic. These both indicate an underlying 'win–lose' worldview and neither style indicates a readiness for teamwork, the mutual give and take that equal partnership demands. However, these reactions can be read as additional information for the relationship therapist interested in assessing the couple's level of equality. The therapist assesses the patterns of sharing at home as well, probing the many different areas that sharing touches: emotional sharing, housework, power, childcare, extended 'kinwork' and all the myriad areas of family life.

Therapists need to be aware that the degree of open conflict can be an indication of the progress the couple has made towards equality, with open conflict demonstrating real movement towards equality, and parallel lives indicating a more stuck position. Understanding this, therapists can be more welcoming of open conflict when it occurs and more able to calm the partners' fear of total relationship disintegration during the transformation towards change.

Therapists aware of the place of the couple in treatment on the continuum of change can better fathom some of the rather strange mutations emerging in modern relationships. A couple, both doctors, requested treatment for the wife's depression. The husband was the epitome of the 'liberated new man'. Dedicated to the family, and to her having her own career, he had stayed at home for one year after the birth of each of their two children. He even regularly brought the infants to his wife's hospital for her to nurse.

As they related their story, it emerged that the wife had actually wanted to postpone having children and had wanted to invest herself in developing a private practice. Her husband's insistence on having children immediately after their marriage was so impelling that she was afraid she might lose him if she resisted. Aside from really loving him, she felt it was not easy to find a man who accepted her ambitions as he did.

Her depression was a result of the unbalanced power structure of their relationship, in which she had little choice about her own lifestyle, and it was a result of confusion about what constitutes an equal relationship. She felt she had no right to get angry with a husband so dedicated to family life and her career. Both partners felt that they had achieved an egalitarian lifestyle, but were miserable.

This couple was difficult to comprehend, as they presented themselves as extremely egalitarian. However, interactions between them were dominated by the husband, who chose the topics for conversations and appeared to have the final word about everything. It was difficult to establish an egalitarian therapeutic relationship with this couple. This difficulty can be used as a cue to couple assessment. According to the couple types presented here, this is a far more traditional power structure, camouflaged as an equal partnership.

Chapter 9

The treatment model

Individual interventions and education about equality

Therapists who want to address gender in marital therapy do not know how to proceed within a social context that continues to reinforce stereotypes and power imbalance. Gender and power influence on marriage is correctly perceived as a reflection of a much wider social inequity towards women. At family therapy conferences, colleagues share their mutual frustration with current treatment models' lack of guidance. Recommendations in the professional literature often comprise vague global protestations, such as 'pay attention to the income and work potential of the spouses and implications for the balance of power' (McGoldrick and Walsh, 1988). After paying attention, then what? What can we actually do?

We certainly do not have to wait for wider social change to occur: together with our clients, we are responsible to invent the conditions for that change by helping couples become friends. By tackling gender and power directly in a strategic, comprehensive, and in-depth manner on the personal level we take a step towards solving the social problem of inequality. We have shown that these issues are at the heart of marital distress and thus we can be most effective in our goal to increase relationship satisfaction by fashioning these issues as an integral part of therapy. Our own ambivalence about changing gender roles, and fear of change, has curtailed our willingness to address these matters head on.

Couples cannot become equal partners without becoming more responsible and androgynous individuals. This involves developing a coherent ideology about fairness in relationships that recognizes the importance of balancing their own with the other's needs. It means equally valuing their own and the partner's unique contributions. In a social context that stresses self-actualization, ethical issues related to fairness are too often forgotten. Teaching partners to strive to maintain a balance between 'I' and 'Us' is an important part of the process.

Does making individual ethical issues a part of the relationship demand prolonged individual psychotherapy? On the contrary; by focusing on both couple interaction and individual partners' personal growth, relationship therapy can powerfully address fairness. Intervention simultaneously in couple and individual issues related to gender and power uncovers intimate patterns of relating that reflect the deepest levels of personality and identity.

In this work we are first and foremost attempting to change the power balance between the partners and release the gender restrictions of stereotypic roles. Both power and gender restrictions limit the degree of ethical accountability in a social system. As the couple relationship moves closer to equality, more equal expression of opinions, feelings and needs necessarily generates increased conflict. Couples then learn to cope constructively as both men and women begin to have an equal say. Treatment of couples can utilize any or all of these three therapy methods:

1 Modifying dominant–subordinate roles through individual interventions and education towards equality.
2 Developing intimacy through an individual focus in couple sessions.
3 Preparation for sharing through couple interaction.

These components can form a stagelike progression for some couples. For traditional couples, all elements are needed and can form a progression: from individual sessions with a focus on education and change in hierarchy roles, to work on the individual with the partner observing, and finally to conjoint work with the couple. Other couples who have themselves moved further on the continuum of change may necessitate only some of the elements. Just as couples move forward and backward in their development of a more fair relationship, so therapy can utilize these components in any order, and with the potential for returning to previous stages as needed.

Thus the treatment plan requires matching the particular circumstances of each couple, which are continually changing as an outcome of the intervention.

INDIVIDUAL WORK: EMPOWERMENT OF EACH PARTNER

The continual balancing of autonomous personal responsibility for monitoring fairness with a high level of relationship commitment is decisive in helping couples move towards equality. Thus, a central focus in this work is on increasing personal autonomy within the context of relationship therapy. Partners need to refocus on the self, and often require a safe place alone with the therapist to start doing this. When changes have begun to occur, continual strengthening of the individual can occur with the partner also present. Therapy involves a concerted effort to break down barriers that interfere with the development of individuality and responsibility in the relationship: ambivalence that is interfering with communicating clear messages, gender roles that constrict behavior; power motives that underlie the politics of the relationship; and personal history that can be brought to bear on all these issues.

Empowerment of the subordinate partner

The less powerful partner in the relationship needs support and help to become more capable of creating a cooperative relationship. While this partner, most often the woman, desires closeness and intimacy, actual friendship with the more powerful partner is not feasible until both partners feel and behave like equals. The subordinate partner often feels unworthy, victimized, abused, childlike, helpless and out of control. It is futile to expect equal partner teamwork when one partner experiences this constellation of crippling emotions. Traditional wives who are terrified of making a mistake and being ridiculed cannot become an equal partner about important decisions. They are not ready to be supportive of their partners when their partners' vulnerable feelings are revealed. When gender identity involves being taken care of, the woman will not be able to take her place as a real friend about many issues.

The less powerful partner needs to work alone with the therapist to increase awareness and take personal responsibility for change in the following spheres:

1 The extent to which he/she has become a victim, and has allowed exploitation or emotional or physical abuse to occur in the relationship.

2 The way gender roles have harmed individual growth and self-esteem, including constriction of personal choice, constricting role prescriptions, not learning competencies usually exhibited by the other gender and poorly handled ambivalence; the ways these gender role problems have reinforced the unequal power balance of the relationship, including lack of entitlement, lack of assertiveness, self-effacement, self-blame.

3 The extent to which anger at injustice has been denied, repressed or redirected, sabotaging the partner's ability to demand change.

4 The extent to which the partner has abdicated personal responsibility for choices made; the dependency this abdication of responsibility has entailed and the price this partner has paid for it.

The subordinate partner has a difficult emotional task in the initial stages of treatment, best undertaken alone with the therapist. The individual sessions allow the subordinate partner to present the real picture of fears, anxieties and low self-esteem, without losing face in the presence of the partner. This is important because the subordinate partner has often come to therapy because of wanting to be taken more seriously, wanting needs to be considered and met.

Uncovering all the barriers to real empowerment of the developing subordinate person in the presence of the partner would only serve to undermine the process of increasing equality. The couple is usually not ready to handle intimate revelations of vulnerability, without retaliation and harm to both. Premature conjoint sessions often reinforce the power structure; at home, the more powerful partner may use material brought up in the session to fortify an eroding position. The couple cannot be induced to having more intimacy than they are prepared for without harming the emerging strength of the subordinate partner.

The process, similar to feminist consciousness raising regardless of which partner is subordinate, results in: an awakening to abuse and oppression in one's own life; an increase in awareness of one's personal involvement in that abuse; the emotional divorce from the role of victim; and a redefining of what is possible in intimate relationships. Anger inevitably arises, sometimes in a sudden and explosive way:

Talia is the obese housewife married to Danny, a successful lawyer, described in chapter 3, p. 74. In joint sessions Talia and Danny's interaction was patterned and rigid: all topics were raised by Talia, but Danny changed the subject, cut her off in mid-sentence, looked away when she got emotional, avoided eye contact and was sarcastic. Inevitably, Talia would start crying, and he would say: 'There she goes again – turning on the tap!'

After she worked alone with me in therapy for two months, Talia improved her self-image. She investigated why she allowed herself to become so dependent on Danny and used therapeutic support to think about her own personal choices and goals. She continued to absorb a great deal of verbal abuse at home, continuing a familiar 'dance' of his lashing out and hurting her, her crying, and his eventual leaving the house.

During a pivotal individual session, she was asked if she realized the extent of the abuse she was willing to absorb. He controlled their money, made all decisions, did not tell her when he was coming home, traveled abroad without notifying her. Unexpectedly, the term 'abuse' seemed to have an electrifying effect on her. Talia had never seen it in that light. The idea that she was being 'abused' was shocking to her. Despite all the pain he caused her, and her suffering in the relationship, the word seemed to categorize her together with battered women and rape victims. The sessions released a great deal of pent-up rage; she was furious at him, and even more angry at herself for not having identified what was happening to her. In her compulsive pursuing of closeness, she had ignored her own humiliation. In exploring other situations in which she had been a victim, she revealed that she had been sadistically dominated by a favored older sister and had accepted this situation as normal. She became angry not just at Danny, but at her mother and sister as well.

From then on she began to experiment in creating limits and gave up her pursuit of Danny. She no longer cried when they fought. She demanded that he notify her when he was planning to be late, saying that if not, she would lock him out of the house. Not believing her, Danny was angry with her sudden demonstration of strength. She actually did lock him out one time. The couple interaction shifted significantly. He no longer put her down, began to listen to her, consulted about his hours and began to share decisions with her.

At some point anger is replaced by pain, due to lost opportunities for personal growth, and the giving up of gendered dreams of being rescued, cared for, and saved by another person. This pain can be accompanied by shame at having allowed oneself to be subordinated, and fear about managing life from a more autonomous role. All these emotional processes are best handled in individual sessions, where they can be worked through in a safe and supportive atmosphere.

Eventually the subordinate partner learns to integrate strengths and weaknesses, so that it becomes more possible to talk about vulnerable feelings with the partner and yet retain the sense of strength gained in individual sessions. When the dominant partner has also worked individually, the potential for intimacy is greatly increased. But even in situations where the subordinate partner has succeeded in changing the power balance without the dominant partner's involvement in therapy, the new balance results in significant changes in their interaction.

The subordinate partner learns why and how they let themselves be dominated. This has to be accomplished without guilt; this is not 'blaming the victim', but empowering the person to feel that things don't just 'happen' without some form of cooperation. The therapist needs to find an appropriate balance between seeing that anyone in an exploitative situation becomes weakened by being in that situation, and seeing the gender and personal history that might predispose the person to have acquiesced to becoming a victim.

Empowerment of the dominant partner

Power is not empowerment; the dominant partner often actually feels powerless. Dominance is a strategy, albeit an unsuccessful one, to maintain control in the face of underlying feelings of helplessness. It is the use of power to bolster a flagging self-esteem and to regain some mastery. Work alone with the dominant partner has several aims. Joining with this partner, we attempt to reach the more vulnerable sides that have been suppressed and demonstrate that their uncovering can be a positive experience.

In dominating, real emotional needs are not met; the fact that this partner is getting more than the other is only relative. It is impossible to measure who is getting more, since both partners in an unequal relationship system feel deprived and empty. When one partner in an intimate relationship loses, both lose. Dominant partners are unaware of how they are losing, how much underlying pain their are experiencing, how lonely they are, and how little they trust human relationships.

Reaching the vulnerable feelings involves getting through the dominance behaviors that have been cutting this partner off from contact. Dominance behavior varied between individuals, and can be identified as the resistance this particular individual puts up to becoming vulnerable. The same behavior could be dominating, or could be assertive; the question is the motive behind the behavior and not the form the behavior takes. A woman previously in a subordinate role may cut her partner off in conversation. This might be an attempt to reach him and not to dominate. Another constantly uses cutting her partner off to stop her from getting close to him. Dominating behavior is used here to resist intimacy.

Dominance behavior can take a variety of forms, including: attempting to impose a certain view of reality, putting the partner down, arguing, cutting off conversation, insisting on one's way, withdrawing, changing the topic, making decisions without consulting the partner, or hiding information from the partner. In effect, any behavior whose motive and function is to remain in control can be seen as dominating. For example:

Sharon and Tom, the traditional couple in crisis who had uncovered a long-term pattern of the husband's affairs, entered a stage in the therapy where Sharon experienced and contacted her rage about Tom's chronic adultery and about never having any influence on him. Throughout the years she had asked for more help in the home and more time with him to no avail. While Tom worked in therapy on his dominating patterns, Sharon withdrew from him in silence at home. She refused to come to treatment for several weeks, saying that she had no partner to work with. This was a reversal of their usual pattern; in the past, Sharon had pursued him and not vice versa. Tom responded to the new situation by entering a power struggle with her, showing the increasing conflict of a couple moving from a traditional to a transitional structure. When she became silent, he let her and did not initiate talks. A stand-off ensued, in which both waited to see who would break first.

His response to her withdrawal (and underlying rage) was examined in individual work; he faced his deep ambivalence about having a strong wife with more influence over him. He had not told her that he was going to the individual sessions, thinking that if she wrongly believed he had stopped therapy she might be induced to give in and talk with him. The long-term price he paid for these kinds of power tactics was explored. He saw that his having affairs all those years was in effect a very similar dominance maneuver: he was attempting to control the relationship and solve the couple's sexual problems in his own way. He decided to reveal to her how much he really wanted her to talk with him, as well as the fact that he was continuing therapy. Their power struggle tapered off and they started to talk again. She soon returned to therapy as well, not needing to express her rage through withdrawal.

The therapist's job in work with the dominant partner is to stop this type of behavior long enough so that vulnerable emotions can be accessed. Stopping dominating behavior necessitates helping this partner identify it. Often the motive of the behavior is out of awareness:

Danny, Talia's husband, tended to interrupt conversations, change the topic, look away for long periods of time when the conversation was difficult for him, and make jokes that were rather derogatory. He did this with Talia consistently, and to some extent with me, a female therapist. In an early individual session I asked him: *'Danny, what do you think it is like talking with you? How do you think Talia feels when you two are conversing?'* He had never thought about this before, and said that probably she felt overwhelmed. I asked if he had thought about the possibility that as long as he cuts her off, interrupts, changes the topic, or looks away, they can never get close. He also had never thought about this and was quiet for a long time. He finally said that this was automatic behavior for him and that he did it without thinking. He wanted to change and was glad that I had told him. He did not want to overwhelm her; on the contrary, he said that all he wanted was for her to be happy and stop all the crying!

Dominant partners are often unaware of their power advantage. They take their positions for granted, and don't see their own manipulations to maintain the structure. They are similarly unaware of the long-term costs to themselves when they 'win', in contrast to the short-term gain of getting their way. While the immediate effects of dominance may be compliance of the partner, getting certain needs immediately met, feeling temporarily powerful or having a sense of control, all benefits are fleeting. In reality, the long-term effects are having a partner who is unhappy and who will retaliate in some way; feeling like an aggressor or exploiter, demeaning the partner, feeling alone, often bored and guilty. There is an underlying fear that the partner will leave. The interaction with the therapist is aimed to teach a new way of relating based on mutuality, with room for disagreement and differences.

The dominant partner has to learn to value feminine traits in the self and partner, such as expression of feelings, intuition, non-goal-oriented 'being' rather than achievement-oriented 'doing'. This partner is often highly goal oriented, and takes for granted all those nurturing behaviors the other performs that allow for goals to be attained. These include housework and care of the children and in-laws, paying attention to the 'petty details' of running one's life and taking care of health-related concerns.

In coming to honor these feminine traits and tasks, this partner begins to accept some responsibility for taking them on as well. Learning to nurture relationships involves locating the blocks to this nurturing. Personal history might have denied access to caring, as often the dominating partner had to be on their own far too early in life.

The fact that the dominating partner emphasizes the masculine traits (regardless if it is the husband or the wife) so valued by society, demands that this phase of treatment is at first carried out in a rational logical mode. We join this partner by using their language and reaching them in evaluating the impact of change. If the dominating partner can be convinced that cooperation is within his or her best interest, there is a chance of creating a real reorganization of the fundamental structure of the relationship.[1]

As part of this approach, the therapist taps into previous experiences this partner has had in sharing. The dominating partner is not dominating in all spheres of life; sometime and somewhere this person has experienced teamwork, sometimes with a same-sex colleague, sometimes with a personal friend. The therapist demonstrates and highlights the difference between hierarchal interactions and equal interactions using prior experiences in teamwork as leverage: the dominating partner can share, but doesn't see it as in their best interest to share with the spouse:

Danny had no experience of teamwork with a woman. However, he did have a law partner. In discussing his tendency to return home whenever he felt like it, without notifying Talia, I asked him whether he would do this to his partner. He said that he doesn't live with his partner so he couldn't imagine it. Attempting to tap into his previous experiences of teamwork, an imaginary situation is set up:

Claire: Let's make up a situation. You and your partner are on visit to a client in another country. You are out to dinner with the client and your partner is back at the hotel. It looks like the dinner will take longer than you thought.

Danny: I think I would probably pick up the phone and let him know.

Claire: Why would you do it?

Danny: He would just wait around the hotel room if I didn't. I guess he might want to go out himself, maybe he would join us, maybe he would want to sleep. Just waiting around for me would kind of tie him up.

Claire: So you would consider his needs. Now let's think what is the difference for you about this situation, and what happens when you get busy at the office, but don't call Talia.

Danny: Maybe it is the same. But I always think that Talia is just waiting around for me. She isn't working and her time is flexible.

Claire: You have told me that you wished she worked and that you are worried that she has no self-confidence. Do you

> think Talia knows what you think about the way she spends her time?

Danny: Sure I tell her all the time. You are saying that maybe her lack of confidence is tied up with this? That she doesn't value her time because I don't?

Claire: I think Talia doesn't value her time enough because she doesn't value herself enough. But how would you feel if she thought you weren't doing anything important?

Danny: Pretty bad.

Claire: Let's imagine that you treated her like you treated your partner – you called her, gave her the sense that her time was as valuable as yours. What effect do you think that might have on her self-confidence?

Danny: I think that is exactly what she wants. But I always thought she was trying to control me. I never thought about it as teamwork. I have a hard time giving her what she asks for . . . I wonder why?

Individual sessions facilitate the establishment of a trusting working relationship, breaking up the automatic hierarchal role-playing that each partner has become locked into. The subordinate partner is out of touch with her/his strengths and, as part of an interactional system, is reinforcing the dominating partner's domination. The dominating partner is similarly reinforcing the subordination of the other. Neither benefits in the long run and thus trigger the other's reciprocal role behavior. Increasing personal autonomy through individual support allows the subordinate partner to bring forth strengths and the dominant partner to access softer emotions in a safe environment.

Metacommunication to shift power patterns

An important tool in changing power and gender behavior is found in modification of the client–therapist behavior. During individual sessions, when a supportive working relationship has been established, the gendered power roles can be changed by focusing on the way they are played out with the therapist. Often these changes are instrumental in leading to change within the individual and between the partners. Gender and power are so outside of awareness that bringing them into focus is a forceful experience. By heightening awareness of interactional behaviors, we are in effect focusing on the 'metacommunication' of conversation, where power issues are encoded.

The way we react in interaction with any individual is partly determined by gendered behavior, and as such makes up the core of our identity. Assuming that gender and power roles constrict and limit interactional potential, the freeing up of alternatives is an exciting experience.

Partners who tend to play the subordinate role use submissive behaviors while talking in therapy about intimate aspects of their lives. People in the subordinate role often focus on their partners in the conversation, to the exclusion of focusing adequately on themselves. This can be viewed as resulting from, but also maintaining, gender role: ignoring one's own welfare and the promotion of own benefit in the conversation as in life. Moreover, this partner remains cut off from contact with feeling powerful, assertive and entitled. For a women, these feelings are threatening to her gender identity and are associated for her with aggressiveness, selfishness, and lack of concern for others. But a man in the subordinate position is also threatened by his own aggressiveness; he may fear being 'macho' like his father, or may fear losing the partner if he is perceived as too demanding.

The subordinate partner also uses a passive language in describing their life and especially in describing interactions with the dominant partner. 'He made me ... ' is a common motif for people who feel victimized, but this kind of passive role also maintains the construction of the victim role.

The dominant partner will bring a dominating style of control into the sessions, and act it out with the therapist. We often encounter the tendency of the man in the individual session to cut off feeling talk and to talk instead about his competencies. He may either dominate the conversational flow or expect the therapist to do all the work, by asking the questions, bringing up topics, intuiting his feelings. He is not nurturing conversation but protecting his own vulnerability. This mirrors his behavior in his intimate relationship. He is cutting himself off from feeling his sense of incompetency in relationships, his fear of showing weakness, and from feeling responsible for relationship.

The more powerful woman partner will behave very similarly with the therapist, demonstrating how power position can preempt gender role. Blocking and labeling these behaviors consistently can change inner experience quite dramatically. Subordinate partners benefit from focusing on the self and from learning to talk in the active voice. Dominant partners benefit when their controlling behavior is stopped and they can access feelings of helplessness.

For example, Talia (in the subordinate position) was deeply unhappy in her own life, but spent all of her individual sessions talking about Danny, demonstrating how inactive she felt. In this example, this overinvolved behavior is targeted, labeled, blocked and the resultant feelings allowed to emerge. Talia has spent about half of her session talking about him:

Talia: Danny is so mean to me. All he cares about is his work, his clients. He cares more about them then me.

Claire: I want to ask you about something we haven't talked about yet. I wondered if you noticed that in the past half hour you have spent more time talking about Danny than talking about yourself?

Talia: No, but he is the problem! If he would treat me nice everything would be fine.

Claire: Perhaps part of the problem is that you have a hard time focusing on yourself, thinking about what would be good for you. Instead, you talk about him ... at least you don't have to feel selfish!

Talia: (quiet at first) ... I was called a show-off whenever I tried to get my mother's attention.

Claire: Many women feel that to think about themselves too much is wrong – they are on this earth to take care of others, and thinking about themselves is too egoistic.

Talia: Yea ... and if I thought about myself, I might get really upset. I mean, what have I accomplished in life?

Claire: I know you wish you had done more, but you know, I wonder if you value having made a beautiful home and raised two healthy sons?

Talia: Danny says that is easy, that any half-wit can stay home with children and he says ...

Claire: That is what I was talking about. You automatically bring him into the conversation. What do *you* think about making a good home for children?

Talia: I think it is worth a lot! I think that maybe it is one of the hardest jobs around.

It is not a coincidence that when Talia realized her tendency to insert Danny into her experience, and when my intervention blocked her from doing this, she contacted first her low self-esteem, based on a devaluing of her feminine accomplishments. It is by supporting these accomplishments (valuing the feminine) that she can start to feel more worthy and eventually stronger. She will be better equipped to enter into an equal partnership with Danny. If the therapist shares her opinion that only by 'making something' of herself in the outside world can she have self-worth, then the necessary support will not be forthcoming. This will leave her more depressed then before, as she is no longer complaining about him, but feeling the lacks of her own life.

The subordinate partner is over-focused on the other. A man in this position may be unable to talk about himself and needs help to contact his strengths, often his devalued feminine side. The subordinate partner, be it the male or the female, is usually the more emotionally expressive partner, but devalues this emotionality as a weakness. Instead, emotionality needs to be relabeled as a resource for the relationship (again, valuing the feminine) and the partner as contributing this needed resource to the relationship.

The dominant partner tends to dominate the conversation with the therapist, making it extremely difficult to contact sensitive material. For example, Danny tended to change the topic frequently. This intervention came after several incidences of topic changing, and after a warm relationship had been established:

Danny: I really don't know what Talia wants, she is so negative that I get closed down . . . I just shut down and I won't budge.

Claire: Do you feel that it is hard to give when you are angry or hurt?

Danny: You know, yesterday a colleague of mine really got me mad . . . he said . . .

Claire: Sorry to interrupt you Danny. I would like to point something out that I noticed, and see what you think. I noticed that whenever we get close to talking about your feelings, you change the topic . . . sometimes you change the topic even when we aren't talking about feelings . . . but especially then . . .

Danny: Really? I did not notice . . . now where was I – oh, yes, my client said that he wanted to pay me at the end of the year . . .

Claire: Danny, it happened again. What do you think is going
           on?
Danny: Well, what were we talking about before?
Claire: How hard it is for you to cope with not knowing what
           Talia wants . . . that you get shut down.
Danny: Yes . . . it really hurts me to know that no matter what
           I do, I cannot seem to make her happy . . . sometimes I
           think she doesn't really love me, even through she says
           she does. I cannot make her happy.

These types of intervention demand close attention to the context
of client behavior. They are only effective when patterns are
identified and their use blocked repeatedly and consistently;
behaviors are labeled often and enough momentum for change is
generated. As with any type of defensive behavior, these behaviors
occur to protect the client from experiencing unpleasant or anxiety
provoking material. In this case, we are focusing on material that
is gender related, and is outside the awareness of the client. The
context will help us determine what is not being contacted. Danny
changed the topic when touching on feelings related to helplessness. Another person may repeatedly put down their partner
whenever their own self-esteem is shaken. Talia tended to bring
Danny into the conversation when she was feeling bad about
herself and her lack of accomplishments. Another person may
switch to talk about the partner whenever anger emerges.

Allowing contact with these previously unexperienced parts of
the self is instrumental in remedying the gendered ambivalence
that disturbs the development of personal responsibility and
empowerment. Each partner is especially upset by behaviors in
the other partner that are related to these suppressed parts. For
example, as long as Talia cannot allow herself to focus on her own
accomplishments and taking time (in the conversation and in real
life) for herself, she will blame Danny for being selfish. As long
as Danny cannot contact his own feelings of helplessness, continuing to dominate interactions to keep the heat off himself, he will
blame Talia for being ineffective. In essence, the partner is blamed
for having that part of the self not allowed to emerge. And that
often is a part denied as inappropriate to gender role.

When we help our clients to focus on their metacommunication,
encouraging their ability to observe their patterns of interaction
in interaction, we also help empower them. Empowerment is

increased by having a choice through having increased alternatives and options. With increased awareness, the addition of new behavioral patterns and the contacting of previously hidden feelings, we help partners get unstuck from rigid power positions.

EDUCATION TOWARDS EQUALITY

Educating couples on equal partnership requires activating the themes generated by the research. It necessitates locating the many stereotypes about equal partnership which need to be debunked; for example, that sharing is a fifty–fifty deal, or that equality compels men and women to give up all differences. Couples come to realize that equality is not based on earning the same amount, nor on pressuring the woman to have a career. Rather they learn about the relevant themes underlying friendship, such as the importance of recognizing and meeting each other's needs, honoring each other's differences, and coping positively with gendered communication patterns. A type of cognitive intervention, this component requires the correct assessment of which preconception might be obstructing the couple's movement towards a more equitable relationship system.

The couple's definition of sharing, their gender stereotyped constrictions and their views on equality in general are conceptually linked to their major areas of distress. The therapist teaches the partners to think about power, how it influences their relationship, the place of friendship in their relationship, the benefits of androgyny and equity, and the costs of oppression and unfair sharing of power. The potential for more conflict in equal relationships has to be squarely faced as a potential discomfort and confusion in relinquishing familiar gender roles.

Therapists can use readings, handouts, videotapes or any other educational methods which generally enhance learning. However, the most forceful educative experiences occur when the therapist locates opportunities to tie couple interaction to one of the central concepts. Here is a brief example:

Shlomo: Etti looked like she needed the day off. You know this summer we couldn't afford to have all three children in camp so she has been staying home with them more than usual. I was planning to be in town. I thought about our talks and I decided that maybe I would stay home and watch the children today.

Etti: I was amazed since Shlomo never initiated something like that ... he has done it, but only when I asked him to.

Claire: I think it is great that you are becoming more of a team. This is an example of how you two can be better friends to each other. What seems most important here is that you, Shlomo, were sensitive to Etti's needs, you took the time and effort to think about what she might require. And you also took the responsibility to do something about it.

Etti: That is exactly right. Now that I think about it, he has stayed with them so often, but I didn't feel that appreciative and I guess I didn't really seem too grateful. He always said I don't appreciate all that he is doing. Maybe that is why I had to ask, I stayed responsible for running everything. I still had the burden of responsibility totally on me.

Much of what occurs in therapy is educational and elucidating all the methods for changing beliefs and attitudes are beyond the scope of this book. However, the following are three ways in which the therapist can focus on attitude change.

Value clarification

As part of the educational component, therapists can implement value clarification. Couples are often unaware of their value system, and certainly of the contradictions in their value system about equality. For example:

Jennifer and Rob (the couple described in Chapter 7) were in a state of crisis due to Jennifer's sudden success in business. Their values about the woman's role in the home were directly investigated; the couple was asked what they believe should be the role of each at home and at work. Jennifer said that she believed that the man should be the main provider, and the woman in charge of the home. Rob said that he did not agree, and that he wanted his wife to be equally involved in supporting the family. Continued probing about these issues revealed that Jennifer was actually ambivalent; she really wanted to be an equal partner, but was both afraid of what her strength would do to Rob, and was unsure about her competency. Rob was also more ambivalent than he had indicated at first. While believing in equality, he was afraid that if Jennifer became financially independent, she could leave the first time they had a really bad fight. He feared that he might leave first. He wanted her to succeed, but also expected her to have primary responsibility for the home front.

The educational component requires the normalization of these agonizing dilemmas and tying them clearly into social change, thereby removing the personal sense of failure and guilt. The therapist can state clearly that everyone would like to have the best of all worlds, 'have their cake and eat it', and that knowing how to give up is a difficult problem for most of us. Discrepancies between stated attitudes and actual sharing that were discovered in the assessment phase can now be more fully discussed. Listing the benefits and costs of maintaining traditional and/or more progressive attitudes towards women can help to clarify competing values and assist partners squarely to face short-term versus long-term results of maintaining these values.

Choice

Together with universalizing and discussing questions about sex roles, the therapist can also empower the couple to make choices about their values. Couples muddle along, sending double messages, conflicted but unaware of how confusing they can be. Articulating and making choices based on awareness increases a sense of personal power:

Claire: Rob, you say that you wish for Jennifer to succeed and make it in this new venture. But you also want her to continue to be at home and responsible for the children. It is natural that you want all of this, we all would like to have the benefits of the old ways and the new ones, with no price tag. But I wonder if it is possible for you to have both here. Can Jennifer be both successful and at home, without sharing the home responsibility with you?

Rob: No, I guess not. But I am uncomfortable leaving all the home responsibilities to the nanny – I don't feel relaxed at work, knowing she isn't at home.

Claire: So I guess you can make a choice here; you can continue on sending the double messages: Jennifer I want your success – but stay home! Or you can choose to ask her to stay home more and give up the work. Or, you could choose to take on more of the home front yourself and help her succeed.

Rob: I am worried about her success – she might get so self-important that she would forget all about us. I know what I want to choose; I have no problem helping out more. I am worried – that's all.

Claire: Can you talk to Jennifer, now, about some of these fears?

Teaching about gender differences

An important theme from the research useful for an educational focus is diversity: recognizing and accepting differences. Most couples in therapy view their problems as based on their differences, instead of seeing their differences as a source of their unique strength. Gender differences appear especially perplexing, as they are experienced both as foreign and related to personality. Men experience women's emotionality with repugnance ('You are being hysterical'); women can feel utterly shut out by men's analytic problem-solving style ('You are like talking to a wall').

Therapists first and foremost point out and legitimize differences; differences can be viewed as expected and positive. It is crucial that therapists are familiar with research about gender, and can point out that many differences viewed as temperament related are actually learned sex roles. Typical differences such as women's verbal skills around emotions, men's high arousal during conflict and tendency to withdraw, men's attempts to problem solve when their wives are upset, women's concern with connection – all these should be readily available in the therapist's consciousness, to be brought up in therapy as they are observed in sessions.

Accepting conflict as normative and beneficial, the therapist highlights and seeks out differences rather than favoring consensus. Comments like: 'You two are quite different about this', or 'Let me sum up some of the differences I perceive between the two of you' set the stage for work on diversity.

The therapist educates about the importance that role

differences play in a healthy social system: 'What would our lives be like if everyone were the same?' or 'Think about your place of work – what is the contribution of differences between people to your workplace?'

The therapist continues to normalize and universalize differences throughout therapy, helping couples to gain some perspective on them. Finally the couple is helped to find ways in which their differences contribute to their relationship:

Talia felt that Danny was uninterested in her life and he felt that she was trying to devour him. The pursuer–distancer syndrome functioned to continue this polarization: the more Talia sought olooonooo, tho moro Danny rotroatod into hic work; tho moro ho retreated, the more panicky she felt and the more she sought his closeness, and the more he retreated . . .

It was pointed out to them that they were very different about distance and closeness: Danny tended to need distance far more than Talia, and was often concerned with maintaining his boundaries, gaining more privacy, and keeping his space. Talia felt responsible for the nurturing of relationships and monitored their degree of intimacy. The gendered nature of these differences was pointed out, and they were asked if they noticed these differences in their friends. Universalizing the differences led to a discussion of what possible benefit they might have in keeping these differences.

At first neither could think of any benefits. They were asked to play out a sculpture in which they were both seeking closeness and another in which they both sought distance. In the closeness sculpture they were quickly brought down in laughter; they had created a couple embracing so tightly that no one had air. The distance sculpture was no improvement; they both had their backs to each other, and no contact whatsoever.

This experiential exercise elicited a discussion of the benefits of difference and their relative intolerance of differences in their lives. They were intolerant of their different styles of parenting, of how they spent free time, and their sexuality. Learning to identify differences, relabel them in a positive light, and appreciating the contribution of these individual 'gifts' became an important theme throughout their therapy.

Role plays can be used to further illuminate differences. For example:

Talia and Danny were asked to role play what they *wished* their communication would be like. Each was asked to play themselves and the other, rotating between two seats. Talia demonstrated emotional talk and a listening response. Danny demonstrated a problem-solving approach with a practical solution. Their different goals for the communication were immediately apparent, and led to a fruitful discussion of male and female differences.

Repetition of the theme of differences needs to occur throughout therapy as we are attempting to modify a basic attitude that couples hold. Coming to view differences as life giving and not life threatening is indeed an important step towards building an equal relationship and cannot be overstated in therapy.

Chapter 10

Couple interventions

CONJOINT SESSIONS WITH FOCUS ON THE INDIVIDUAL

As a way to bridge the move from individual sessions to joint couple work, or as an intervention in its own right, couples can experience deeper levels of intimacy when they have the opportunity to watch their partner in individual sessions.

The notion of 'shared experience' as prerequisite to friendship is the basis behind this intervention. Partners have not built up adequate sharing of their worlds due to gender segregation, lack of trust, fear of betrayal, rigid gender roles and power restrictions. However, being able to get inside the experience of the other is at the root of wanting to share; as friends we want to help out as much as possible, we cannot exploit our friends without losing the friendship.

A powerful intervention, the viewing of each partner at work in therapy, opens up a level of sharing not previously experienced. Couples are introduced to the rationale for this intervention: equality as demanding shared experience, listening, allowing the other to be different from the self, and personal autonomy. The sessions are structured as follows:

1 Each partner has the experience of being the focus, with the other listening, taking turns over time.
2 The partner in the 'hot seat' (working on self) faces the therapist, with the other partner sitting as far as possible out of view, or at least not facing the partner, and not too close.
3 The partner listening in is not allowed to react at all, but is given a pad and pencil to write reactions to the sessions.

4 The session ends with fifteen minutes of feedback and inter-action between the two partners and the therapist. In this section, the listening partner can ask questions and react to the session. It is not seen as 'therapy' in that no one issue should be pursued in depth, nor should the partner in the 'hot seat' have to defend him/her self.

The therapist needs to be active in creating and setting up this structure. The partner in the 'hot seat' needs to be protected from involvement with the partner, from partner responses or from any distraction to focusing on the self.

At first, most couples are intensely uncomfortable with this format, as it demands a level of intimacy not experienced previously with the partner. Thus, the partners will tend to look at each other for reassurance or feedback, and continue their natural patterns of interaction. If the therapist waits, allowing the regular interaction configuration to persist, it will be far more difficult to create a new structure. Thus, the initial therapist intervention is crucial; it is up to the therapist to establish the new pattern.

Once the couple have settled into the new structure they find it liberating. The partner in the 'hot seat' can explore, reveal and work without interference. The partner listening and writing is free really to hear and look at the partner without having to react. While the content of the session is individual, the effects occur on the interactional level; this is a form of relationship counseling, despite the fact that one partner is silent for threequarters of the session.

The therapist needs to be aware at all times that this is couples therapy. The partner listening is processing, hearing and integrating a new view. The partner talking is talking for the self, but in the presence of the other. This prepares each for intimacy that is not immediately dependent on the other's response. Self-disclosure is undertaken for the self, and the reactive preoccupation with feeling secure, getting approval from the partner, or fear of being criticized is reduced.

The therapist aims to have each partner experience that side of the other that has been hidden from view; usually the gendered role behaviors prohibited. Women have the chance to be openly assertive, powerful, clear, and convincing. Men have the opportunity to reveal hidden doubts or weaknesses. Men have the chance to hear what women really endure in their multiple roles, the threats to self-esteem routinely absorbed, and the lack of control of their fate imposed by more powerful figures. Women hear the loneliness of the 'provider' role, the exhaustion experienced in having to present a facade, and the thwarted need for closeness experienced. Each can hear what the other really encounters as a man and as a women, without demands or complaints. For example:

Talia in the 'hot seat' with Danny listening

Talia started her session by continuing to complain about Danny's lack of attention to her, his self-absorption, and his inconsiderate behavior. However, questions by the therapist about her feelings, thoughts, and inner experiences led to her talking about her childhood. For the first time in their marriage, she revealed her abuse as a child, and then tied it into her sense that she could not influence Danny.

She explored her gendered belief that it was up to him to make her happy, that as long as he was cruel to her she had to play the reciprocal role of victim. She reflected out loud that perhaps Danny was right about her; maybe she was worthless. However, she ended by saying that she deserved more, that she was worth better, and that maybe she could make something out of her life regardless of what he thought of her.

In his feedback to her, Danny said that he was touched. He did not want to destroy her self-esteem, and stated that he had been so rough on her because he was trying to push her to do something with herself. He felt very frustrated that his good intentions had turned out so badly.

Danny in the 'hot seat' with Talia listening

In the next session, Danny began by expressing anger at Talia. He was fed up with her complaining, her lack of satisfaction with him and with life, and her pessimistic mood. Nothing seemed to satisfy her. Asked what this reminded him of, he shared his childhood experience of frustration at not being able to help his widowed and impoverished mother. A concentration camp survivor, his mother brought him and his sister up alone in the slums of Tel Aviv by taking in clothes that needed mending. His earliest memories were of sitting under the sewing machine, hungry, but not wanting to disturb her work. He remembered going off to play in the streets for hours, feeling helpless and angry that she had to work late into the night.

He then related this sense of helpless rage to how he feels when he is impotent to help Talia. He gets furious at her that she puts him in the same position he felt with his mother; watching her pain and unable to do anything about it. Exploring his gendered idea that it is up to the man to make a women happy, he began to imagine what life would be like if he could allow Talia to make her own way in the world. He said it would be a relief.

In her feedback, Talia expressed some anger. She was adamant that Danny was not responsible for her life, and that he was patronizing her by taking charge and then demeaning her for not being good enough. She clearly wanted him out of the parental role. But she also said that she had not realized how much he actually cared about her welfare; all she experienced was the criticism.

The therapist's job is to keep the focus on the self and not the partner in the bulk of the session. However, it is also helpful to tie in whatever feelings were experienced and shared from the past to the present reaction to the partner. Gendered beliefs that are at the root of mutual disappointments can be highlighted as they interlock and explain the way both partners place unrealistic expectations on each other. In the above example, both Talia and Danny suffered from the effects of their mutual belief that it is up to the man to make the women happy. Talia was constantly a helpless victim to her disappointment; Danny was frustrated and angry that Talia was not letting him feel effective as caretaker.

In their first session with me, Danny had complained that Talia was not interested in his work. He was hurt that when he had an important court appearance she would forget and not even ask about it. After they worked individually in the presence of the other, Talia suddenly and spontaneously started tracking his court appearances. She asked about his day, showing interest in his life. Sharing his inner world resulted in an increased desire to share his work world as well. As she showed more interest, he began to share more of his problems at work, as well as his successes. He shared his financial dilemmas, and began to appreciate her 'good head' with figures.

Often concrete sharing spontaneously occurs in the context of increasing friendship. Suddenly behaviors that were 'markers' for partner caring and the focus of bitter power struggles, are given freely as gifts to a person now perceived more as a friend.

PREPARATION FOR SHARING: FOCUS ON COUPLE INTERACTION

Comunication training

Joint sessions have a special role in helping couples try out equal partner behaviors within the context of couple interaction. There is no substitute for this, as sending home partners with no practice in negotiation, convincing, and problem solving around real issues means taking a risk. Only by watching the couple actually try to behave as equal partners can the therapist see if they are ready for this kind of teamwork at home. Every relationship therapist knows about the gap between what the couple believes about their interaction and what the therapist sees. Thus it is common for the couple to state that they communicate about an issue; when the therapist asks to see that communication by having them work together while the therapist watches, the lack of real communication skill becomes evident.

Communication training is useful here. All methods of communication training are used while the couple are interacting with each other; the therapist is watching as a coach. Listening skills and paraphrasing are important, as are all the standard elements of couple problem solving, such as defining the problem and generating solutions.[1]

Helping the couple to become an independent team, the therapist fills the role here of consultant and coach. It is always tempting to give brilliant interpretations, but the majority of this work should be done alongside the couple, while they focus on each other with the therapist there to support that work. Therapist interventions can also highlight themes pertaining to gender and power as they are reflected in the couple's actual interaction.

Deepening gender empathy through sculpture

Gender and power constrictions are limiting and debilitating, not allowing each partner to realize their full potential. The subordinate partner is fearful of losing the partner, of being left, or of not being able to cope on their own. The dominant partner is lonely, isolated, and mistrusting. Fear of being exposed leads to holding on to defenses even when wearing heavy armor becomes exhausting. A couple was asked to create a relationship sculpture showing how each perceives their interaction. The wife had herself down on the floor cowering fearfully, but arms reaching out trying to catch the fleeing partner. Her internal experience of the sculpture was primarily of fear. Her husband sculptured himself with arms raised above his head, demonstrating a leadership position, with his wife behind him, trying to hold him back. However, his hand kept dropping in fatigue. His internal experience was of exhaustion, and not power.

Gender empathy through sculpture makes these feelings manifest to the partners, while concomitantly understanding how difficult change really is. What needs to be elucidated is what each partner wants and needs from the other, and yet cannot articulate. Partners need first to experience the empathy they never got, in order to know what they want.

Alter ego role play

As the couple interacts around their problems, attempting to deal with their individual issues, unspoken gender assumptions continue to block effective communication. Knowing these barriers the therapist stands behind the partner talking and vocalizes these underlying gendered fears.[2] For example, Talia and Danny are discussing money:

Talia: I want to be included more in decisions about money; I don't even know how much savings we have, where the money is saved, nothing!

Danny: You never wanted to know ... there is no problem showing you the bank statements. It isn't a secret.

Talia: I see the bank statements every month! I am the one who has to run to the bank and pay the bills. That isn't the problem at all.

Danny: So what is your problem? You know a lot, so what is it you want?

Talia: I guess what I want is to influence you about things ... you just decide without consulting me to take money out, move it around ... like it is your money.

Danny: Well, isn't it my money? I earn it! When you start working it will be your money too. No problem!

Claire [standing behind Danny, speaking for him and then getting assurance that his feelings have been accurately expressed]: I need more support about money from you ... you always say that you want me to consult. But you leave me with all the burden of earning the money. That seems unfair; on one hand I have to do all the earning, but I have to share the decision-making!

Talia: Well, maybe. But don't you think that I 'earn' as well by taking care of the house? Isn't that worth money?

Danny: Yes it is, but I need you to share the worries, not just the decisions.

Talia: How?

Danny: I would like it if you would ask me about our financial situation, and not just when you want to buy something big. I want you to know exactly what is going on.

Talia: But that is exactly what I have been talking about ...

Danny: I am not talking about knowing about our savings. I mean to come and initiate talks about it, show interest, and not just once a year ... I mean all the time.

Talia: It would never work ... you would think I am a nag ... you would just push me away.

Claire [standing behind Talia, speaking for her and getting assurance that her feelings have been accurately expressed]: I don't know how to be your friend. I feel double messages coming from you – like now, I do want to do what you ask, but I am afraid of crowding you, of making you feel pressured by me.

Danny: I guess I am not really clear. I will have to think about this.

The alter ego method is inserted within the flow of discussion between the partners, in order to further the expression of feelings on a deeper level, as well as to help the couple move beyond stuck points to more productive problem solving.

Role switching and dialogue with partner

Another technique to help couples communicate better around issues that touch on gender is to have each partner role play the other. Playing the role of someone of the opposite sex, they have the experience of contacting unaccustomed feelings and can better appreciate the other's dilemma. Like the alter ego method, this is carried out as part of the interaction when communication falters.

While partners role play each other, the therapist 'interviews' the person (playing the other) about feelings and ideas that the partner might be having. Couples playing the other do not easily enter into the real experience of the other. Often they both initially present stereotyped cardboard roles. If the partners are left alone, they can go to a more profound level and reach clearer understanding of the other on their own. If not, and the therapist sees that they are stuck representing this rather fixed image of the other, interviewing by the therapist will help them begin to experience the other in more depth:

Talia [*playing Danny*]: I am sick of your complaining and nagging. I need for you to be more appreciative and caring of me, all you do is ask and ask, you never give anything!

Danny [*playing Talia*]: I never give anything? I only give, I never take ... I feel so abused, I feel used by you. You think a maid could replace me, that is how much you value all I have done.

Claire [*interviewing Danny playing Talia*]: Talia, what is it like for you to feel that you give so much, and that Danny just doesn't appreciate it?

Danny [*playing Talia*]: It feels bad ... frustrating. I guess it makes me want to give less.

Claire: So, what happens then?

Danny [*playing Talia*]: Then ... then ... well ... I guess what I do then is make sure you suffer! I complain and complain and complain.

Talia [laughing, breaking role]: I sure do make sure you suffer, don't I ?

Danny [laughing, breaking role]: Yea, you sure do!

The therapist here facilitates the couple dialogue by making sure that each truly understands the other's experience. This increases their sense of friendship, and consequently their willingness to work together to compromise and find a solution.

Convincing and negotiating

When power is unbalanced, one partner is usually at an advantage by being better at convincing than the other. This partner usually feels more autonomous than the other and can be more forceful. The male partner usually has more experience in forcefully stating his position and attempting to influence the other directly. Most women are sorely lacking in convincing skills, feel unentitled to use them and are disadvantaged in negotiation with their partners. They feel bullied when they perceive their partners becoming overwhelming, take their partner's forcefulness as coercion, and feel personally hurt by this behavior. To use it themselves feels like attempting to dominate. Women are especially at a disadvantage because of the emotional baggage they bring to conflict. Taking conflict personally and as a threat to their connection with the man, their upset reduces the chance of negotiating and compromising. Emotionality paves the way for having one's opinions disregarded as they get buried in tears and recriminations.

One of my first experiences with this issue was about ten years ago. This incident has not only stayed with me since then, but is shared often with couples in treatment. I was leading a group with a forceful, dynamic and assertive woman colleague. From the start she was more talkative, easily held the floor, made numerous interventions and helpful comments. Over the course of the group meetings I began to feel smaller and smaller; finally I hardly spoke up at all. Eventually I talked to her, objecting that her forceful leadership style was pushing me out and saying that I felt I had no contribution to make at all. She said: 'Do you think that I should become smaller so that you can feel bigger? How about you dealing with me?'

Women need to learn to be more personally powerful themselves, and to take the conflict inherent in asserting themselves in a more playful manner. Rather than seeing conflict as a dangerous activity, women need to get into the fray with more of a game-like way, making up for all those years with dolls and girlfriends while men learned self-assertion playing ball on a team. Becoming comfortable with convincing goes beyond simple assertion. It implies taking on a cognitive set in which attempting to change the other's opinion is redefined as contributing to the relationship and not just the self. Thus convincing becomes far more than just trying to get your way, but comes to be viewed as a contribution: maximizing your input into the couple relationship system.

For equal partners everything is open to negotiation. Having no prescribed roles means constantly coming up with creative negotiated solutions. If the couple takes conflict as a sign of distress, getting even more upset about it, they have created a new set of problems for themselves. They are in conflict about the conflict. Equal partners have a more carefree attitude about conflict – many even enjoy the sparring involved.

One very touching aspect of work on convincing and negoti-ating is that men can become women's mentors around these skills. Whereas before therapy the husband used his superior negotiating skills to win arguments, this model allows husbands to become their wives' teachers. When the power balance shifts, and the dominant partner gives up the win–lose orientation to the intimate relationship, there is an emerging wish to be a friend. For men, this can be translated into the training of their wives in negotiation. When the female partner is willing to be trained, accepting that the husband has a resource she doesn't have, but is willing to share it, the couple begins to benefit from their differences:

Claire: Danny, you have said that you and your law partner are able to negotiate differences. What exactly do you do that makes this possible . . . do you think you could share this with Talia?

Danny: Sure . . . well, for one thing we aim to get to a compro-mise we both can live with. I always say that when one of us is too happy about the compromise, it probably isn't a good one. We both have to give up something. And also, we don't get all involved personally – after a particularly hard meeting, we go out for a beer. We make it clear to each other that nothing is personal.

Claire: Talia, what do you think about this?

Talia: I think that if we could do it, it would be great. I guess I can hardly imagine going out for a beer after a fight. I usually wind up crying up in the bedroom for hours. I think it would be wonderful.

Emotional expression

While often the male partner is more skilled in convincing and negotiating, the female partner is often more attuned and able to verbalize feelings. Just as the husband can mentor the wife in becoming a more forceful communicator, so the wife can mentor her husband in feeling expression. The therapist can intervene to help both focus on this skill and in helping the woman take the role as teacher of change, instead of nagging and demanding change.

A surprising number of women want emotional expression from their partners without being able to remain on the emotional level themselves. Many women are so ambivalent about their emotionality that they do not send clearly emotional messages, but may express raw emotion and then evade it by becoming critical, demanding, or talking about details. In this way they curtail their own ability to become their partners' mentors.

Sharon is the betrayed wife described in the Introduction who discovered that her husband Tom had been having affairs since the start of their marriage. In this session, she complained that Tom had never listened to her feelings. I asked her to express these feelings while facing him. The couple demonstrated how both partners avoided the expression of deep feelings, although Sharon is quite able to express her feelings when asked to. This example shows that when Sharon was helped to stick with her feelings, she reached Tom and got the listening she wanted. He began to imitate her by expressing his feelings more directly as well.

Sharon: Tom, you cannot imagine how all this has affected me. I am so hurt, I cannot tell you. How could you do this to me? If I loved someone, I could never sleep around like you did. Why did you do it?

Tom: I told you last session – I explained it to you.

Sharon: You see . . . you don't listen to my feelings!

Claire: Sharon, you started by talking about how you feel, but then got into asking him for answers. Stick with your feelings for a while and let's see what happens.

Sharon: OK. Tom, not only have you hurt me, I feel frightened. I feel frightened because I feel so alone. I thought I knew you, and now I realize I never did. I feel alone, and unloved. That's it, I feel unloved. I feel unappreciated and used. All those years I was staying home with the children, I thought that you were at work. I thought we were together. I spent all that time at home, thinking that you were taking care of the business, for all of us. And now I see that you were abusing my trust. I feel used, I feel stupid, really stupid.

Tom [crying]:   I never meant to hurt you, really. I do appreciate what you gave, I just had my own needs and I felt I could not talk to you ... I feel awful, I want you to know I never stopped loving you. I felt alone too, having to hide everything.

Claire: Sharon, do you now feel listened to?

Sharon: Yes I do. I feel that he is with me.

Claire: Sharon, you are very good at expressing your feelings and you can teach Tom how to do this. But you need to stay with those feelings, not to avoid them. Maybe you think he won't be able to take it?

Sharon: I guess I have a hard time believing that he really wants to know what is going on inside of me.

Tom: Of course I want to know, I always wanted to know. I felt lonely all these years myself.

Women given permission to be emotional can easily do so. The listening and caring that women so desire often is forthcoming when they stick with these feelings assertively, without complaining and attacking. 'I feel very alone' has a very different impact from 'You don't listen'. But it would be naive to think that it is just the expression of these feelings that can elicit listening from a dominant partner. Without prior change in the power structure of the relationship, and gendered prohibitions and constrictions, husbands are enticed to withdraw from the uncomfortable experience of contacting their wives and their own feelings.

Another issue to track is women's reaction to their husbands revealing their feelings. Women are not used to handing the direct expression of their husbands' vulnerabilities. While very much wanting to share their partners intimate lives, when their partners do finally open up, some women become paralyzed. Not practiced in supporting men, afraid of shutting him down again, worried about making him feel worse, women will sometimes just sit there and stare. It is important to continue supporting both partners at this stage, as they enter new territory. Women do have skills in nurturing those in pain and they need permission to use them with their husbands.

When men do open up and reveal vulnerable feelings, they come in contact with their dependency on their partners. This is not an easy task, and contradicts their masculine role. They may reconnect to their early dependency on their mothers, which may be quite threatening. They can feel stupid, weak, and worried that they will lose their partners' respect. Sensitive handling of the transition towards novel androgynous behaviors is crucial to the success of therapy. When partners begin to experience intimacy without the detrimental results they feared, they have taken an important step towards becoming friends.

Chapter 11

Treatment of the traditional couple
Putting the wife in charge

A distinctive characteristic of the traditional couple requesting relationship counseling is that the relationship upset is experienced primarily by the woman. Her feelings are markers reflecting the rigidity of the power imbalance and gender restrictions in the relationship. The wife 'wears the symptom' as gender stereotyping dictates that she express the emotions for both partners. The husband usually denies having personal problems, projecting them on to his wife through criticism and blame. He may experience signs of physical stress, or avoid dealing with conflict through alcoholism, workaholism, or escape into affairs. By wearing the relationship problems she increases her vulnerability to his power manipulations and decreases her self-esteem. The husband may refuse therapy, or refuse to make changes, charging that she is making a fuss about nothing. A woman in this situation can feel quite desperate, since nothing she does or says seems to move him. But it is precisely this lack of influence that is at the root of their relationship problem.

The therapist working with traditional couples is faced with a thorny predicament: the very issue that causes the most distress is also the one most sensitive to confront. How can we ethically meddle with the traditional role structure without impinging on our clients' autonomy? The answer is that therapy aims to empower both partners so they they can renegotiate their roles and lifestyle. They may then choose to continue the 'traditional' role structure (husband works outside the house; wife stays home with the children) but within a relationship structure of equality.

LILY AND LEON

Lily and Leon, Israelis in their early thirties, both came from poor Moroccan immigrant families and both had experienced emotional and physical deprivation growing up in the slums of a major city in Israel. Leon's father committed suicide after immigrating from Morocco, while Lily's father was unemployed due to his alcoholism. Both saw their mothers as sustaining the family and their fathers as pathetic and weak. For both, this was a reversal of the way things were supposed to be.

Brought up in a traditional Middle Eastern patriarchal subculture, both dreamed of giving their children a 'normal' family life. They wanted desperately to be middle class. For them that meant that the father went out to work and was able to provide his wife with the privilege of staying home. For Lily and Leon, attaining this lifestyle signaled victory over their childhoods. Both were proud that Leon's success in his electrical appliance company meant that Lily could mother their two children as they both desired.

This couple experienced relationship problems before marriage and Leon had six months of individual counseling from a local social worker to help him overcome his fear of getting married. He found the prospect of commitment to a woman terrifying, sure that he could not succeed where his father had apparently failed. Convinced that as a man he had to be the sole provider, Leon did not feel up to this rather daunting task. The counseling left his sex-role stereotyped beliefs untouched, but helped him overcome his anxiety. He not only married, but filled the primary provider role well. He viewed the previous counseling as successful, vowing never to again be in the humiliating position of needing therapy.

His image of a good husband and father remained rigidly gender stereotyped. Not having known his own father, he conjured up an idealized man who was very sure of himself, made all the decisions, never expressed weakness, was self-centered, dominating and forceful. Filling this role to his best ability, Leon also viewed himself as responsible for 'making' his wife happy. Any bad mood or complaint on her part was viewed by him as a threat to his success as a man. Needing therapy again was a defeat for him.

His stormy history had left him sensitive and introspective, tending towards anxiety and insecurities. Trapped in the macho masculine role that did not really fit his personality, Leon was chronically depressed, which his persona demanded that he hide from his wife. In his view, a real man is not dependent on a woman. He had no idea why he was unhappy and assumed Lily must be at fault. He was fulfilling his side of the bargain and if things were not working at home, then his wife must be failing in her role.

Lily was actually extremely competent at homemaking and was also known in the neighborhood for her helpfulness and kindness to others. She did all the housework and was totally responsible for the children. Over the ten years of their marriage, she became increasingly depressed. Her unhappiness was a mystery to her and to Leon, as they both thought that she had the perfect life. Both assumed that she had a weak character, that she was inferior to him in intelligence and that her moods were ruining their home-life. She had no patience with Leon and the children, withdrawing from their demands, especially when Leon was angry and hostile to her.

Their referral for marital therapy was the result of her depression. She cried constantly, was increasingly apathetic and detached, disappearing into the bedroom to be alone for hours. Lily went out less and less, so that she also felt guilty about ignoring her duties to the wide extended family and to needy neighbors. However, depression reduced her activity level and kept her home.

Gender stereotypes did not allow Leon to share emotional problems. Unable to express his feelings, he released his confusion and unhappiness by raging at Lily. It was easy to be critical of her functioning; she was perfectionistic and easily became guilty. As she became more moody, she functioned less well in her homemaker role. Neither partner perceived her moods as connected with his temper. Viewing her as the emotional backbone of the family, they both thought that if she would be happy, so would he. In effect, the traditional lifestyle so desired by Lily and Leon was a disappointment for them. Rather than questioning their assumptions, they both blamed Lily for their unhappiness.

The social context impacted on this situation. In the last ten years, the dominant cultural norms in Israel had become more career oriented. The housewife role no longer signals having arrived and women were generally expected to contribute in paid work outside the home. Lily now found little support for her ideal vision of homelife, as most of the women she knew held outside jobs. Lily came to see herself as having accomplished nothing much in life.

Without her bad moods, Lily's role mandated that she be available for the needs and whims of others. Through her depression, not only could she focus on herself, but she could deflect Leon's depression as well. His anger at her let him disregard his own internal sadness; Lily's symptoms met real emotional needs for them both. In this way, Lily went on doing the emotional work of the relationship, to her own detriment. This was not a stable system and Leon's anger often got out of control. Eventually it was Lily who asked for help.

Phase 1: conjoint sessions to establish treatment contract

Leon brought Lily to me since she did not have her driver's license; she had been planning to get it for years. He expressed willingness to come to treatment to help her, but did not think that they had a problem as a couple. He was convinced that as soon as she snapped back to her old self, everything would be fine.

Getting her to feel fine presented me with a bind. Both viewed a strong woman as a dominating one and saw their mothers as having to be strong because of the husbands' weakness; a strong woman was for them an indicator of family problems. Within this construction of power, Lily had no room to grow as an individual, limiting how 'fine' she could feel. Like many couples, they wanted the symptom to disappear without tampering with their relationship. They expressed worries about changes, both noting that most couples they knew were unhappy, that they really did not know what to expect from marriage any more.

In a situation of confusion and lacking in clarity, the therapist's being completely frank is critical. The couple's problem was presented to them directly as their attempt to make the transition to a more equal partnership, albeit in a dysfunctional manner. Their difficulty in meeting society's changing situation resulted from their traumatic histories, which predisposed both partners to pessimism about men and women being friends, and to idealizing the traditional middle-class family. This definition of their problem was then used to spell out their options, the risks involved with therapy and the value underpinning this type of work. For example, this reformulation was delivered at the end of the second session:

Claire: I would like to sum up some of the things I have learned about you from our first session. And I would like to use this chance to explain some things about this therapy. How does that sound?

Leon: I wonder how long it will take to get Lily back on her feet?

Claire: I am glad you mentioned Lily's problems. I need to relate to who has the symptoms here.

Leon: Isn't it clear that Lily has the problem?

Claire: A lot of couples who come in for therapy are busy with the issue of who has the problems ... which is actually another way of saying who is at fault. But isn't it possible that neither one is at fault? You mentioned that you are confused about marriage. Well, I think that most couples today are confused and that we live in a very confusing time. You both mentioned not wanting to repeat your parents' marriage. You both had very traumatic family lives, and it seems to me you have done an amazing job in creating something different for your children. But society is changing and what might have seemed right for you when you married, may not fit today. We see women going out to work and sometimes earning even more than the man. Men are more involved with their children. Times are changing so fast, it is bewildering.

Leon: You said it ... I don't know anymore what I am supposed to do ... Lily says I should be helping out, but she wants me to earn all the money too. I come home exhausted and she is mad that I am not taking on more! I don't know what she wants from me.

Claire: Most couples today feel that the messages they get from their partners are contradictory. We want changes, but we also want the security of the past.

Lily: I never thought that other couples are confused like us. It is kind of a relief that you are saying this ... I thought I was doing something wrong.

Claire: I think that you are both experiencing the normal confusion of modern times, and I think that you are trying to cope as best as you can with some pretty difficult social changes. One of the major changes is that couples today

	want to be good friends to each other, something you have said did not exist in your families.
Lily:	It was never a ambition for them, but it certainly is for me.
Claire:	Right . . . do you think you could be happy Lily seeing Leon as there to provide economically, but not to be your friend?
Lily:	I always wanted him to be my friend. But that isn't what he wants from a relationship!
Leon:	Who said I don't want it? I need a friend too. But you have been too depressed to be my friend, or anyone's friend for that matter.
Claire:	So you both feel that friendship is important. But I need to tell you what I mean by friendship, so you can think if this therapy is right for you. Friendship can only occur between equals. That means two people who have equal influence, who make decisions together, who share experiences with each other . . . it also means two people who take a lot of personal responsibility for seeing to their own happiness and for helping their friend be happy as well.
Leon:	Why wouldn't we want that? It sounds good.
Claire:	Because it also has some risks. If we take friendship as a primary goal for this therapy, it means making sure that both of you feel strong. Both of you would have a sense of choice. I see that you both want the marriage, and I hope that it works out the way you want it. But when you choose to work towards equal partnership, there is no guarantee about what choices will be made.
Leon:	I do not want Lily with me because she feels too depressed to make choices. I want her to choose to be with me.
Lily:	I can't believe he said that . . . that makes me feel wonderful! [Turning to Leon] Is that really what you want for me?
Leon:	Of course I do.
Claire:	It is my sense from what you have told me, that your idea of what it means to be a man and to be a woman have limited how close friends you could be. Many men and women need to learn how to communicate with each other to be friends, something our parents did not really teach us.

The risks of increased choice need to be spelled out so that the couple can make an informed choice. A primary safeguard in not impinging on clients' values is consistently and openly to specify the values underpinning therapy, and the benefits and risks involved in adopting new values. We work towards increasing choice from the outset, as each partner reflects on the therapy offered, making a conscious choice about whether to continue. In this example, Leon's choice to continue was affirming for Lily, clarified values and built an initial alliance for future work.

Choice was increased in considering intervention methods. Lily obviously needed a great deal of support to clarify what she wanted, to overcome the guilt feelings behind her depression, and to release some of the anger she was suppressing. Lily was boycotting the homemaker role, without taking personal responsibility for her revolt. This work is best accomplished in individual sessions. However, her nurturing role dictates that the relationship should come first, and her difficulty in focusing on herself was a reflection of the basic problem. A direct suggestion that she have individual sessions would appear as an agreement that she is indeed the problem. Offering relationship sessions would signal that the relationship comes first, denying Lily the support she needed.

The entire problem of the traditional wife is reflected in this seemingly trivial decision: does she have the right to ask for attention directly for herself, without having to resort to becoming symptomatic? The notion of empowerment, and expanding choice, directs us in finding a solution. Lily was put in charge of making the choice about how to begin the therapy. The therapeutic model was explained: the options of individual work alone with the therapist, individual focus while the other observes, or conjoint couple sessions, were carefully described. Lily was asked to chose which she thought would be of most benefit to her as both partners saw her as having the problem. This strategy allowed me to join the couple's definition of reality, while using their frame of reference to continue furthering Lily's personal autonomy. Leon seemed surprised that Lily, given her bad emotional state, was being given such an important decision. He was willing to go along, Lily seemed delighted and asked for therapy alone. She had already started the process of transformation and needed support. Regardless of her initial choice, following each session she would have been asked how she wanted to proceed. After only three sessions, Lily requested a move to individual work with the partner observing.

Phase 2: work alone with Lily

The rapid movement Lily made in her three sessions confirmed that she wanted to alter many aspects of her life, but had been stuck in a passive role. Her negative evaluation of the gifts she brought to the relationship, her low self-esteem, had limited her ability to push for change. During the three individual sessions with Lily, I worked to help her value her feminine accomplishments: providing a stable and warm home atmosphere for Leon and the children, devoting herself to extended kin and neighbors, and caring for the home, were all given serious attention and re-labeled as achievements that went unappreciated. At first, Lily resisted these expressions of support from me; devaluing the feminine, as well as compliments from her female therapist. She countered that she earned no money, she had not made a career for herself, and that Leon was far more competent.

I asked why she, a woman, compared herself with Leon? Did she expect to be exactly the same as him? Were there areas of expertise in which she felt especially competent as a woman? These questions were provocative for her. Wearing the lens of gender, she begin to think about her basic assumptions; about her view of masculinity and femininity, about equal sharing and about the nature of the friendship she wanted. She had assumed that she was totally responsible for the home, and yet was subtly competitive with Leon. Looking for unique strengths, she realized that she was especially good at handling many different things at one time, while Leon could focus only on one thing at a time. She was able to cook, take care of the kids, and help a friend on the phone. She joked that Leon got nervous if you asked him a question while he was occupied with something.

But after the laughter, the awareness of unfairness in the relationship appeared. This is a natural progression. As contributions are valued, consciousness of their previous devaluation leads to anger. She began by showing some mild irritation at Leon, who was 'not very nice' to her. I asked her what this meant. Lily portrayed some very demeaning behavior: he blew up and attacked her verbally in front of other people if she even slightly annoyed him; he disappeared from the house for hours without telling her where he was going, and he insisted she have sex with him regardless of whether she desired it. Eventually she confided that he hit her. He especially hated to be misunderstood, and lashed out physically when she did not immediately know what he wanted. She had protected him and the family image by never having revealed this secret. Telling this to me was an important first step in shifting her alliance to herself and her own welfare.

Her mood shifted. Lily was no longer depressed, but she was very angry. She felt incapable of demanding more respectful behavior, saying that she felt very helpless around Leon, although she did not know why. Helping Lily move from this position to one of power meant dealing with a role learned way before she married. Lily had learned to 'manage' men, but never to confront them. The cultural stereotype of female power in her North African family allowed her to run the home while making sure that Leon felt stronger than her. This meant agreeing to decisions she did not support and accepting abusive behavior as her fault.

Lily's lack of power was deeply ingrained, culturally conditioned and a profound part of her identity. Rather than take up this issue directly, I thought it might be more effective to target how her helplessness translated into in-session behavior with me. Lily tended to talk in a passive voice during her sessions, and especially when discussing Leon she used the passive language of the victim: 'Leon made me feel ...' or 'he got me all upset'. Her internal dialogue did not allow her to feel powerful: she rarely used the word 'I' in a clear and differentiated manner, using the passive voice in describing actions. By labeling and pointing out the passive voice, asking what she felt, thought, or wanted to do, Lily strengthened her sense of self. Her language became more forceful and assertive in the session with me.

In this brief example, her developing ability to focus on herself allowed her to access internal resources and strengths inherent in the traditional feminine role:

Claire: You say that you don't think you know how to set limits, right? And that is why you let Leon behave in a disrespectful manner?

Lily: Yes, when he yells at me in front of the kids, I have no idea what to do, he just shuts me up ... no, I just shut up in silence.

Claire: I saw that you just changed from using a passive to an active way of talking ... that is great!

Lily: I thought about what you said ... it is true that I often
            feel that Leon is doing things to me, rather than I play
            any part.
Claire: What would you do if someone yelled like that at your
            children, would you sit back in silence?
Lily: Of course not! I am a lioness about my kids ... I went
            to the teacher the other day to complain when I heard
            that she had been rude to my daughter ... I am very
            direct about things like that.
Claire: And if one of the kids yelled at you like Leon does?
            Would you choose to be silent?
Lily: Silent, no ... I limit my kids ... I see what you mean. I
            can be pretty forceful when it is about my children.
Claire: When the children are rude to you, it is about them or
            you?
Lily: I guess I think it is for them, so I can place limits. I can't
            do that for myself.
Claire: We just spoke about how you use the passive voice ...
            You just said 'I can't do that for myself' ... are you sure
            that it is really 'can't'?
Lily: Of course not ... maybe I don't want to ... I guess I
            think that if it is for me, it is not nice to be so strong,
            but it is fine when it is for the children. I do know how
            to do it ... Maybe I need permission to do it with Leon?
Claire: You need permission, from me, or ... ?
Lily: I need to give myself permission to do it. Of course I
            could stop him, but I don't allow myself to do it.

Lily began to perceive how much power she had handed over to
Leon, and that while she might behave assertively with her children, she chose not to with her husband. As Lily began to consider
the possibility of asking for a respectful attitude towards her, she
spontaneously brought up and began to confront the barriers that
women face when they contemplate change. She pointed out that
Leon made the money, and that he had used this fact to control
her. He did not always come up with the amount he promised,
and she was worried he might punish her trying to set limits by
not giving her enough to run the household. She also realized that
she harbored deep fears that, if provoked, he might become even
more physically aggressive, putting her in real danger.

   It is often a shock for women to comprehend how much their
behavior is constrained by fear. One by one, she contacted all the

obstacles to her taking action. My role was of validating these real obstacles, while thinking together with her about additional options. What could she do if he became more aggressive, and how would could she respond if he withheld money. More than the problem-solving function, it was my intent to support her ability to cope with change, whatever it might bring.

After the rage, grief emerged. Her father had beat her, and she had never overcome the fear and anger she associated with men. She felt inferior in Israeli culture; as a woman of Middle Eastern background, due to her dark skin and her sense of shame about her family history, she was sure she could not make something of herself outside of the role of mother and wife. She sadly realized that she had not looked for work outside the home because she could not face the 'male world'. Her 'choice' of a traditional lifestyle was greatly influenced by her fear of failure in the world of work.

At this stage it is important to universalize and normalize: woman who confront their fears tend to blame themselves for their cowardice, adding more pain and further reducing their self-esteem. Lily was relieved by the insight that many women in her culture face real danger when they stand up for themselves. There were good reasons that it felt frightening to Lily to think about being an equal partner. The slow process of patiently bringing up her fears, coupled with receiving support, allowed her to get free. It also demonstrated her underlying resilience and strength.

Phase 3: individual work with the partner present

Lily, ready and eager to confront Leon, was demanding changes at home. While she was ready for conjoint sessions, I knew that Leon was not nearly as prepared. Leon lacked options as much as did Lily: the primary provider role was the only one he could envision. However, not having had the individual support, nor the needed trust in me, he did not feel confident to allow her to be strong. There was far more open conflict between the couple than before. Leon was both threatened and intrigued by the 'new Lily'. He liked the fact that she was no longer depressed, but was intimidated by the fact that she demanded real changes. She faced him squarely, asking him to stop interrupting her, putting her down, using verbal or physical violence. Lily wanted respect, and was determined to get it.

This is a crucial turning point in couples therapy, often leading to a surge in demands on the husband. The new equilibrium depends on how this transformation is handled. Were Leon to become defensive, scared or unable to cope, he might withdraw from conflict and confirm Lily's worst fears – that there really is no way she could be strong and have a relationship as well. However, if he could positively incorporate her push for change, her gratitude and satisfaction would greatly strengthen their relationship. The transformation going on in therapy mirrors the changing social condition of women. Unlike 'real life', the therapy situation offers the potential for modulating rate and impact in a way that rarely happens spontaneously. The therapist can have an effect on the way the husband processes his wife's demands and on helping him overcome barriers to adapting to change.

While Lily was ready to take on Leon directly, I slowed the process down by asking Leon if he wanted individual sessions or felt ready for working individually with Lily present. Leon wanted the latter. Lily was the first to be the focus, allowing Leon to observe and become a participant in Lily's transformation. He had the safety of distance (in his role as observer) and the intimacy of closeness (in vicariously experiencing Lily's process of change). My confronting and challenging Lily allowed Leon to gain a new respect for her, and calmed his fears that I might be on her side:

Lily: I find myself so humiliated that at the end of the month I don't have enough for the household, and I have to come begging to Leon for extra. It seems like my failure and I feel kind of scared of his reaction.

Claire: Do you see the money earned as his money?

Lily: Yes, although now that you say it that way, I do make a contribution . . . but it doesn't earn money . . . so I guess I never thought about it as 'our' money.

Claire: I wonder how much you both would have to pay if you needed to be replaced . . . could you both afford someone to do all the things you do?

Lily: No, of course not, there isn't anyone who would anyway, but it would cost a fortune. I wonder why I have to go begging like that?

Claire: 'Have to' is the passive voice – can you think about your own involvement in this?

Lily: I don't have to . . . I am kind of scared of Leon and I find it hard to ask him directly for things. But in reality, the checking account is in both our names. Theoretically I could take out what I need. I never even brought it up though. Leon and I started off this way and it just sort of continued. He gives me a certain amount each month and I have to manage with that. I always thought I should be grateful that the amount has gone up and felt bad that I don't seem to manage. But the expenses are going up all the time too.

Claire: What would happen if you were to try to negotiate a change about this with Leon ... could you start to manage the household money, would you want to?

Lily: I am the best person to do it! I know all the expenses and I have a good head for numbers. I think in the end we would save because I would take responsibility for the amount I take out. Now I feel like a child, asking for 'extras'; I don't know what we make, I don't know what we could afford. I want to know, I want to be involved. But I have to overcome my fear of talking with him.

In processing Lily's session with Leon, he commented that her fear amazed him. For the first time he revealed directly that he was tired of having everything up to him and thought he would welcome her being more involved in the finances. He never understood why she waited for him to 'hand out' the money as she could take out what she needed directly from the bank. Like Lily, he had slid into a pattern that did not make sense.

Often the dominant partner is unaware of the fear he inspires, feeling himself controlled by the negative interactions. Leon did not like the thought that his wife was frightened of him. He admitted that sometimes he was rough with her, but that was because he actually wanted her to fight back; this was his way of trying to strengthen her! Lily was amazed at his logic, finding it hard to believe. This is a common rationale the dominant partner gives for using aggressive methods of control, without paying attention to the actual results.

I noticed that after having observed Lily working alone for a session, the atmosphere between the partners was softened and more peaceful. Leon agreed to work with me individually, with Lily observing the session. It was in this format that he could safely look at the roots of his dominating and aggressive style.

An example from his session shows the move from couple to individual focus:

Claire: You say that you sometimes get angry at her, hoping that she would fight back?

Leon: I don't like to see her scared! It makes me really angry and I try to get her to stop crying in her room and deal with me.

Claire: Does it work, do you see her getting stronger when you yell at her?

Leon: No, it seems to have the opposite effect . . . she gets more silent and withdrawn, which makes me even angrier! I hate having that effect on her. I feel totally misunderstood . . .

Claire;   So you are saying that when she is unhappy, so are you?

Leon: Yes, that is very true . . . I feel bad when she feels bad.

Claire: I wonder if feeling misunderstood is a familiar experience for you?

Leon: Well, now that you ask . . . when I was young I suffered from a bad stutter, and I was always very sensitive to whether I was being understood. I somehow expect Lily to understand me and when she doesn't, it drives me crazy.

Claire: How do you feel when she gets silent after you have shouted at her?

Leon: I feel bad . . . very alone, like I did when I was little. My mother always took my tormentor's side. She was trying to be both mother and father and was worried I would be a sissy. I never felt support from her. I guess I feel like that, and it makes me angry.

Lily had never seen Leon reveal weakness, nor talk about himself for more than a few moments at a time. During this session she listened carefully, taking copious notes. Her post-session reflections were helpful as she felt that she now understood him better. She still did not want to be his 'punching bag' but she felt that she was willing to work together with him to stop his abusive behavior. Leon continued gendered behavior by trying to place the burden of change on Lily:

Leon: I really want to behave better with you . . . I don't want you scared of me. I wish you would stop me from getting out of control.

Lily: Well, OK. I guess I could try to stop you.

Claire: Wait a minute ... Lily, I wonder if you really want another chore? Do you want to be a policewoman, trying to stop Leon from getting angry at you? Do you want to take that kind of responsibility?

Lily: No, I don't. I think he should stop himself. I do enough in this relationship. I just automatically say yes to whatever he asks!

Leon: But, I do need to be reminded, or something. I really don't know when I am getting too rough.

Lily: I don't mind letting you know when you are starting to get aggressive. I can signal you, but you have to be responsible to stop.

Leon: I think that might work.

Claire: I think it is really great the way you two just negotiated an agreement. You both are bothered by an interaction between the two of you. Instead of either blaming each other, or letting one of you carry all the burden of change, you just figured out a way to be friends and solve the problem fairly.

Assumptions about division of roles restricted their emerging equality. The therapist's ongoing task is to identify gender rules that are limiting their ability to have a fair relationship and reinforce the emerging ability to behave as equal partners. When barriers to friendship are removed, equal sharing of tasks emerges spontaneously.

Phase 4: conjoint sessions and follow-up

The therapy with this couple concluded with two conjoint sessions in which they dealt actively with other conflicts and worked to deepen their degree of intimate sharing. Educational methods were used to highlight and consolidate ideological changes that came about due to the increased fairness in their marital system.

Leon did not require more individual work, saying that he could talk openly with Lily about his worries about money, problems at work and anger at her. As a matter of fact, he suddenly discovered the pleasure of intimate friendship and wanted to tell her everything. Both partners in traditional relationships undergo a process of change, but not at the same time nor at the same rate. Change in one partner often threatens the other, triggering anxiety, which then becomes the impetus for reciprocal change and mutual growth. At this point it was Lily who needed help in absorbing the change. As Leon opened up more, sharing his painful history, the insecurities he carried and his fears about providing for the family, Lily had no idea how to respond. Often women who are anxious for their partners to open up simply stare in amazement, having no idea what to say when their husbands reveal weaknesses:

Leon: I am tired of having to act like I know everything, have all the answers. I walk around sad all the time. I want to be able to lean on someone too!

Lily: So what can I do?

Leon: I don't know, I really don't.

Claire: Lily, do you feel that if Leon tells you what is bothering him, that you have to solve the problem?

Lily: Yes ... I guess when he talks about his worries, I think he wants me to come up with a solution. I don't have an immediate solution.

Claire: Leon, is that what you really want? Would you like to have Lily come up with solutions to your problems?

Leon: [talking directly to her] No! I would feel bad actually ... like you were showing me what I have been doing wrong. But I don't know either what I want from you!

Couples need help in creating new ways of comforting each other. It comes as a surprise for many to discover that 'just listening' or 'just asking questions' constitutes support; many think they need to come up with a brilliant solution to be helpful. Couples can be emotionally ready to be friends, but still need to learn some skills. In a situation of power hierarchy, straightforward behavioral tools, such as listening skills, are resisted. When power and gender blocks are removed, couples are eager to learn.

This couple moved from a traditional power structure to equal sharing with a relatively low level of conflict. Leon was far more ready to change than Lily expected. A practical person, he fully grasped that his own welfare was tied to hers, and that for him to be happy she needed to be happy. With this notion firmly in place, there is more motivation to contribute to and invest in the partner's requests for change, leading to a confirmation that, indeed, the partner's satisfaction leads to an increase in one's own well-being.

The therapist's role here is to emphasize these changes, abstracting the principles behind them and helping the partners to develop and consolidate an equal partnership ideology:

Lily: Leon always said that the family came first. But this is the first time that I really believe it.

Claire: Can you say what it is that makes you feel this? What exactly has changed in Leon's behavior?

Lily: Well, he seems to notice things that need to be done ... and I don't have to tell him to do them as much any more. He makes suggestions that are helpful now, not critical. Like yesterday, I had to find a babysitter, but Leon was the one who thought of my cousin who is home from the army. Suddenly it wasn't only my problem.

Claire: I think what you are saying here is that you see Leon sharing the responsibility, the real emotional burden, of what goes on at home? He is no longer your helper? Leon, what is it that makes you want to be more responsible?

Leon: I don't really know. If we are talking about the babysitter ... yesterday, I remembered how I felt when I was stuck at home last week because we had not found a sitter and Lily had to go visit her mother. I remember thinking then that if we had thought about getting a sitter beforehand, maybe I could have gone out too.

Claire: So, what I hear you saying is that because you can feel what it is like to be in Lily's shoes and you understand her experience, that you want to become more responsible?

Leon: I never used to understand what caused her so much tension. A few days at home with the children fixed that!

Claire: I think this is important. As both of you share more, you will more and more be aware of what it is like to be in the other's shoes. That will help you continue to share, out of real understanding for your partner. That is the basis of your friendship.

Therapists who are cognizant of the themes underlining equal partnership, will see them slowly emerge as couples become more cooperative. The need for consolidating through labeling cannot be overemphasized. Because sharing behaviors need to be grounded in a new ideology of fairness, and because partners are unconscious of the changes underpinning their actions, the therapist plays an invaluable role by pointing out these changes.

Two months after terminating the therapy, Lily called to say that she was considering taking a job, and was excited about the prospect of going out to work, but she was also pregnant. No longer incapacitated by fears, nor held back by depression, she was appropriately concerned that she could not go out to work at the same time as she was caring for a new baby. Lily had made up her mind that she wanted to try. She asked for a few more sessions to communicate more effectively with Leon. There would no doubt have to be a major reorganization of their homelife, with far more sharing on his part. In two additional sessions they used me as a coach in their negotiation of new schedules and roles. Again, Leon surprised Lily in the degree of his support for her ventures, demonstrating the tenacity and courage that had helped him move from his impoverished childhood to his present accomplishments. It was obvious to me that as this couple worked to overcome obstacles to sharing, they gained enormous respect for each other as good friends. Their view of conflict had changed and they appeared to have accepted its inevitability.

CONCLUSION

As the traditional couple moves towards equal sharing, partners experience repeated transitions and the need for continual negotiation. Therapists can be most useful by offering the possibility of ongoing support. There is no 'cure' for these marital crises, nor should there be; the potential for growth and development is endless. Couples are encouraged to return for short interventions around points of change, to think of conflict as natural and to work preventively.

Traditional couples differ as to their ability or need to change. Not all reorganize as totally as Lily and Leon. Some of these couples remain traditional in sharing household and childcare, but become better friends, with more intimacy and sharing of decision-making than before. These couples may return for more therapy at a later stage, or may themselves negotiate further shifts in their roles.[1] Other couples respond with more conflict, as the dominant male partner refuses to accept the changes the partner wants.

Some of the issues related to the therapeutic handling of intense crisis are taken up next.

Work with traditional couples focuses on empowerment and choice needed for the couple to be friends. The question the therapist needs to ask openly is: do both partners in this relationship feel that they have freely chosen their lifestyle? Barriers to free choice are removed by shifting power structure towards equality, and removing gender constrictions. In this case, Lily's reevaluation of her feminine role focused on learning to value her feminine accomplishments. A new understanding of power led to an awareness of how imbalanced the relationship had become, unleashing the anger to fuel her transformation. Empowered by taking more personal responsibility for change, Lily was helped to remove further barriers to free choice of her lifestyle. She decided to go out to work.

Her emerging sense of self triggered changes in Leon, who was rather choked in his attempt to fulfill a stereotypic masculine ideal. However, he needed help in accepting Lily's transformation and in learning constructively to hear her anger. Expressing his own 'feminine' side, his vulnerable feelings, was a step in his own empowerment. Leon could chose to share only when he was able. to expand his image of masculinity and incorporate more androgynous traits. By increased shared experiences, this couple moved towards establishing the sense of friendship that then served to support future changes in their lives. They clearly had made the 'quantum' leap to a subjective appraisal of their relationship as fair. Further lifecycle changes were negotiated within the context of a mutual need to maintain the relationship as fair.

Chapter 12

Treatment of the transitional couple
Overt and covert power struggles

Transitional couples are characterized by a decided shift in the wife's power, a rejection of the traditional role of wife, and the attempt to create a more equal structure. The shift in the traditional power structure creates a vacuum and leaves these relationships vulnerable to power struggles. Straining to maintain fairness, couples often rely on methods that only intensify tension, such as fifty–fifty accounting. Partners can differ between themselves on the degree to which sharing is desired, as well as on their definitions. Often there is a gap between their aspirations and the constrictions of deeply held gendered beliefs. Couples may sincerely want to share household chores, but the wife wants things done her way, or the husband resents being told what to do. Sharing may evaporate when the outside world impinges in the form of increased work demands on the husband, or when the couple experiences internal structural change, such as the birth of an additional child.

In short, couples in transition experience all the contradictions and lack of clarity inherent in a major social passage. Women at this preliminary stage of empowerment rarely perceive that they have a choice of lifestyle and instead feel driven to prove they can 'do it all'. Unilaterally rejecting the unfair burden of doing all the emotional work of the marriage, they may fear getting too intimate with their partners. Always the possibility of regression towards a more submissive role and loss of personal autonomy, threatens in the horizon.

Men in these relationships want friendships with their wives, but seldom have the necessary intimate relationship skills. While verbally stating that they are willing to share the housework and childcare, few are prepared to be equal partners. Standards for housekeeping may be lax, they are not ready to take up the slack left by the wife in the emotional domain, or they may be uneasy about their masculinity. As one man complained in therapy: 'It feels like we are two men married to each other'.[1]

For transitional couples in therapy, the question of who is in control becomes essential. Resisting domination, but having no models of equal partnership, the female partner may wind up using dominating tactics herself. She may sustain the threat of leaving to stay in control and exact conditions she wants. The male partner struggles to maintain control by passively resisting the work of the marriage. There are husbands who just cannot learn to separate the white laundry from the colored pieces, keep forgetting to wipe around the sink when they do the dishes, and cannot seem to master the fine art of using the microwave. No matter how many times the wife explains what kind of attention she needs, he does not give it. Rather, he may employ a variety of maneuvers to get his partner to pay him more attention. Drinking, getting depressed, or developing any symptom that mobilizes his wife to attend to him and ignore her own needs, are all common for husbands at this stage. Covert power struggles underlie many daily life negotiations.

Relationships obviously do suffer, and the 'progression' towards equality can look more like a regression. If the tendency of the couple is towards avoidance of conflict, they institute parallel lives, with one or both partners finding fulfillment outside the marriage. If the tendency of the husband is to counter his wife's increased independence with active resistance, open conflict will ensue. However, the impetus for change exists within the couple relationship: therapists do not 'push' towards a fair friendship, but facilitate movement on a path the couple is actually already following. Couples differ in their degree of being stuck, which in turn demands different intensity and duration of intervention. Many of the most difficult cases are stuck in chronic parallel lives.

PARALLEL LIVES

There are cases of parallel life couples where the relationship truly has ended and the therapist's job is ease its demise. But for many, the relationship has more life than might appear. Couples are stuck in not wanting to copy traditional patterns, but having no prospect or hope of anything better. The tendency towards with-drawal results from avoiding the pain of a conflict they do not know how to resolve. Avoidance effectively hides how much the partners are still connected and how much potential for inflicting misery there really is.

This type of couple is difficult to treat as the wife has found alternative and safer sources of satisfaction: in work, affairs, children, hobbies, or friends. For these women, the pain of trying to be close seems greater than the gain avoidance offers. Interestingly, it is still most often the wife who asks for therapy, a gender stereotyped behavior. Yet she is also deeply ambivalent about change. In transitional relationships, both partners have a curious blend of traditional and egalitarian beliefs, making them confusing to understand. At the crossroads of change, women are especially confused, and in turn confuse their partners, and dilute the forcefulness of their attempts to create change. Sending mixed messages, women want to liberate themselves from the confine-ment of the submissive wife role, yet also want to hold on to and enjoy its benefits.

If the woman does not clarify whether she really wants to be in the relationship, this question becomes the hidden agenda, sabotaging all change attempts. Therapy can easily be the focus of the wife's confusion. The sessions become the bearer of intimacy, while the wife acts out her need for autonomy through resistance to tasks, learning of new skills, or attendance of sessions. When she is clear about what she wants, she brings the full weight of her personality to help create the changes she needs.

The therapy case described here illustrates therapy with a parallel lives couple. Therapy lasted over one year, with fairly distinct but turbulent phases, as the couple moved from parallel lives to open conflict, and eventually to an equal partnership. To the degree that avoidance has become chronic and longstanding, therapists should expect the crisis of the open conflict stage to be more intense. The therapy is informed by an understanding of the ambivalence both partners experience about changing gender roles and, especially, the necessity for distancing that the transi-tional woman feels. Most often, her fears of intimacy are founded on both her history and the difficulty her partner has in supporting her real autonomy. Treating the transitional couple demands heightened sensitivity to the complexity inherent in bringing progressive ideals into line with daily life reality.

HADASS AND HAIM

Hadass and Haim are an Israeli couple in their early forties, with two teenage children. A senior executive in a private investment corporation, she makes a large salary and wields a great deal of influence at work. He runs a small family business, making less money than she. Married under unusual circumstances twenty years earlier, both had tragically lost their first partners at a young age. Haim's wife died in childbirth and Haim found himself a single parent to a newborn daughter. Hadass had lost her childhood love in a road accident after only two years of a childless marriage.

They met and spent a great deal of their time talking about the grief they shared in common. Haim, having no experience with taking care of babies, was reliant on the goodwill of female kin, whose patience was wearing thin. Hadass was not only willing to care for the child, she wanted to move in with him. A single male parent with a newborn is so uncommon that Haim never got over the feeling of gratitude that he had found a woman who was willing to mother his child. Throughout their marriage, while competently caring for their children, Haim never felt independent in this area. Gender restrictions kept him dependent on the presence of a female for this important role.

In hindsight, Hadass claimed that she did not really fall in love, since she was still mourning her first husband, and mostly saw marriage as a practical solution to her current predicament. Her first husband's parents wanted her to share their mourning by spending all her free time with them. Although broken-hearted, Hadass wanted to get on with her life. Getting married was a way of maintaining her freedom.

Hadass requested marital counseling. She related that they had been unhappy for at least fifteen of the twenty years they were married. For the first five years they were close and had a good emotional connection. She felt they shared equally in the care of his child. But when they had their own first child, Hadass became totally caught up in parenting, dominating all decisions about childcare. She knew that Haim felt pushed out of the home. He complained that he had become Hadass's 'helper', but Hadass felt she could not modify her behavior. In response, he became more involved with work, traveling for extended periods. Hadass felt abandoned and she cut herself off from him, finding alternative emotional connections elsewhere.

For many years they led parallel lives, with mainly the children as a link between them. She went out almost every evening (seeing her lover and friends) while he stayed with the children. While she had an active social life, he had none and centered all his social contacts in the family. She found others far more interesting, rarely sharing any of her life with him. Clearly she had far more power; they made love and talked only when she was interested or willing, and over time her consent to contact diminished. A family man who could not envision divorce, Haim remained indebted to her and his protests at her coldness had little impact. They had tried counseling upon his request, but after six sessions Hadass ended the therapy, saying it was not helping them. Haim reluctantly accepted the situation.

Around the age of 40, Haim suddenly started craving more attention from Hadass. His complaints became more persistent, but his way of seeking connection was in asking a lot of questions and initiating more sex. Hadass was decidedly not interested, felt smothered, and became openly rejecting. He responded with intensified pursuit. Hadass requested therapy as their alienation grew increasingly more hostile and uncomfortable.

Phase 1: work alone with Hadass

During her first sessions with me, Hadass put Haim down, deriding his lack of social skills, his deficient intellectual and cultural knowledge, and his emotional insensitivity. She felt she could predict every response he made and found him very boring. She was convinced that there was no point in investing in the relationship as she had a satisfying emotional and physical relationship with her long-term lover. For reasons unknown to her, she could not make the decision to divorce, despite the obviousness of this choice. Hadass had the resources, economic and social, to live on her own and while there was no apparent reason for her staying in the marriage, she requested relationship counseling.

The major goal in this phase of therapy, which continued for three months, was to empower her to make a choice and commit herself either to improving her marriage or leaving it. She revealed that she had hidden her long-term affair from her previous therapist, making any real progress impossible. With me, her first few sessions were reflective of her confusion; she talked exclusively about Haim (albeit negatively). Her ambivalence was reflected in confusing demands from me. While presenting only the negatives of her relationship, she challenged me to understand what she could not grasp, why did she stay. I assumed that Haim received similarly puzzling messages and that a part of Hadass, rejected and split off, needed Haim.

Hadass had traditional female characteristics, superimposed on her firm commitment to equality for women. She perceived herself primarily through relationships and, in a manner characteristic of many women, actually found it difficult to allow herself to focus on her own needs. Her underlying tendency to lose herself coincided with a dominating style. She appeared almost egocentric, but was actually struggling to maintain her independence.

My initial hypothesis was that Hadass had been profoundly wounded by Haim's withdrawal from her over the previous fifteen years. Ambivalent about equally sharing the parenting role, she had expected him to stay involved, but on her terms. His typical male avoidance of this central conflict was deeply hurtful to her. It may well have reactivated abandonment feelings experienced with the loss of her first husband.

Understanding the transitional woman means grasping the fear of dependency. Traditionally, it has been men who fear intimate dependency. For similar reasons, liberated women do not want to find themselves too needy. Hadass could not allow herself to reveal her dependent feelings, neither to herself nor to Haim. She not only accepted his distancing, but outdid him in this avoidance strategy, resulting in separate lives. When the wife does not fulfill the traditional role of emotional caretaker, no one does it.

Empowerment dictated helping her focus on herself, and especially legitimizing her own needs. Strengthening her sense of entitlement would eventually lead to an acceptance of dependency as part of intimate relationships. At this early stage it meant legitimizing her right to have therapy for herself and resisting her confused requests for relationship work. I reiterated that it was her right to make up her own mind about what she really wanted. Not only did she express relief, but she admitted that this was exactly what she wanted (but had been unable to express directly) from her last therapist. We contracted for work alone, giving her the time to explore the meaning of her relationship with Haim and come to her own decision.

Hadass described her relationship with Haim in extreme terms, making her inability to leave seem inexplicable. Paradoxically, the cognitive distortion of viewing the situation as all bad hampered her ability to make a decision. To be able to decide, and give up options, we have to know what we are losing. Her difficulty in admitting her dependency on Haim was making it hard for her to see him as having any positive virtues. Understanding that Hadass occupied the overbenefited, dominant position in their relationship hierarchy makes her behavior comprehensible. The dominant position person resists awareness of being dependent; realization would destroy the illusion of power and control.

In effect, Hadass required Haim to have the life they had built, which allowed her to have a full-time career, two children, a stable home, as well as an exciting lover and interesting friends. Becoming conscious of dependency is not an easy goal for a dominant position person. The key to accepting dependency is learning to value the feminine. As long as Hadass did not value the work Haim did at home and the importance of his supplying her with a stable home, she would not understand what was keeping her with him.

The dominant person often denigrates feminine attributes in general: dominance in our culture seems to be related to extreme masculinity. Hadass presented an image of a rational, logical person. These characteristics made her a leader at work. In therapy, it made touching emotional topics impossible. Whenever the conversation approached her feelings, she changed the subject. Early on she declared, 'I will not talk at all about the past, but only the future', controlling the therapy, and ruling out all the pain experienced in her life.

In the dominant position, Hadass had split off her emotional, soft, and feminine side from her competitive, rational, and masculine side. With her husband she was the epitome of the sex-role stereotyped dominating and exploitative male. Her feminine side found exclusive expression in a rather sex-role stereotyped way with her lover. Their relationship had gone on for ten years, but he would not commit himself to her. He played power games with her around time and place of meetings, demanded more attention from her than he gave, and kept her wondering when the she might next see him. With him, she occupied the role of the traditional wife, always wanting more than she was getting. The fact that he was married meant that her fear of being dependent could be kept under control; there was no real danger that her lover would want to live with her.

Hadass was not getting her emotional needs met in either relationship. In neither could she focus on herself: her real fears, wishes, or needs. In each she brought only a part of herself, playing a role and exaggerating different sides of her personality. Her ambivalence about the feminine role needed to be brought to awareness. Empowering her to make a choice about her life depended on increasing her sense of personal authority, which can only occur by integrating and valuing her feminine side, allowing her dependency needs to emerge.

The two main methods used for increasing awareness and valuing of her femininity were: education about power, gender and equality; and work on her in-session behavior with me. Educational interventions were direct, cognitive and appealed to her rational, logical side. Work on our relationship was more indirect and emotional for her, and introduced her to the benefits of focusing on herself and on feelings.

Education about the concepts of fairness, equity, power and the model of friendship was straightforward. For example, we discussed power, its effects on people in general, and the way it might interact in her relationship. I wondered if Haim was afraid of making her angry, intimidated and inhibited in her presence. She had noticed that he was more open with other people, and that he seemed insecure around her. She noted that in general people seemed hesitant around her, and the notion of power position was helpful to her.

Using themes related to equal partnership helped clarify why she stayed in a marriage she thought unrewarding. The concept of fairness proved to be especially significant for her:

Claire: Do you think that you have been fair with Haim? We talked about how important fairness is in marriage ... what do you think about fairness in your marriage?

Hadass: No, I don't. Now that you mention it, I think it is true. I feel I am not fair to him. I actually feel quite disturbed about it. I never could quite put my finger on what it was, but that is it ... I really feel that I haven't been fair! He does do all the housework, took off all the time when the children were home sick, he is always willing to cook, all that stuff. I know he is devoted, and I know I am not.

Claire: Why do you think it might be important, this feeling that you haven't been fair to Haim?

Hadass: I think that perhaps it is one reason I can't leave. I feel that I haven't been fair, and that he gets the raw end of the deal, so I found it hard to give him one more blow.

Claire: What would being fair mean to you?

Hadass: Well, I think that I would have to tell him about my lover – which I never would do. So I guess that is why I feel so stuck. I can't tell him the truth, which isn't fair ... you know, if he knew, he might decide to leave. This way I am keeping him there, not letting him have this fact about me. He thinks that no matter how distant we are, I am faithful. He would never accept my affair, he would want a divorce.

Claire: So perhaps you are keeping him there. But that only means that you need something from him. It means that your not being able to leave might not be as irrational as you think. You might actually be doing something that makes some sense. Let's look at those things you get from him, that maybe keep you from being fair with him.

Hadass: I guess I need him to make me feel secure.

In similar discussions, Hadass became aware of being exploitative and developed a grasp of how Haim's position in their hierarchy might influence his behavior. This opened up a new way of looking at him. Until then, Hadass had viewed his personality as fixed and stable, not influenced by the context.

The second method used with Hadass was an analysis of in-session behavior with me. From the start, she either dominated the therapy, or sat back and expected me to figure things out for her. Hadass had no idea how to work as a team; at work and at home, she was the boss. And just as she had not invested much work in her relationship with Haim, she did not invest much on her own with me. Her idea of work in therapy was that she would present me with the problem, and I would come up with a brilliant solution.

It was also difficult to establish a relationship with her; she installed a sense of uncertainty, leaving me not sure from session to session if she would return. Hadass had no intention of letting herself become dependent on me. She tended to be abrupt, quickly interrupting when she felt she understood something, making a 'Come on, get on with it' kind of expression. Hadass dismissed anything that appeared obvious to her, but still sat back and expected me to come up with some enlightening explanations.

I used the confusion I felt with her as a guide to what Haim probably felt: quite intimidated in her presence and unsure of what she really wanted. Hadass used these tactics when we were discussing something potentially painful; in this way, she would cut me off and try to take control of the session. As I accumulated instances of her maneuvering out of uncomfortable moments, I was increasingly secure in my hypothesis that her rather superior manner was designed to keep from touching her feelings. These observations were then shared directly and honestly with her. For example:

Claire: I wonder how you might feel about this issue?

Hadass: [sounding annoyed] I already told you what I felt!

Claire: I would like to share some of my feelings with you right now . . . is that OK with you?

Hadass: Sure . . . go ahead.

Claire: I have noticed that you seem kind of impatient with me right now. I feel rather intimidated with you when you cut me off like that . . .

Hadass: Oh, I am sorry, I know that I am kind of rough, my workers have told me . . . I really am sorry!

Claire: I wanted to tell you, not because I am hurt, because I am not, but I am thinking about when you do that . . . I have noticed that you do it mostly when we talk about feelings . . . like now, we were just talking about how scared you are about divorce.

Hadass: I never noticed that . . . yes, well, I am more than scared, it makes me feel like a failure, it makes me feel really bad [starts to cry] . . .

These kinds of interventions can have an immediate and powerful impact in approaching previously hidden affect. This method also brought Hadass and me to several instances of conflict between us, bringing more emotionality into the therapy sessions. The method of working on in-session behaviors helped her contact feelings, but those feelings included a great deal of anger, much of which was initially directly at me. In this example, I was blocking her talking either about Haim or her lover, noting how difficult it is for her to focus on herself:

Hadass: Then Rony (the lover) said that he wasn't really sure if he wants to leave his wife. He is so confused!

Claire: I was just noticing again that somehow we are back on Rony, and have left off talking about you ... do you notice that as well? Do you want to do that?

Hadass: Well what on earth do you expect me to talk about! I hate what he is doing to me, and you know that, I hate it when you stop me from talking about him! I hate you both ... look, I am sorry I said that, I didn't mean it!

Claire: I think you did, and I think it is fine that you can tell me how you feel. I know how hard it is for you to tell Rony how angry he makes you, but I think it is good that you can tell me. ... You know, I might have made things too hard for you, telling you all the time when you focus on others, and I am sorry. Perhaps I have been confusing, even inconsistent. On the one hand, I have tried to make this a safe place for you, where you can really be yourself. On the other hand, I have made it hard for you to talk about Rony, which is what feels natural to you.

Hadass: Yes, I think it is true that you are sending me mixed messages. ... You know, I can only get angry at Haim ... he is the only one I am not afraid to lose ... do you think that is another reason I might be staying with him? I do feel sometimes that he sees the worst of me and he still wants me ... so, it makes me feel kind of safe ... I guess I do feel safe with you too.

Claire: I am glad you feel safe with me. I wonder why your anger is the 'worst' of you? What is wrong with anger?

Hadass: I never was allowed to get angry, not at my parents, not at anyone. I have to be nice ... don't I?

Claire: Do you 'have to' be nice? What would happen if you start to be yourself?

The fact that she could express anger at me, and that I was willing respectfully to consider the possibility of my being wrong, eventually led to a sense of equal partnership with me. She stopped her vacillating between being rather contemptuous or handing over all responsibility to me. More as a team, we investigated how her dominating style might impact on Haim. Eventually she realized that she didn't respect Haim because he expressed feelings easily; for her, that kind of behavior indicated weakness, which she did not admire. Typical of women, the feeling that she had the hardest time accepting was anger. Once she could accept that in herself, she was able to accept and respect feelings in general.

The combination of education about the equal partnership themes and tapping her emotional, feminine side through my blocking behaviors, led to her willingness to talk about the past. Her history explains some of her need to cut off from and bury her feminine feeling side. Not only had Hadass lost her first husband, but she had experienced the traumatic stillbirth of a child. For her, emotional survival involved the suppression of feelings, carrying on bravely as in battle.

Going back further, I learned that she was the only daughter of intrusive and needy parents, who favored their two sons and attempted to make her their caretaker. In response, she cut herself off from her own needs and feelings in order to care for them. She developed a dread of the price close relationships exact, and an underlying sense of the unfairness that, as the only female child, she was sacrificed to this role. Later losses only served to confirm her fears. Her personality determined her power position in the relationship, with each reciprocally reinforcing each other.

As Hadass focused on herself in therapy, she first asked for changes from her lover. She wanted to know when she would see him and she asked that he make more efforts to accommodate to her busy schedule. Her lover resisted and insisted on maintaining the status quo in which his needs predominated. This led to a real crisis between them, an ultimatum from Hadass, and eventually to her lover's decision to leave his wife. He then became quite dependent on her. Suddenly Hadass felt rejecting. Her repulsion tended to confirm my hypothesis about her difficulty with dependency, but she was quite disturbed by her response. She honestly tried to face why, after all those years of pursuit, when she got him – she no longer wanted him. She realized that she could not respond to emotional requests from a man, but had formally been protected by her lover's distancing behaviors.

Hadass began to consider more seriously her role in creating the emptiness of the marriage. She saw that she was now pushing her lover away as she did Haim. Our egalitarian relationship allowed her to examine this in her therapy sessions. For the first time, she talked openly about her fears of being dependent on a man, of compromising her freedom, and her fears of loss if she let herself get too close.

Contact with her past, its pain and her true feelings, actually strengthened her sense of herself. Finally freed of her dependency on her lover, she chose to improve her marriage. I suggested that Haim now come in for joint work. Haim was eager to begin therapy, saying that he would do anything to make their marriage work. He had noted Hadass's increased interest, and wanted to know what to do to win her over. Hadass was doubtful that they were ready to meet together with me, but was willing to try. She had never confronted him directly with her feelings, had many secrets, and was not sure which ones she was willing to reveal.

Phase 2: conjoint sessions

Two attempts at conjoint sessions proved her correct. Their behavior in these conjoint sessions was patterned and rigid. Haim stubbornly insisted that Hadass was not trying hard enough, that if she would only try more, they could be close. Hadass remained silent, hiding her secrets. Neither were able to talk in the other's presence: Haim and Hadass had avoided talking about so many important issues that they were extremely ill at ease sitting together. An attempt to train communication skills was a failure; they did not do the homework, changed topics, and used silence to avoid the exercises. It was obvious that conjoint work was premature for them. Hadass had 'chosen' her marriage, but had no idea how to start building a relationship with someone who was virtually a stranger to her.

They were even more uncomfortable with individual sessions with the partner watching. Any kind of intimacy was blocked, and only work alone with Haim seemed possible. Discussing the dynamics of a shifting power structure, I prepared them for the changes that could occur if Haim focused on himself through individual sessions. Understanding the stormy transformation in achieving a new power balance, I foresaw that individual therapy would probably open up conflicts that had never been expressed, resulting in Haim becoming increasingly angry. Both said that they had nothing to lose. While none of us were aware of how violent the anger between them would be, my having prepared them was decisive in helping them weather it through.

Phase 3: work alone with Haim

Whereas Hadass's behavior in therapy was dominating, Haim's was almost obsequious. For him, Hadass was perfect; she was intelligent and sensitive, while he saw himself as not very smart and rather boorish. He said he was not at all angry at the way she spurned him, but he was hurt. Haim presented a picture of someone who tried hard, and could not understand why she kept on rejecting his attempts to be intimate. He acknowledged that they had never been close, but could not understand why they should not be able to build a new relationship. This basic position, which I was to hear repeatedly, was that she was not trying hard enough. If she would just try, it would all work out. For him, everything was a matter of motivation.

Haim did not himself lack motivation. He took almost endless abuse from Hadass and kept on trying. For him, she could no do wrong. Throughout the first three individual sessions, he never deviated from an almost worshipping stance with only superlatives to say about her. The blatant unfairness of their relationship was screened out. For example, while he was primarily responsible for taking care of their children, she was openly critical of his ability as a parent, contradicting him in front of the children and giving him orders about how to deal with them. She made it clear that she was in charge and he was her helper. He felt humiliated, but accepted this behavior, glad that she was willing to talk with him at all.

His behavior with me mirrored this compliant attitude: he was attentive to my every word, stopped talking the minute I said anything, agreed with everything I said, smiling constantly. He seemed cut off from the gravity of the situation. He had never openly challenged Hadass about anything, had never argued with her. When upset he would drink and was currently drinking himself to sleep every night. He was afraid to let her know how hurt he was, lest that make her reject him even more.

Haim's submissive behavior was deeply rooted in his unhappy childhood. The only son of Holocaust survivors, he got nothing of emotional sustenance from either parent. His mother was rarely home, in a manner similar to Hadass, as she was a compulsive card-player. Haim had no sense of anger about this and would accompany his mother to her games just to be in her presence. He hardly remembered his father who worked long hours.

Haim's denial was a survival mechanism; what he got was enough for him. At the age of 11, his parents sent him away to a kibbutz boarding school, visiting only infrequently. In a wooden manner, Haim related how he waited each weekend, in the hope that they might visit. However, he told me that he really understood them: the long taxi ride, the time taken away from their rest, all seemed logical reasons for them to abandon him.

His masculine gender role reinforced this ability to do without. As a boy, he had been a street child, given to stealing and hanging around with tough older boys. As a man, he prided himself in his ability to perform under conditions of hardship, saying that he needed very little from anyone. He had no friends, and never felt he needed any. He had no explanation why, at the age of 40, he suddenly felt needy.

For the first month, he blocked any attempt I made to tap into his discontent, returning to his basic stance of not understanding why she did not try harder to want him. Agreeing with everything I said, he took absolutely nothing in. Nothing I said aroused any angry feelings, nor did he deviate from his standard position. For example, in telling me about their sex life, he described how she brusquely pushed him away and how he kept on trying. I commented on how frustrating that must be for him, to which he pleasantly agreed. He then returned to his pet statement: 'But Hadass just isn't trying hard enough; if she would just try we could have a fine marriage.'

It became more clear why Hadass was so frustrated with him. Nothing much reached him, he maintained his 'party line' no matter what was said, but in a subtle manner he put Hadass in the position of villain. All this was done indirectly; he was so good that it could only be that she was bad. Using an understanding of power positions and the fact that the submissive partner can only express anger indirectly, it is possible to discern a subtle power struggle at play. Haim was afraid of expressing animosity in a direct manner, but had developed a style of expression that drove his partner crazy. I could feel its impact on me.

Much of his behavior was not loving, but actually quite hostile. For example, his insistence on sex no matter what was going on between them was more than insensitive, it was also hostile. When she wished to be alone, he insisted on talking. His behavior placed Hadass in the position of constantly being the rejector and constantly in the wrong.

Significantly, despite her dominating behavior, Hadass could not influence Haim. His passive resistance and suppressed rage found expression in his almost obsessive pursuit of her, no matter what she did or said. Without openly confronting their mutual animosity and covert power struggle, they could not expect to reach the state of friendship. Both somehow expected to go right on to their having good feelings together, without confronting what was going on between them. It was only by bringing this indirect power strategy into the therapy that real change could occur.

The direct educational approach had minor impact. Haim could not see why anger expression was necessary in a relationship; he had never allowed himself to be angry directly at anyone who really mattered to him. A power analysis of their situation and the placement of friendship as a major goal interested him, but had no effect on his behavior. He felt fearful to do anything that might alter the delicate balance between them which was a closed system.

Focusing on his in-session behavior proved to be the key to Haim's transformation. By professing to understand and agree with everything I said, Haim repeatedly returned to his pet idea that Hadass was not trying hard enough. There was no give and take between us and nothing I said seemed to matter. Pointing this out to him, I shared how discouraging it was to feel that I could not affect him in any way. I wondered if this might be what Hadass felt with him as well. After several such interventions, Haim's behavior changed; he started to open up and really listen:

Haim: Yesterday I tried to talk with her again, about us.
Claire: And how did it go?
Haim: Terrible! This time she stopped me right away, said she had decided that she was no longer going to discuss our relationship with me, that these talks don't go anywhere. But it is all I have! All I want is to know what is happening with her, she won't share any of her life with me.
Claire: Do you have any idea why she won't talk with you?
Haim: Not at all. I think it is very reasonable to want to know how we are doing ... I think she is wrong to stop me.
Claire: Haim, we have talked a lot about why she might not want to talk about your relationship – did any of what we said make sense to you?

Haim: Sure, lots of things. But I just think she should try . . . it is all motivation, you know. If she would want to try, then we would be just fine, but she doesn't want to.

Claire: Haim, you know, I am getting frustrated again . . . much like in the last session. You say that you understand her behavior, but then you go back to saying she should try harder. I feel like all our talks have no influence on you at all . . . do you think that this is what Hadass might feel as well?

Haim: Yes, I guess so . . . you know, I don't want to understand her!

Claire: Yes, I agree and I am glad you are willing to look at that. What do you think that is about?

Haim: I don't know . I just know that somehow I feel that to understand her is wrong. I don't want to understand her.

Claire: Do you think that for you, understanding her might mean agreeing that she is right?

Haim: Yes, I think she is wrong in how she behaves to me. Why should I try to understand her behavior?

Claire: You sound rather annoyed with her.

Haim: I am annoyed . . . no, I am angry at her! We could have a wonderful family life and she is ruining it!

Claire: Tell me more about the anger . . . when did it start?

Haim: I have been angry at her for a long, long time.

Hadass was convinced that Haim was not intelligent and that his tendency to repeat himself was because he had virtually nothing to say. Using a power analysis, Haim's almost obsessive repetitions became understandable as a form of passive resistance. As he opened up, an excellent ability to comprehend and utilize abstract ideas was revealed. Haim enjoyed trying to understand himself and Hadass; he turned out to be rather good at it. His potential for an intimate relationship developed as he applied his intelligence to this new understanding, coming up with many astute observations about both of them.

Haim began to develop a life of his own, apart from Hadass and the children. During the next two months, he began to make new friends, joined an exercise class and started going out frequently. Realizing that people actually liked him, Haim began to question the portrait Hadass and he had developed about him.

Threatened by his emerging positive self-esteem, Hadass told him that no one can develop friendships in such a short time, that they were probably very superficial in nature. Moreover, he had no right to leave the children alone in the evenings. As Haim focused more on his own welfare, Hadass resisted and protested. However, Haim continued to invest in himself, and found support through the therapy.

As she resisted, Haim persisted and even escalated his demands for fairness in the relationship. For the first time Haim openly asked where she was going at night, an obvious question he had studiously avoided asking. Suddenly, he switched from extreme compliance to active rebellion. His transformation was gender stereotyped; his anger was expressed aggressively. Openly hostile towards her, he challenged her right to dominate the relationship and asserted his right to pursue his own interests.

Hadass responded by intensifying her dominating tactics. She stayed out till the morning hours, gave no account about when she would be home, and refused to talk to him at all, even about the children or practical matters. Their relationship quickly turned into a battlefield, with both refusing my offer of conjoint sessions to try to confront their hostility through understanding and awareness. They seemed to be saying to me: 'Don't disturb this process with therapy!' However, Hadass requested individual sessions to help her think through her reactions.

I was able to remind them that the crisis had been predicted and to give it meaning through an explanation of shifting power dynamics. My interventions consisted mostly of soothing through these explanations, and directive attempts to limit the damage. The latter became more difficult as Haim touched unknown aggressive sides of himself: he was provocative, critical and openly contentious with her. Their fighting, so different from their previous years of avoidance, was heard around the neighborhood. At one stage I arranged a brief separation for several days, to insure Hadass's safety. My relationship with both allowed them to rely on me and allowed me to limit the extent of the destructiveness of the process.

This stage came to an abrupt end in a surprising manner. Unknown to me, Haim had hired a private detective, uncovering Hadass's affair. Moreover, he discovered that Hadass's lover was also being unfaithful to her. This rather shocking information precipitated a shift in their power structure as suddenly Hadass was confronted with painful previously unknown facts. Her lover, for years her escape from intimacy with Haim, had apparently constantly lied to her. Wounded, she resolutely ended that relationship and turned back to her marriage. Simultaneously furious at Haim and yet somehow feeling that he had rescued her, Hadass privately expressed relief to me. Inconsistencies in her lover's behavior became understandable, and she began to face the essential emptiness of that relationship.

Phase 4: conjoint sessions and the development of friendship

For the first time, they both requested conjoint sessions, showing their new ability to deal directly with conflict. It was nine months after therapy had begun, and a very different Hadass and Haim came to that conjoint meeting. Hadass was clearly in a great deal of pain, and cried for most of the session. Haim was still openly furious, blaming and enjoying the power reversal. Both partners were facing the underlying alienation and lack of friendship in their marriage.

However, they had now endured a difficult crisis and were still together. Paradoxically, this was actually the first time they had mutually shared a meaningful experience in many years. The threat now was in simply reversing the power structure, with a triumphant Haim dominating a conquered Hadass and no real improvement. The issue was brought up directly with the couple in the first session as part of the discussion about goals:

Claire: So what do you think we should aim for at this stage of therapy?

Haim: I think that Hadass owes me an explanation – I want to know all about this affair, how long it was going on, everything.

Claire: Hadass, are you willing to open all this up?

Hadass: I think I should have some privacy about my life.

Haim: I don't think you have any right to privacy! You haven't earned that right!

Claire: The danger I see confronting you two here is this: previously Hadass was dominating in the relationship, and Haim, you felt you had no influence on her. Now, it appears that you have gained power. But the question is, how do you want to use it? Would you now like to have a reversal with Haim dominating Hadass? Haim, do you want Hadass feeling forced by you? What kind of a relationship do you two want?

Haim: No, I really don't want to dominate. I just don't know how to proceed here. I want us to be friends, but I am so angry.

Hadass: I cannot build a friendship with Haim if I am in the wrong ... I think that he has just as much responsibility as I do in having created the marriage we had. I refuse be the bad one any more.

Claire: Friends can openly handle conflict between them. Let's see what each of you think friendship would mean to you ... what kind of friendship would you like to have? How would you handle differences as friends?

The change in roles was especially evident when Hadass requested that we return to communication skill training, tried unsuccessfully a while before. For the first time Hadass was investing in the relationship and was suggesting a constructive method in an active voice. Her role as Distancer had altered, and she began to take responsibility for her share of the relationship work. This had a major impact in softening Haim's rage. While previously unable to articulate it, Haim was angry at the unfairness of having to be the guardian of the relationship. Her new willingness to do the emotional work, later demonstrated by her real investment in the communication exercises given, reassured him that he had an equal partner.

Using communication training, I helped them first process the difficult crisis they had experienced. After learning to paraphrase and reflect in an active listening mode, they were asked to make recordings of conversations at home. The purpose of the talks was for each of them to have a chance to tell the other about their ordeal. They were asked to use the time to learn about each other at a pace suitable to each; the development of friendship was based on shared experience, and they sorely needed to expand their ability to share. Hadass found these conversations very difficult as they demanded a level of sharing she had never experienced.

These tapes were used in the following sessions to analyze how they were progressing towards friendship. Their attempts to listen empathically were highlighted, and when they became judgmental or blaming, this was pointed out. They were asked to replay an interaction during the session, this time using listening skills. The alter ego method was used to deepen the level of intimacy:

Claire: In this tape you Hadass are talking about your feeling pressured by Haim to get close all the time. Could you just continue this discussion right here?

Haim: I want more time with you Hadass, I have felt so lonely these last years, I just want to get to know you again.

Hadass: I don't want to be told what to do by you ... I will open up when I am good and ready!

Claire: [standing behind Hadass's chair, talking for her to Haim]: Haim, I feel pressured when you ask so much from me so soon ... I need more time, and to take things at my own pace.

Haim: I know that and I want to give you the time you need. I just have a hard time holding back.

Hadass: That is what I need to hear!

Their discussions soon began to focus on their core conflict: Haim wanted more closeness while Hadass wanted the right to her privacy. This conflict reflects the changing gender issues that fueled their parallel lives and is typical of transitional couples. Hadass is concerned about losing herself in a relationship, as women traditionally have. As a transitional women, she wants the freedom to focus on her own needs and is distrustful that she can do this and be intimate with Haim at the same time. Haim wants the intimacy previously rejected by men, but he has a hard time letting Hadass control the interaction and allowing her to determine the level of intimacy according to her needs. His demands control the interaction according to his need for closeness. Through therapy, Hadass first had her need for boundaries legitimized, without resorting to distancing or dominating tactics. Haim had his needs for intimacy legitimized, and learned to seek friendships outside the marriage. He then learned to seek intimacy with Hadass without pressuring her for closeness on his terms.

The gender explanation was clearly stated and they were helped to see this issue as a common one for couples in a time of social change. The message was that they were different and have different needs, yet they each had a right to have their needs met. As equal partners, conflict around these differences should be expected. In the future, they would have to renegotiate their needs continually, and they could not expect simple one-shot solutions.

In time, their negotiations expanded to cover a wide variety of other issues: household tasks, who stays home when someone is needed there, and how much time each can spend in individual pursuits. For Hadass and Haim, their entire relationship had to be renegotiated, using the give and take of bargaining, and not unilateral and oppressive power tactics. As equals they were able to do this without either one feeling victimized.

CONCLUSION

For many couples, wives' increased power creates disequilibrium in the relationship. Women themselves are uncertain as to whether they can be intimate with men and still hold on to their identities. One common motif for therapy with all transitional couples is legitimizing the right, and establishing the ability, for the female partner to maintain her self within the relationship. Often, the 'new' man's emerging need for closeness is used subtly to dominate. Men have not always developed the necessary emotional independence to be close without controlling the partner. These emotional tasks demand a high level of personal autonomy and clarification of gender roles.

When transitional couples begin to experience open conflict, it is in the context of unclear gender roles. Women in conflict cannot use their power of expertise in the home, while men cannot use their power of economic clout. This makes the conflict rather chaotic. The process is not patterned, nor is the outcome predictable, making conflict all the more threatening.

In the case of Haim and Hadass, their prolonged alienation leading to parallel lives was a solution to these seemingly insolvable problems. Hadass experienced extreme gender ambivalence, playing rigid roles with both her husband and lover in an attempt to maintain her autonomy. Haim was dominated by his fear of loss and ill equipped to deal with a strong partner since he rejected anger as a legitimate emotion. His transformation to an empowered stance took the route of domination, the only role for power he knew. Teaching both partners the egalitarian alternative proved to be pivotal in helping them find a way for both to be strong within the relationship.

Therapists working with transitional couples need to appreciate the uncertainty of changing gender roles. This means slowing down the pace of change, establishing a firm supportive relationship with each partner, and continually empowering them through choice each step of the way. Real change in gender roles is evolutionary, although there is certainly an element of revolution as well. Appreciating the depth of change experienced by partners in transitional relationships is crucial in helping them to move beyond either parallel lives or open conflict.

Lily and Leon have a lot in common with Hadass and Haim. Labeling relationships as traditional or transitional should not obscure the fact that all couples deal with similar concerns. Fears about intimacy, the lack of communication skills, and unrealistic beliefs are typical in most long-term relationships. These last two chapters have attempted to emphasize the different ways in which couples at different places on the continuum of change respond to therapy. Individual histories and personalities interact with the couple power dynamics to create unique stories and patterns.

Common to couples is their uneven absorption of changing gender roles and power structures since relationships reflect contradictions in the wider social sphere. Sometimes it appears that people are asking themselves to be all things at one time: to fulfill all the traditional gender roles while simultaneously to be equal partners. In this sense, men and women are in the same boat and can share the confusion with empathy and understanding.

Therapists are similarly affected by these confusing messages. The case examples demonstrate that awareness of gender and power starts with the internal monitoring going on inside the therapist and that transformation begins within the therapeutic relationship. The concluding chapter will focus on how the therapist's use of self determines how much equality a couple will absorb through therapy. Couple change is constrained by the therapist's level of growth and development. In the final analysis, it is the therapist's understanding of gender, power, and equality that most helps couples to remove the barriers to change.

Chapter 13

Issues in training and supervision

It is clear that attaining equality in intimate relationships goes beyond dividing up chores, but relates to the very fabric of the relationship, determined by the ability of the individual partners to be friends. Given the persistence of sex-role stereotyping and gender discrimination, this is no small feat. As such, therapy aimed at equality in couple relationships demands more from the therapist than learning a new set of skills. It might be said that work towards equality in relationships goes to the core of the therapist's beliefs about relationships in general, the role of men and women in society, as well as the therapist's own freedom from cultural stereotypes. The teaching of couples and family therapy usually touches on the trainees' life situation and history, but focusing on gender, power and intimate relationships seems to stir up more intense personal reactions. This can blur the boundaries between the professional and the personal, making it hard to remain neutral and focused on the couple in treatment. Supervisory groups that make gender and power central variables tend to become emotionally charged, quickly delving into and stirring up the trainees' own lives.

As the 'self of the therapist' is so entangled in these issues, linking the training experience to the social context of gender and power is crucial in helping professionals to maintain the balance between subjectivity and objectivity. By locating the personal in the political and by maintaining the dialectic between these poles, a synthesis can be found in which therapists working with couples come to a deeper understanding of their own reactions to gender and power issues. Through this connection they are able to empathize with their clients' difficulties. Just as the partners in therapy come to anchor their own relationship problems in the wider social context, gaining strength from this broader perspective, so the therapist comes to see personal life experiences reflected in clients' struggles. Holding on to this connection, without losing the distance that more abstract understanding gives, helps foster an equal partnership with the couple.

As therapists undergo their own personal transformation, themes related to the process of equal partnership are revealed. This chapter will examine some of the processes which occur during training in the model suggested by this book. These mirror many of the teaching issues that have been discussed by other feminist family therapists and touch on common struggles in the development of gender and power consciousness. They include the dilemmas in changing deeply ingrained beliefs, in learning to be sensitive to the clients' gender issues, in developing awareness of one's own gendered restrictions in behavior, and in fostering movement towards the therapists' ability to equally empower men and women.[1]

The process of change that trainees experience reflects themes that arise in the movement of relationships from hierarchy to equal partnership. The training group is a collection of individuals with gendered socialization histories and interpersonal dynamics nurtured by a common social context. Gender and power constrictions impact on the group in a manner similar to their impact on the couple. As the expert, the trainer/supervisor models the process of empowerment by openly sharing knowledge and self-disclosing personal information which increases the learners' range of alternatives, leading to a sense of personal and professional efficacy.

Each therapist comes into the training group with a unique and uneven mixing of traditional and egalitarian values. The trainees, ambivalent about change in sex roles, are also personally caught up in reforming their own relationships and have only to varying extents made peace with feminism. It is by working through this confusion that the training experience reflects the transformation of clients towards greater empowerment by expanding conscious choice and making the process a shared and understandable experience.

UTILIZING TRAINING GROUP DYNAMICS

Just as couples can become stuck by dividing up and projecting different attitudes about gender, so training groups can quickly become polarized in stimulating but diverse ideological battles that blur common individual ambivalence. In general, group roles are often allocated which symbolize exaggerated aspects of various individual reactions to the group experience: one member dominates the interaction as a leader, another draws criticism as a scapegoat, while a third maintains harmony by playing the peace-maker. While stabilizing the group, rigid adherence to roles ultimately stymies personal growth and can result in group stagnation.

Internal ambivalence about change in women's roles similarly translates into projections of exaggerated positions: one trainee extols the virtue of androgyny, another expresses the dangers in blurring gender differences, while a third insists on remaining neutral, saying that gender is a personal matter. With mixed sex groups, the men might be defensive about change, while the women take on the position of advocates of progressive values. When there is one sex only, the same roles are still divided up between the members. This dynamic is especially evident in the beginning stages of work where anxiety is high and projections are a way of initially managing intensely uncomfortable feelings that threaten the group's existence.

The supervisor/trainer's role is to legitimize and universalize the underlying shared confusion about changing gender roles, knowing that as individuals become more personally responsible for their own ambivalence, they expand their readiness to learn. To this end, care is taken that material about gender and power never be delivered in a dogmatic educational fashion, promoting either compliance or resistance. Rather, presentation of research about women's subordinate position in marriage needs to be balanced with reflective questioning demonstrating the real therapeutic dilemmas. Provocative questions that demand continual rethinking of basic issues in couple therapy stimulate the development of an examining and open atmosphere. There is no one right answer to these quandaries.

For example, the training group need to grapple with dilemmas such as:

• Are we therapists primarily responsible for maintaining the family system, or are our loyalties primarily with the welfare of the individual members?
• What happens when there is a contradiction between the two? Even if we believe that power inequality underlies many

couples' presenting symptoms, does that mean we have the right to modify the structure of the relationship when the couple may not have asked for help with this?

• Are we as therapists advocates of the two-parent intact family, or do we foster the acceptance of any lifestyle?

When feelings are intense and positions appear rigid, training groups can benefit from using the 'fishbowl' structure, in which an inner circle is formed. For example, all the men can talk in a small circle at the center of the room, with the women trainees positioned around them in an outlying circle; they then switch, so that women have the chance for discussion with the men observing. Participants are often amazed by the different climate of the two groups and the way gender influences the type of discussion held.

This method can also be used for those who hold a certain ideological position, such as those who think therapists have a duty to work specifically towards equality watching those who believe that therapists do not have the right to intervene in lifestyle issues. By exaggerating these polarized projections of our internal ambivalence, rigidity is reduced, with options and alternative ideas emerging spontaneously.

In general, the early stage of training in gender and power issues needs more structure than later stages. Ideally therapists would begin with a theory course in women and families, which would include the feminist critique of family therapy. More often, the supervisor/trainer is faced with a heterogeneous group, having varying degrees of previous preparation. To create a common language, it is helpful in early meetings to bring in experiential exercises that introduce ideas and stimulate personal involvement and thinking. The following are examples:

EXERCISES ON GENDER AND POWER

1 Name two of the most masculine people you know, and two of the most feminine. You can choose from films literature, pop stars, etc. What adjectives describe these people? Which adjectives fit you?[2]

2 Sit opposite a partner and begin a conversation to get acquainted (about five minutes). Now continue this conversation, but pretend you are the opposite sex (about five minutes).

Discuss this experience with your partner: what felt different playing the other gender? What does this mean to you?

3 Choose a partner and sit opposite each other. Take turns role-playing a conversation you are having with a daughter or a son. What would you tell your child about what you want them to be as men or women? After the role play, discuss messages you received from your parents (overt and covert messages) about they wanted from you as a man or a woman.

4 Gender 'survival' messages: start by warming up with cutting out pictures from magazines that say something about gender. Then, in pairs, share lists you made of five or six messages for either gender that you learned about intimacy, bodies, dating, showing emotions, family life, chores, activities for girls and boys, world of work, older men and women, such as: 'Boys don't play with dolls'; 'Girls are not as good as boys at math'; 'Men are served first'; 'Women are more emotional than men'. Sitting opposite a partner, discuss the following questions:

- How are your lists different/same?
- Which 'survival' messages are OK, which do you still have some use for?
- Which 'survival' message(s) of either of you show up in therapy settings, work settings, at home?
- Which 'survival' message(s) has the most impact on you in your work as a therapist (either as you incorporate it or push against it in some way)?
- In the therapy models that you work with, what echoes do you hear of various gender 'survival' messages?

5 Circular questions related to gender: sample questions are given on the exercise sheet to help model possible circular questions related to gender. For example:

- If your mother (father) had worked outside of the home, how do you think family relationships might have been different?
- If you had been born of the opposite sex, how do you think your life would have been different as a child?
- If you were a different gender, how do you think your style as a therapist might be different?
- If you were a different gender, how do you think clients might react differently to you?
- If you were growing up in the 1990s, how might your parents

have taught you differently about being a boy/man, girl/
woman?
Have each person write five or six questions, and then sit with
a partner and ask each other these questions.
6 Any or all of these questions can be used to stimulate discussion about gender and power in therapy:

- Do you use nonsexist language in sessions, report writing,
supervision?
- How do you address stereotyped sex roles in sessions?
- What are the ways you keep in touch with what you your-
self were taught about gender?
- How do you work with your own values about gender in
therapy?
- How do you work with the role of women as often the
primary contacts with the social service network?
- In what ways are models of therapy that you use gender
biased? How have you modified or changed the models?
- How do you bring the larger sociopolitical, economic and
historical context of gender into the treatment context?
- What kind of gender issues do you find in your work setting?
How do these issues affect your therapeutic work?

EQUAL PARTNERSHIP THEMES AND
SUPERVISION/TRAINING GROUPS

The supervisor/trainer models equal partnership principles by
making the themes of equal sharing manifest in leadership style.
As a model of egalitarian values, the trainer needs continuously
to monitor the level of sharing in the group, and fairness in
attention to different members. Moreover, teaching the equal
partnership themes located in this model can be enhanced by
practicing them in the group, and then by pinpointing how the
themes can be used to establish equality in any social system.
Themes that come up most often in supervisory groups include
power, sharing group tasks, and accepting diversity.

Power

How are group decisions made? The supervisor continuously turns
decisions back to the group for discussion, such as which kind of
cases they will discuss, the way the group will be structured, time

allocation, vacations, etc. To the extent that the supervisor/trainer increasingly shares authority and empowers the group members to take responsibility for the direction of the work, the participants will come to understand the dilemmas of shared power better from the inside.

The supervisor searches out potential points of choice that can be shared with the participants. For example, in working with a trainee emotionally caught up in a case, the supervisor took the opportunity to ask the trainee whether she wanted to work on her emotional reactions, or deal with the 'how to' of managing the actual session. The trainee chose to go with work about her emotional response, but said that she wanted to reserve 'extra time' during the next session to get some more practical help with the case. The other participants supported her, although it meant her getting more than her fair share of attention. In this sense, equal partnership principles are demonstrated as the entire group learns to cope with *changing needs of the members*. These ongoing decisions empower the trainees to feel more responsible for the process by becoming aware of choices they have.

What kind of model of authority does the supervisor present? To the extent that there is self-disclosure of personal reactions, open sharing of ambivalence about changing gender norms, and recognition of participants' competencies, the supervisor/trainer fosters an equal sharing of authority. The message is that the supervisor does not have all the answers, is struggling with the same issues, and relies on other members for their input and help. In one supervisory session, a scheduled couple did not show up for the live supervision and none of the other participants had prepared a case for presentation. The supervisor decided to present a case of her own, asking the group to supervise her. Not only was their supervision excellent, but their feedback later showed this experience to be a turning point for the group. Their comments showed that the level of trust shown to them, and their suddenly realizing that they had a lot to give to their supervisor, enhanced their sense of professional ability.

Sharing group tasks

The training group has its own tasks to accomplish. Some of the tasks are instrumental, such as the preparation of reading material, presentation of cases, scheduling couples for live supervision, bringing in videotapes for observation, and preparation of refreshments. Other tasks are more emotional in nature, such as sharing emotional reactions, caring for trainees who are treating a difficult case, maintaining the emotional climate of the group, dealing with group conflicts. The tendency in all groups is for role development, so that certain members take on the caretaking roles while others do more of the instrumental tasks.

The supervisor/trainer monitors and comments on the division of labor in the group and asks for feedback about the subjective sense of fairness. Working together with the members continually to maintain equity, the themes are demonstrated and the similarity to the sharing work that needs to occur in couple relationships is highlighted. Conflicts between group members are initially handled by the supervisor, who articulates and models the theme that conflict between equals is to be expected and accepted. As soon as possible, group conflicts are turned over to individual members for resolution.

A trainee who experienced some anger at another trainee's comment, which appeared to her to demonstrate a lack of sensitivity, was asked if she would deal with her anger directly with the other trainee, who expressed her own willingness to work in front of the group. While their interaction took about fifteen minutes of the group time, it was important in delivering several messages: that conflict can and should be dealt with and then put to rest; that the emotional climate is important and can be monitored without the group becoming mired in group process issues; and that the responsibility for handling conflict can be equally shared between the two people who had the conflict.

Accepting diversity

Groups have as much trouble in accepting differences between members as do intimate partners between each other. The tendency in groups is for pressure towards conformity. The supervisor/trainer fosters an egalitarian atmosphere by pointing out differences between the trainees: in theoretical approaches, styles of therapy, personality, and practical solutions to cases. By legitimizing and emphasizing differences, the idea that differences are a resource is promoted in the group process and tolerance for difference grows, paving the way towards a more egalitarian atmosphere.

Gender differences are openly discussed as typical gender inter-actions are enacted within the group. The male trainees often dominate the discussion, with the females taking on the role of good listeners. In one supervision group, the men were asked to just listen for an hour. This seemingly innocuous directive was extremely effective in arousing intense emotions related to gender issues: the ambivalence of the men, as they felt both relief and fear of their own passivity; the anger of women, as they contacted their previous oppression and discomfort with sudden responsi-bility. These and other reactions mirror client reactions to change: the discomfort of men who suddenly feel they are being pushed into the background, and the uncertainty of women who suddenly feel powerful.

Exploring the theme of diversity leads to opening up differences often buried in groups, such as identifying the experiences of minority members and their feelings of isolation in the group. In one training group, the only Black trainee in a group of seven was asked if she could discuss her feelings about being the only person of color in the group. The supervisor drew anger from the group by challenging the group's desire to see everyone as 'the same'. Eventually, awareness of the discomfort felt about articulating differences helped these trainees better to grasp and overcome their own reticence about naming differences between men and women in general, and between the partners they were helping.

The other themes related to equality similarly develop during the group process in supervision/training situations. The supervisor/ trainer who can pinpoint and utilize these themes helps trainees to experience them firsthand, increasing their comprehension of the processes needed for attaining equality. In addition, maxi-mizing attention to these themes appears to foster the develop-ment of a well-functioning training group in which equality for each member is the norm, empowering each person to offer their full potential to the group.

THE LEARNING PROCESS

Learning new attitudes, ideas and skills involves a stage of 'unlearning' which is both exciting and disconcerting. One of the first stages involves recognizing the present lack of clarity of concepts. While well versed in the rhetoric of women's liberation, few can concretely envision the way equality between the sexes would actually look in the daily life of intimate relationships. Politically correct catchwords are commonly used without careful attention to establishing a common definition and a clear vision.

Therapists rarely have the opportunity to articulate their own views on equality. One might presume that equality is based on having equal resources or power, while another assumes that equality means equally dividing up household tasks; they could discuss a case without recognizing that they hold different operational definitions. Their different views could influence their objectives for treatment. The first therapist might focus on the wife's working, her access to money, and her involvement in decisions. The second may pay more attention to the wife's weariness, overwork in the home and lack of assistance at home. Many therapists just assume that their definition of equality is the standard one.

In the first stage of training in gender and power, these issues related to definition need to be made central. For example, a trainee brought this case to supervision:

A middle-aged couple, a second marriage for both, had been negotiating marital conflict. When they first came in for therapy, the wife was overfunctioning in the home, while the husband was more involved with children from his first marriage. The wife was doing all the housework and childcare, and was feeling overwhelmed, while the husband was often out of the home. After ten sessions, the husband was far more involved in homelife and the couple had begun to share the running of their home. As a matter of fact, the husband had taken on all the cooking and preparation of meals.

The therapist eagerly encouraged the couple to think about termination and had repeated often during the sessions prior to supervision that she felt the couple were ready to try going without treatment. Supervision was requested when the couple called 'SOS': they were fighting terribly again and felt they had returned to their starting point.

In reviewing the case in group supervision, the therapist could not understand what had happened, since in her view they were a great team. In reviewing her definition of equality, she revealed that in her own life she was currently angry that her husband was not sharing more of the housework. This therapist was very impressed that the client husband was so involved. The sharing she wanted meant role-sharing of actual behaviors, and she especially meant men doing traditionally female tasks at home.

The lively group discussion led to a multitude of diverse definitions from the trainees, each reflecting personal life situations, values and philosophical world view. The therapist realized that she had been prematurely assuming a positive therapy outcome, based on her own wishes for a certain kind of sharing she herself wanted but lacked in her personal life.

The therapist returned to the couple to find out more about *their* definition of equality. She discovered that the wife was not at all happy about the sharing of household tasks, as she didn't feel that she was doing what she liked to do. As a matter of fact, she felt she was the superior cook. However, not wanting to hurt her husband (nor her enthusiastic therapist), she had quietly submitted to the arrangement, grateful that he was involved at all. She herself didn't know why she was so angry, as she watched her husband taking over the territory she perceived as hers.

In talking this over with the therapist, she came to see that the wife wanted more control, but not knowing how to do that, she had abdicated control altogether. This left her feeling powerless, and even more confused, since she was supposed to be happy. The therapist then helped the couple talk directly about sharing, to arrive at a joint definition. The wife, using negotiation skills, convinced her husband that for her, sharing meant sharing control about who does what. The who does what was less important to her than having an equal say in this process. These discussions then revealed that the husband had been imposing his view on the wife for some time, and that the wife was more resentful than she first had realized.

They terminated therapy after six more sessions, in which they had to work through the anger of the wife at having submitted to her husband's wishes for so long. Eventually, they created a subjective sense of fairness in both partners by increasing equal decision-making and sharing of tasks based on each partner's needs and preferences. The therapist reported to the group that the wife had taken back the cooking.

Learning about gender, power and equality comprises a reexamination of previously learned theories, as well as the clarification of personal definitions. The feminist critique of family therapy has much to offer in terms of adding a new way of viewing the field.[3] Hare-Mustin's groundbreaking article (1980), 'Family therapy can be dangerous to your health', led the way for others who have criticized sexist assumptions of family theory and practice.

Family therapy developed within the social climate of the 1960s, primarily by male theoreticians and therapists, and reflects family norms before post-modern feminist influences. Family therapy interventions are often gender biased, either overemphasizing or underemphasizing sex-role influences. An example of the former is valuing the husband's career without paying equal attention to the wife's work. The latter bias can be seen when divorcing partners were treated as if they faced the same struggles, despite the relative impoverishment of wives after separation. Theories in family therapy reflect society's overvaluing of masculine traits. These include an emphasis on individuation and separation, rather than on connection and caring. Not enough attention has been paid to housework and the details of daily life, with an overfocusing on more global processes, such as 'enmeshment', 'boundaries', 'differentiation' and other abstract ideas that do not take actual content into account.

The systemic conceptual basis of family therapy has extolled 'circular causality', blurring the power differences in families, making it seem as if family members influence each other equally. The potential danger is to ignore women's real lack of options in the wider society that impact on her ability to persuade her partner. This can lead to blaming the victim of incest or physical violence for her part in causing the abuse. Interventions that demand change from the woman equally from the man ignore her actual helplessness and lack of power.

There is a decided tendency to overfocus on the woman in family therapy as she is more compliant, speaks the therapy language of feelings, and is more motivated to change. Overfocusing on the woman can lead to demanding more change from her. Finally, family therapy has been accused of being ethnocentric: ignoring gender and power in marriage has fostered an idealized image of the intact two-parent heterosexual marriage, implying that other alternative family structures (one-parent, lesbian, single or coinhabiting couples) are 'other' and thus deviant. These assumptions serve further to limit women's power by making alternative lifestyles appear less worthwhile than staying in marriage.

Many of the current problems of the modern family are problems of gender and power, but family therapy has tended to individualize these issues, making personal history too central and social conditions too peripheral. Thus, supervision gets caught up in the details of individual and couple histories, without reference to the social context that plays such a powerful role in the problem.

The process of reexamining cherished and accepted ways of doing things can be unsettling. Trainees experience their own internalized sexism as well as anger at societal injustice. This can be especially difficult for experienced therapists. As products of a patriarchal society, we all devalue the feminine in ourselves and others to some extent. For each person, internalized denigration of the feminine has its own expression.

For one therapist, there is discomfort when the wife becomes too emotional and cannot be easily returned to a more rational position (although the same therapist will turn to the wife for clarification of feelings or emotional support for family members). For another, there is impatience when the wife goes on about the 'petty details' of the household, ignoring the seemingly more important larger issues. One therapist concentrates all her energy on bringing in the resistant husband, making it seem that the wife cannot manage a situation on her own. Another turns to the wife when talking about the children, but to the husband when talking about finances. One therapist asks the husband if the hour for the next session fits his busy schedule without asking the wife the same question, or turns to the husband when talking about the bill. Another presents a case as 'Mr Jones and his wife', without thinking of the sexist language used.

The list is endless and the point is that increased awareness of sexism includes heightened awareness of the idiosyncratic expressions of sexism reflected in doing therapy. In effect, there is no way that a therapist can tackle these questions without becoming aware of how they impact on the self.

THE FEMALE THERAPIST

Training in equal partnership has an especially powerful impact on the female therapist. Close up to these issues, she is often in the process of transforming her own life at the same time as she works to help couples. The trainee may be a single career woman, facing sexism at work, difficulty in the arena of finding a partner or facing social disapproval if she wants to remain single. She may be a re-entry mother, worried about how her family is faring as she goes back to work. She may be a lesbian who is experiencing ambivalent feelings about working with traditional heterosexual couples. Or she may be a woman in the process of divorce, wondering if she will recover emotionally and dare to be in another relationship. No one in training is neutral about gender and women's subjectivity offers a welcome resource and a chance to experience personally what the couple is experiencing.

Women therapists have to cope with issues common to women in relationships. As women, they have been socialized to care for others' emotions and speak a language of feelings. This obviously is a benefit in treating couples, but makes relating to men more difficult. While men therapists relate better to their own gender clients, women have an added problem that male therapists do not face. Men clients have been found to be defensive with female therapists, which was not found for female clients and their male therapists. In effect, women face their own and their male clients' ambivalence about female authority.[4]

The female therapist needs to overcome the limitations of gender stereotyping herself in order to work towards equality with couples. She benefits from having faced her own tendency to split her masculine from her feminine sides. Many female therapists have a hard time believing that they will be perceived by men as feminine if they are also seen as strong and assertive. Some can allow themselves to be powerful at work, but not at home. Others will be powerful with women clients but not with male clients. In various ways, women therapists suffer from the social stigma attached to forceful women: their role demands their being directive, but their gender socialization fosters indirection and passivity with male authority. They handle this by not integrating their strong and their vulnerable side, keeping these seemingly contradictory traits in separate compartments.

Overcoming this dynamic is especially crucial in establishing a positive therapeutic alliance with both partners and helping the couple to weather the difficult and conflictual transition to more equally shared power. Female therapists have many points of conflict in achieving these aims.

One crucial issue is whether the female therapist herself *believes that equality with men is possible*. If she has never experienced it in her own life, and is pessimistic about what men are capable of, she may not envision a true partnership for her clients. Her goals are limited by stereotypic beliefs (which appear to her as self-evident truths): men are not as capable as women in expressing their feelings; men are very childlike and their feelings need to be protected; men are threatened by a strong woman and cannot face direct confrontation. This is not to say that men are not similarly conditioned by these types of restrictive beliefs, but that when their female therapists cannot see beyond them, the chance of helping men move on is minimal.

Another issue women therapists share with their female clients resolves around their internalized image of 'female destructiveness' and deep ambivalence about anger expression. When anger is expressed in the therapy session, the woman trainee may become uncomfortable. She experiences the wish to stop the conflict, although she may be aware that it is beneficial for the partners to explore their anger directly. For some trainees, anger in the female client is harder to accept, as it stirs her own repressed rage and prohibitions about being 'not nice'. For others, anger in male clients makes her fearful, as it is associated with the danger of male aggressiveness.

For example, after an unexpected and unplanned break of several weeks, a female therapist described how she helped the wife work through her anger at the therapist for having 'abandoned' the couple. Only during supervision and upon questioning did it become apparent that the therapist had totally ignored the husband's anger, which he had then turned against the couple's teenage boys. This triggered a new understanding for the therapist of how afraid she was of male anger, how she had not helped this man express his rage about many issues and had subtly undermined progress by keeping conflict to a minimum.

While female therapists understand cognitively that conflict can be beneficial and that transformation necessitates experiencing angry feelings, their unfamiliarity with direct anger expression gets in the way. Often the supervision group needs to take up this issue directly to help female therapists work with anger and to help them be able to confront clients when necessary. For many female therapists, being confrontational is seen as antithetical to being nurturing and as rejecting the client. Seeing that confrontation can be loving takes developing a new attitude towards the assertive sides of the personality, often demanding personal growth and change in the therapist.

For the female therapist to help couples become friends, she has to know how to be a friend herself to men. She needs to be aware of her internal reactions when men clients cry and feel helpless and to have worked through her own internalized devaluation of these 'weak' feminine sides appearing in men. This may mean looking at how she feels about herself when she cries, or how she looks at men in her life when they feel helpless. The group experience can help women therapists monitor their tendency to protect men from painful feelings, and their tendency to expect the female partner to do the same. It is not uncommon in live supervision to find that after a particularly effective intervention, in which the husband directly reveals neediness, the wife and the female therapist have absolutely no idea what to do. The female therapist may worry she will embarrass the male partner by observing his pain, or that he may become angry with her if she comments on it. Or the female therapist and the woman partner may have established a subtle collusion to protect the man from facing difficult issues.

The supervisor can help overcome these gender problems by using role play situations to have women trainees speak directly to the male experience in a new and unfamiliar way:

> The female therapist was describing an impasse with a couple in which the therapist perceived that the husband was resisting therapy and rejecting her. The supervisor asked the trainee to role play the situation, with another trainee playing the husband:

Trainee: I was wondering how you feel about Tal (the wife) crying just now.

Husband: She is overly emotional, that's what I think!

Trainee: You sound like it is uncomfortable for you to hear her emotions?

Husband: Are you kidding? Me, uncomfortable? I have absolutely no problems . . . none.

Trainee: But it sounds like perhaps it isn't easy for you to listen to her crying?

Husband: I just told you, I am just fine.

This type of interaction is frequently repeated, in different forms, between male clients and their female therapists. The result of miscommunication, based on lack of appreciating the male experience, can lead to a coalition between the female client and therapist, which further alienates the male partner. Here the supervisor can help by *role playing the male client, playing a 'fantasy man' who is able to express some of the hidden assumptions and experiences of the male client*. The female therapist has coped with the underlying issues directly:

Trainee: I understand that you feel fine, but perhaps it is hard for you to see your wife cry?

Husband   [played by supervisor]: I hate being pushed to talk about my feelings ... it makes me very angry

Trainee: What about it makes you angry?

Husband   [played by the supervisor]: I don't like to be pushed in general. And I get the feeling that you are looking around for problems ... I have learned to try to be positive about life, and here you are focusing on the negatives!

Trainee: So you feel that it is rather unhelpful if I focus on what hurts?

Husband   [played by the supervisor]: I came in here to get some answers, and all you do is ask questions about problems! I would like concrete help about what to do, not to commiserate about bad feelings. How is that going to help?

Trainee: I see what you mean. But do you think that Tal feels like you do?

Husband   [played by the supervisor]: No, she is like you! She wants to talk about feelings all the time. But I hate seeing her cry, it seems like self-pity and just drags her down.

Trainee: So maybe that is one of the issues we need to deal with here ... that you and Tal might feel differently about how to deal with problems?

Husband   [played by the supervisor]: Yes, I think that would be an important issue to deal with.

The supervisor helped the trainee to empathize with the husband by gaining an appreciation of the gender differences that were impeding her work with the couple. When female therapists become more empathetic, they paradoxically become more able to confront the male client. It is as if only by touching the male experience can the female therapist make the needed connection with the male client and use it then to confront him. Female therapists who remain intimidated by their male clients are those who fail to comprehend the unique and different experience of being male. They have a harder time seeing the male client as an equal partner in the therapy, either trying to placate him by paying too much attention to him, or avoiding him by interacting more with the female partner.

In confronting issues related to gender and power, the female therapist has to face the considerable effort that may have gone into coping with sexism in her life as a professional woman. The female therapist may resist facing how angry she really is. Working past the rage, she expands her ability to deal with the male client as an equal, and concomitantly develops her own self-esteem and sense of competence. She has more understanding of what the female partner is coping with and is less likely to expect that the female partner can make changes in the relationship without the other's active commitment to change personally. These changes are essential if she is to be helpful to couples who are moving towards equality themselves.

INTEGRATING EQUAL PARTNERSHIP GOALS

This book is a result of a personal search for a way to introduce work on gender and power to therapy with couples. Trained in behavior therapy, I rely on training in communication, problem solving, and contracting as major tools. Today, these remain the foundation from which I build. Couples are rarely skilled in listening and expressing their deepest emotions, focusing on problems through adequate definitions, or able to negotiate changes in their lives. Most relationships seem to benefit from increasing these important competencies in partners.

Later training in structural and paradoxical systemic family therapy, in intergenerational approaches, experiential approaches and objects relations thinking greatly enriched my work. Like many therapists, who are exposed to these and other theoretical orientations, the development of my work in couples therapy resulted in a mixing of different lenses and tools.

Where does work on gender and power fit into this process of blending and integrating?

Targeting equal partnership as a major therapeutic goal can offer an *umbrella for integrating other approaches to work with couples*. In the area of family therapy, *Structural Family Therapy* (Minuchin, 1974) similarly offers an overriding conceptualization of family structure that allows the therapist to analyze power and hierarchy between parents, children and extended family and the resulting lines of communication, coalitions and boundaries issues that hierarchy determines. For example, in a family where the mother and daughter have formed a coalition, leaving father out, the structural family therapist will realign mother and father as a bonded unit, and work to create a hierarchy between the parental and child subsystems. Tools from other approaches, such as paradoxes, drawings, contracts or genograms, are all useful in helping to achieve this overall structural change.[5]

The ideas proposed in this book for helping couples to be friends similarly focus on the *structure of relationships* as central, allowing the integration of a variety of orientations to restructure power imbalance and overcome the restrictions of gender socialization. Since individual responsibility and growth within the couple relationship is important as well, object relations and intergenerational work can be helpful in strengthening personal autonomy in the partners, helping to impart the strength to change the relationship power structure and overcome gender restrictions. Experiential role-playing and creative methods similarly can help partners deepen their aliveness and intimacy, and helping to energize towards change. Paradoxical interventions can help couples become unstuck, allowing movement to a further point along the continuum of change. As couples move into the stage of open conflict, communication, contracting, negotiation and problem-solving training within a behavioral tradition are all appropriate.

With equal partnership as an overriding goal, the relationship therapist can chose interventions which help the couple in their movement towards friendship. However, these must take place within the context of an egalitarian relationship between the partners and the therapist. The crucible for change is within this relationship: here equality is first tasted, for many for the first time, and new vision is born of what is possible. Interventions that manipulate and help the client in ways that are not explicit have no place here; they are not compatible with the development of an equal partnership between clients and therapist. Some of the paradoxical methods that neither share the meaning of the technique with the clients, nor concern themselves with the way prescriptions are interpreted, are *not* isomorphic to the process of equal partnership. Insight needs to consider an important byproduct of any method to change power and gender patterns.[6] Methods that empower both partners by encouraging them to be *active agents* in their own change help free couples from gender constrictions and power imbalances.

There are many ways of reaching equality when this goal is adequately clarified and operationalized. As we can view equality between partners as a multifaceted and flexible process, we can also view the work towards equality in relationships as allowing a variety of approaches. The couple might choose a dual-career lifestyle, or to have one partner at home with small children. The therapist may use individual or couple interventions and may integrate methods from different theoretical orientations. There is no one 'right' lifestyle, nor one 'right' method. There is, however, an overriding concern for equal rights and opportunities, and the chance for each partner to fulfill their individual potential within the relationship. This essential goal thus organizes the entire therapeutic process, including choice of subgoals and methods, giving the therapist the clarity of vision to utilize the rich diversity of approaches that are available.

Notes

INTRODUCTION

1 Qualitative research has been proposed as an important tool for understanding families and family therapy by Moon et al. (1991). My study utilized 'Grounded Theory' analysis, based on symbolic interaction theory and described extensively by Glasser and Strauss (1967) and Strauss and Corbin (1990). The interviews were semi-structured, a research approach in which questions are planned in advance, but the data-gathering conversation itself determined the course of the interview. I was also influenced by the developing notion of 'feminist interview research' as described by Reinharz (1992) The methodology used in my study has been reported more extensively in Rabin (1994).

2 The findings of my research, and the resultant therapeutic model, appears highly congruent with the work of social psychologists studying all close relationships (i.e. see Berscheid and Peplau, 1983; Perlman and Duck, 1987). These researchers see all dyadic relationships as parts of a larger system and search for similarities between the processes involved in close relationships. It would thus be expected that future development of the therapeutic model described in this book should be in applying principles of equal partnership to all close relationships, such as homosexual relationships, parent–child relationships and friendships.

1 GENDER, POWER AND CONTEMPORARY RELATIONSHIP TENSION

1 Marital therapy textbooks vary to the extent to which this changing social context is viewed as important to treatment. Some of the texts that directly take up the issue are: Brothers (1992); Crowe and Ridley (1990); Goodrich (1991); Goodrich et al. (1988); Luepnitz (1988); Perelberg and Miller (1990); Solomon (1989); and Walters et al. (1988). Many other texts, oriented to specific approaches, tend to ignore gender and power: Baucom and Epstein (1990); Freeman (1992); and Scharff and Scharff (1991).

2 Talcott Parsons (1954) proposed that men need to detach from their early identification with their mothers and anything female, leading to 'compulsive masculinity', boys 'refuse to have anything to do with girls', and basically to reject tender emotions as a defense againt feeling too much like a girl. Jukes (1993) in *Why Men Hate Women*, and Hafner (1993) in *The End Of Marriage*, both discuss in depth the precarious nature of male identity based on envy of women and the need to control women's sexuality. In *The Courage to Raise Good Men*, Silverstein and Rashbaum (1994) propose that true self-security in men will only develop when they can embrace their feminine sides. This will only occur when young boys are not forced to cut off from their mothers and when mothers allow closeness to their sons without fear of 'emasculating them'.

3 Women experience built-in contradictions between a sense of self-esteem and a sense of femininity. Edwards and Williams (1980) have shown that men and women are often thought of as opposite sides of a duality – with masculinity connected to activity and competence and feminine traits connected to warmth and expressiveness, but not strength or competence. If we lived in a society that valued 'feminine' traits equally to 'masculine' traits, women would not be faced with the impossible dilemma of either feeling feminine or feeling good about themselves. Women experience built-in contradictions between a sense of self-esteem and a sense of femininity. A large body of research in psychology (for example, Broverman *et al.*, 1972; Edwards and Williams, 1980) shows that the feminine side is devalued and that women's self-esteem consequently suffers. Thus women face a unique paradox not faced by men; their very femininity is connected with low self-esteem, but being more masculine opens the way of social criticism.

4 Safilios-Rothschild (1981) proposes that men react negatively to the disclosure of women's strengths and withdraw from their protective role, consequently making the women feel insecure and rejected. Also, as women increase in competence outside of the home, competition for achievement and income between the partners could occur. Men who are threatened by a successful wife and who feel competitive with her report decreased marital satisfaction and their wives feel a reduction in marital happiness as well (Hiller and Philliber, 1986). Fendrich (1984) found that the more money husbands make compared with their wives, the better these husbands feel about themselves. Thompson and Walker (1989) in their review of hundreds of studies, concluded that there is something about the 'symbolic meaning' of wives as co-providers that is distressing for many men.

5 Benin and Agnostinelli (1988); Crouter *et al.* (1987); Russell and Radin (1983); Staines and Libby (1986) are all empirical studies showing that women and men are in disagreement about sharing. Equality in marriage is a goal more for women. Although women benefit from work outside the home, with no harm to children (Crosby, 1991), men don't always see women's work as positive. Baruch and Barnett (1986) found that husbands view their wives' careers as causing more stress than their own. Harrell and Andrew (1986) found that weekly liquor

consumption in men was increased by dissatisfaction with wives' work. They entitled their article: 'Does women's liberation drive men to drink?'. Weiss (1987) shows that men tend to view women's work as something they do for themselves, and their own work as a contribution to the family.

6 Crosby (1982) studied a diverse sample of workers in Newton, Massachusetts. Male and female workers, equivalent in terms of job prestige, family situation, age, education, hours worked per week and commitment to their jobs, were far from equivalent in terms of salary. High salary men earned an average of $9000 a year more than women in their category, while lower salaried men earned $5000 a year more than women. Lips (1991) reviewed the literature on power in the workplace. She documents the continued presence of discrimination at work in many important areas.

7 Ironically, it appears that attempts to achieve equality in the divorce process have severely penalized women. In *The Equality Trap*, Mary Ann Mason (1988) has shown how judges now take the position that women with children can support themselves as well as men. In most divorce cases, women do not receive alimony, and 'no-fault' divorce often leaves homemakers and female workers with children virtually impoverished.

8 Colwill and Josephson (1983); Guimond and Dube-Simard (1983) found that people who identity strongly with their group are the most upset and dissatisfied when they perceive that group to be collectively deprived.

2 THE EGALITARIAN ALTERNATIVE

1 Scanzoni *et al.* (1989) have located two family paradigms, based on different values and norms: the conventional and the equal partner marriage. In the conventional, there are two types of arrangements with similar basic norms. In the traditional family the wife stays home with the children. Whatever decision-making occurs is not supposed to undermine the capabilities of the husband to provide for the family's economic needs. He must always be allowed to subordinate family responsibilities to job demands. Since many women are now working, the emerging conventional paradigm also includes a 'junior–senior' partner arrangement, in which the woman contributes financially but her work is still viewed as having less centrality than his. In both the traditional stay-at-home mother family, and the junior–senior partnership, the mother is primarily responsible for the home.

Qualitatively different and in contrast to these two types of conventional families, there is the equal partnership in which norms are:

1 Everything is negotiable except the principle that everything is negotiable.
2 The ultimate goal of joint decision-making is justice and caring.
3 Each partner cultivates the capability to function effectively in both home and work.

2 Equity theory, as an outgrowth of social exchange theory (Thibault and Kelley, 1959) offers an explanation about how a sense of justice is maintained in intimate relationships. Research on how intimate partners maintain equity feelings over time shows couples take different aspects of married life into account in subjectively concluding that their input in the relationship is equal to their gain. These areas include varied contributions and rewards: personal contributions and rewards, such as intelligence or physical attractiveness; emotional contributions and rewards, such as love and understanding; day-by-day contributions and rewards, such as equal decision-making or practical help (Brehm, 1985; Traupmann *et al.* 1981).

3 Beginning with Jesse Bernard's famous 'his and her marriage' (Bernard, 1972), marriage has been shown to be related to higher mental health symptomatology for women than for men. More recent work demonstrates higher mental health risks for married women than married men (Steil and Turetsky, 1987). Current research shows that marriage continues to be an oppressive and unfair social institution. The research literature on women and the family uniformly documents the extent of sexism in modern marriage. For example, empirical reports show that wives do not have equal say in decision-making (Mirowsky, 1985) and have less financial power than should result from their increased earnings (Blumstein and Schwartz, 1983; Stamp, 1985). Both partners tend to view the husband's work as more important than the wife's (Steil and Weltman, 1991). Wives take on more than their fair share of household tasks and childcare, and carry an unfair share of the burden of emotional support and communication in marriage as well (see Thompson and Walker, 1989, for a review of this literature).

4 Power and gender are socially linked to the extent that men tend to have greater access to concrete resources, and other sources of external power and tend to occupy higher status roles than women. While men may cede many daily decisions to their wives, they tend to retain the overall 'power to decide who decides' (Perelberg and Miller, 1990) and continue to dominate the majority of decisions in married life (Pahl, 1989; Scanzoni, 1972). Male power is not always overt, but deeply embedded in existing structures, such as patterns of interaction between partners, drawing on expectations, rules and roles. However, it appears that male dominance, with regard to control of money and decision-making, is connected to lower marital satisfaction for both partners (Pahl, 1989). Despite this, male dominance appears the norm for heterosexual couples (Falbo and Peplau, 1980). Studies confirm that in marriages where the wife dominates the verbal communication, self-reported marital satisfaction is harmed for both partners (Gottman and Levenson, 1988; Miller and Rogers, 1988). However, independent observers rated videotaped interactions as less productive when the husband dominated the conversation (Miller and Rogers, 1988). To understand these findings, we need to see a distinction between making overall decisions and dominating verbal interactions. A possible conclusion is that men tend either to dominate in their intimate relationships with women, or withdraw from them. Women prefer to

have their partners involved in decisions, and are willing to pay the price of having their partners dominate rather than having their partners avoid interactions and marital decision-making. However, both partners pay an overall and long-term price in marital satisfaction when men dominate.

5 Egalitarian couples have been found to perceive themselves as having better communication than other couples (Pollock *et al.*, 1990) and also appear to invest more in improving their relationships (Altrocchi, 1988). They also invest in individual growth. People who hold egalitarian views were found to be more individualistic and self-reliant (Jackson, 1967) and tend to be high in leadership qualities. However, it appears crucial that both partners agree with the need for egalitarianism, as it is the agreement about equal sharing that is most predictive of marital satisfaction (Peplau, 1983). When the couple disagree about it, it is the egalitarian attitude of the husband that predicts whether the couple will be maritally satisfied. That is, an egalitarian husband married to a traditional wife is more likely to be happily married than a traditional husband married to an egalitarian wife. When the husband is egalitarian, the couple is as happy as couples who agree about being egalitarian (Li and Cadwell, 1987). Nicola and Hawkes (1985) found two variables of central importance to marital satisfaction: the husbands' egalitarian attitudes and the wives' self-concept. Since women today are attempting to strengthen their self-concept by increasingly pursuing their own interests, it is the support offered by the egalitarian husband which makes this possible. Empowerment means that both partners are supported in their growth. However, traditionally, women have been 'the woman behind the man' in nurturing his growth and development. What is new in egalitarian couples is the fact that the husband promotes the wife's growth as well.

6 There is a trend towards more egalitarian attitudes among partners today, but this does not seem to reflect a significant change in actual sharing behaviors (Blair and Lichter, 1991; Kimball, 1983; Thompson and Walker, 1989). Husbands of working wives do fairly the same proportion of household work as husbands of women who stay at home. Gilbert (1988) concludes that only a small percentage of dual-career marriages are actually egalitarian.

3 FRIENDSHIP

1 Given the importance of understanding equal partnership, it is surprising how few direct studies exist of these kinds of relationships. There are far more studies of the inequality in most marriages than of those which study egalitarian marriage. Most studies on equal partnership find successful and unsuccessful egalitarians. The following researchers located two types of relationships; those in which equality was achieved and those 'near equals' who were still struggling: Altrocchi and Crossby (1989); Coltrane (1989); Haas (1982); Hiller and Philliber (1989); Pollack Die *et al.* (1990); Schwartz (1994); Smith and

Reid (1986). Recent unpublished quantitative research in progress in Israel demonstrates a strong correlation between the degree of equal sharing of power and household tasks, and the degree of marital satisfaction (Berman and Rabin, 1995).

2 The Roman philosopher Cicero wrote of a friend as a 'second self' (1898). Aristotle describes friendship as 'a single soul dwelling in two bodies' (quoted in Diogenes, 1925) while Emerson (1951) called friendship 'the masterpiece of nature'. The idea that the marriage relationship is primarily companionate is a move away from the view of marriage as an institution based on roles (Mace and Mace, 1988) and towards a view of marriage as primarily a relationship based on a commitment to mutual growth and personal satisfaction. Schwartz (1994), in her study of egalitarian couples, uses the age-old standard of platonic friendship and finds it is the foundation of equal partner relationships.

4 SHARED POWER

1 This and other exercises for couples can be found in Susan Campbell's (1980) book, *The Couple Journey.*

2 This study appears to confirm the major thrust of Silverstein and Rashbaum's 1994 book, *The Courage to Raise Good Men.* Their point is that women in their role of mothers are crucial to the necessary changes needed in gender roles. Premature distancing from the mother, an institutionalized rejection by both mother and son in the name of fostering masculinity, is proposed as a major force in sex-role stereotyping of men. Distance from the mother is translated as distance from the internal feminine; emotions or anything soft that reminds men of their mothers is likewise repudiated. My study does corroborate that it is the men most comfortable with their femininity who were most bonded to their own mothers.

6 ASSESSMENT

1 In a unique study of marital power and the presence of symptoms, Bagarozzi (1990) predicted that it was the less powerful partner in an unhappy marriage who would be the one most likely to develop a psychiatric symptom. He found that 84 percent of the couples who identified one member of the dyad as being symptomatic conformed to this hypothesis. Mirowsky (1985) found a direct correlation between lack of marital power in decision-making, and the development of depressive symptoms, in both men and women.

2 This case is taken from a recent article by Rabin *et al.* (in press) describing a treatment package using gender and power issues in the context of a new behavioral approach called Functional Analytic Therapy (FAP).

7 TYPES OF COUPLES SEEKING THERAPY

1 This couple was observed at the Maudsley Hospital Couples Therapy Clinic. The author would like to thank Dr Michael Crowe for his cooperation in allowing me to watch therapy sessions at the clinic. As with all couples described in this book, names and identifying information have been changed to insure confidentiality.

9 THE TREATMENT MODEL

1 There is a long tradition of this kind of logical convincing, which is exactly what women need to learn to do with men. In *The Republic*, Socrates proves, through logical argument, that justice is not only more virtuous than injustice, but also more profitable (Warmington and Rouse, 1956).

10 COUPLE INTERVENTIONS

1 Therapists helping couples to work towards equality need to be able to train couples in the communication skills needed for competent problem solving. The literature on marital enrichment has the best material available to help relationship therapists incorporate this aspect into therapy. Many programs exist, and can be creatively inserted as structured exercises into the counseling:
   1 Gordon, L. (1993) *PAIRS*, a four-month course in marriage enrichment.
   2 ACME (The Association of Couples for Marriage Enrichment), PO Box 10596, Winston-Salem, NC, USA 27108.
   3 Lederer, W. (1981) a five-week program for relationship improvement.
   4 Dinkmeyer, D. and Carlson, J. (1984) *TIME for a better marriage*, a marriage enrichment course based on Adlerian principles.
   5 Luecke, D. (1981) *The relationship manual*; a 27-session course in marriage enrichment.
   6 Miller, S. *et al.* (1988) *Connecting*; a communication training approach for couples.
2 Work around gender is greatly enhanced by awareness of common differences in communication style between men and women:
   1 Women tend to focus on relationships and others, men on tasks and themselves.
   2 Women seek closeness and men tend to seek space and privacy.
   3 Women talk about relationships with friends while men like to do things together, often without talking.
   4 Women seek approval in the conversation, while men do not.
   5 Women can talk about emotions more easily than men, except those that pertain to feeling good about themselves
   6 Women worry more than men, and men tend to minimize problems.

7 Men express their anger more easily than women, who tend to suppress it and try to please.

8 Men seek attention more than women, who give more attention than men.

9 Getting respect is important to a man, and he will tend to interpret behavior as disrespectful more easily than women, who are more concerned with being liked and tend to interpret behavior as unloving.

10 Men talk more in public, women more in private, and in intimate conversation, men tend to expect women to fill the conversational space.

11 Men's language is more direct and less tentative than women's, so that women see men as aggressive while men see women as insecure.

12 Men are more decisive and do not share the decision-making process easily, while women share their doubts and questions before they have come to a decision.

13 Men tend to give advice while women tend to be empathic.

Some of the popular literature on gender differences can be helpful in increasing therapists' awareness and ability to be empathic: Evatt (1992); Glass (1992); Gray (1992).

11 TREATMENT OF THE TRADITIONAL COUPLE

1 There is an interesting study that addresses the question of whether traditional couples can be as happy as equal partnership couples. Altrocchi (1988) studied a sample of traditional and equal partnership marriages, looking at degrees of marital distress, patterns of decision-making power, and emotional sharing. He found that indeed traditionals can be as satisfied with their relationships as equal partner couples. However, this only occurred when these traditional partners evidenced sharing of emotional intimacy in an equal manner. When husbands shared equally in initiating conversations and emotional closeness with their wives, the traditionals and egalitarians were similar in their level of happiness. Altrocchi selected his sample of traditionals carefully, so that they tended to be couples who firmly believed in the traditional lifestyle. Yet, even when both partners agree that the husband should be in charge of decisions, the marriage works far better when there is friendship.

12 TREATMENT OF THE TRANSITIONAL COUPLE

1 An interesting study of homosexual and lesbian couples in Israel, living together for at least five years, sheds light on some gender differences in intimate relationships. While the lesbian couples shared housework

and the emotional work of their relationship in a highly egalitarian fashion, the homosexual couples showed the absence of these competencies. The men reported far more often using the services of a maid to clean the house. When they had fights, both partners tended to withdraw from conflict. One partner tended to take the role of creating closeness, without the equal sharing of this role reported by the lesbian couples (Mizrachi, 1994). On the other hand, the homosexual couples took care to arrange their financial future (wills, joint ownership of property and savings) in a way not found in the lesbian couples.

13 ISSUES IN TRAINING AND SUPERVISION

1 There are many excellent books and articles emerging about gender and family therapy, which touch on issues about training and supervision. However, there are only a limited number of articles that have taken on the issue of training exclusively. These include: Bogard (1990); Chaney and Piercy (1988); Roberts (1991); Storm (1991); Wheeler *et al.* (1985). These articles contain specific guidelines, programs or exercises for the teaching of gender in family therapy.
2 Exercise 1 was developed by Ayala Pines for her workshops on gender roles. Exercises 4–6 can be found in Roberts (1991).
3 Some of the best texts and articles offering the feminist critique of family therapy today are: Brothers (1992); Goodrich (1991); Goodrich *et al.* (1988); Lueptnitz (1988); Perelberg and Miller (1990); and Walters *et al.* (1988). Reading the following can facilitate discussion about women in families: Baber and Allen (1992); Badinter (1989); Hafner (1993); Hochschild (1989). The following help in understanding the equal partnership alternative: Crosby (1991); Ehrensaft (1987); Hiller and Philliber (1989); Scanzoni *et al.*(1989).
4 Warburton *et al.* (1991) carried out a study of male and female therapists in family therapy. They found that women therapists concentrate more on the man in the family than do male therapists. However, the man is more likely to be defensive with a woman therapist than with a male therapist. Faced with a woman therapist, a man is less likely to give up control. In addition, these researchers found that women therapists tend to become defensive with their defensive male clients in family therapy, starting a cycle of resistance that may impede progress. They recommend that women therapists become more aware of gender issues and that they work both to limit their inherent tendency towards passivity and their reaction of defensiveness with male clients.
5 Family therapy schools of thought influence each other in a reciprocal manner. An examination of the different approaches shows that the centrality of work on power hierarchy, originally espoused by Madanes and Haley (1977) and Minuchin (1974), today finds expression in almost all approaches to family therapy (Gurman and Kniskern, 1991). Moreover, therapeutic approaches that have ignored or rejected power as an explanatory variable have come under attack as ignoring human experience and as a potential limitation of the systemic perspective

(Dell, 1989). Recent constructivist approaches to family therapy (White and Epston, 1990) are congruent with seeing power in couples as a jointly constructed world view. Goodrich (1991) has pointed out that the process of exclusion of certain world views (i.e. the woman's version of reality) closes off the development of alternative stories or solutions. Alternatively, empowerment can be seen as the process of developing and allowing a wide range of personal narratives to be created and recognized, without the limiting forces of gender and power. The centrality of underlying sex-role stereotyping and power hierarchies is congruent with most major family and couples therapy approaches.

6 Wile (1981) has criticized some of the strategic systems approaches to couples therapy as having a 'sense of opposition', involving seeing family members as being duplicitous and manipulative, as using 'ploys' or games to get what they want. He posits that concealed within the notion of family systems is an implied theory of human nature, which is viewed as helpless (i.e. controlled by the family systems), dependent (i.e. dependent on the family), resistant (i.e. opposed to all threats to the family system), and irrational (i.e. not responding to logic or reason). To further empowerment of individual members, the theoretical orientation has to have at its basis a respect for the individual's ability and desire to change.

Bibliography

Adams, J. (1965) 'Inequity in social exchange', in L. Berkovitz (ed.) *Advances in experimental social psychology*, vol. 2. New York: Academic Press.

Aida, Y. and Falbo, T. (1991) 'Relationship between marital satisfaction, resources and power strategies', *Sex Roles,* 24(1/2), 43–56.

Altrocchi, J. (1988) 'Happy traditional and companionship marriages', 69, 434–42.

Altrocchi, J. and Crosby, R. D. (1989) 'Clarifying and measuring the concept of traditional *vs.* egalitarian roles in marriages', *Sex Roles,* 20(11/12), 639–48.

Antill, J. K. (1983). 'Sex role complementarity versus similarity in married couples', *Journal of Personality and Social Psychology*, 45(1), 145–55.

Apter, T. (1993) *Professional Progress: Why Women Don't Have Wives*, London: Macmillan.

Associated Press (1993, June) 'Who do you want to be on an island with?', *Seattle Times.*

Baber, K. and Allen, K. (1992). *Women and Families: Feminist Reconstructions*, New York: Guilford Press.

Badinter, E. (1989) *Man/Woman: the One is the Other*, London: Collins Harvill.

Bagarozzi, D. (1990) 'Discrepancies and symptom development in spouses: an empirical investigation'. *American Journal of Family Therapy*, 18(1), 51–64.

Bagarozzi, D. and Wodarski, J. (1977) 'A social exchange typology of conjugal relationships and conflict development', *Journal of Marriage and Family Counseling*, 3(4), 53–61.

Barnett, R. and Baruch, G. (1987). 'Mothers' participation in childcare: patterns and consequences', in F. Crosby (ed.), *Spouse, Parent, Worker: On Gender and Multiple Roles*, New Haven, Conn: Yale University Press.

Bateson, G., Jackson, D. and Haley, J. (1956) 'Toward a theory of schizophrenia'. *Behavioral Science*, 1, 251–64.

Baucom, D. H. and Epstein, N. (1990) *Cognitive–behavioral Marital Therapy*, New York: Brunner/Mazel.

Benin, M. and Agostinelli, J. (1988) 'Husbands' and wives' satisfaction with the division of labor'. *Journal of Marriage and the Family*, 50, 349–61.

Berman, O. and Rabin, C. (1995) Equal Sharing and Marital Satisfaction, Unpublished manuscript. Tel Aviv University.

Bernard, J (1972) *The Future of Marriage*, New York: World.

Berscheid, E. and Peplau, L. A. (1983) 'The emerging science of relationships'. in E.B.H.Kelley, A. Christensen, J. Harvey, T. Huston, G. Levinger, E. McClintock, L. Peplau and D. Peterson (eds), *Close Relationships: Perspectives and the Meaning of Intimacy*, New York: Freeman.

Blair, S. L. and Lichter, D. T. (1991) 'Measuring the division of household labor, *Journal of Family Issues*, 12(1), 91–113.

Blumstein, P. and Schwartz, P. (1983) *American Couples: Money, Work, Sex*, New York: William Morrow.

Bogard, M. (1990) 'Women treating men', *Family Networker*, May/June, 54–58.

Brehm, S. (1985) *Intimate Relationships*, New York: McGraw-Hill.

Brothers, B. J. (ed.). (1992) *Equal Partnering: a Feminine Perspective*, New York: Harrington Park Press.

Broverman, I., Vogel, S., Broverman, D., Clarkson, F. and Rosenkrantz, P. (1972) 'Sex-role stereotypes: a current appraisal', *Journal of Social Issues*, 28(59–78).

Burgoyne, C. (1990) 'Money in marriage: how patterns of allocation both reflect and conceal power', *Sociological Review*, 38(4), 634–65.

Campbell, S. M. (1980) *The Couple's Journey: Intimacy as a Path to Wholeness*, California: Impact.

Canarton, S. (1992) 'The rise of the conscious feminine', in B.J.Brothers (ed.), *Equal Partnering: a Feminine Perspective*, Binghampton, NY: Haworth Press.

Cancian, F. and Gordon, S. (1988) 'Changing emotion norms in marriage: love and anger in U.S. women's magazines since 1900', *Gender and Society*, 2(3), 308–42.

Chaney, S. and Piercy, F. P. (1988) 'A feminist family therapist behavior checklist'. *The American Journal of Family Therapy*, 16(4), 305–18.

Christensen, A. (1988) 'Dysfunctional interaction patterns in couples' in P. Noller and M. A. Fitzpatrick (eds), *Perspectives on Marital Interaction*, Philadelphia: Multilingual Matters.

Cicero, M. (1898) *De amicitia*, New York: Century Company.

Coltrane, S. (1989) 'Household labor and the routine production of gender', *Social Problems*, 36(5), 473–91.

Colwill, N. and Josephson, W. (1983) 'Attitudes towards equal opportunities in employment: the case of one Canadian government department', *Business Quarterly*, 53(1), 89–91.

Creek, J. and Hogan, R. (1982) 'Self-concepts, self-presentations and moral judgements', in J. Suls and A. Greenwald (eds) *Psychological Perspectives on the Self*, vol. 2, Hillsdale, NJ: Lawrence Erlbaum Associates.

Crosby, F. (1982) *Relative Deprivation and Working Woman*, New York: Oxford University Press.

Crosby, F. J. (1991) *Juggling: the Unexpected Advantages of Balancing Career and Home for Women and their Families*, New York: Free Press.

Crouter, A., Huston, T. and McHale, S. (1987) 'Processes underlying father involvement in dual-earner and single-earner families', *Developmental Psychology*, 23, 431–40.

Crowe, M. and Ridley, J. (1990) *Therapy with Couples: a Behavioural-Systems Approach to Marital and Sexual Problems.* Oxford: Blackwell Scientific Publications.

Darling-Fisher, C. and Tiedje, B. (1990) 'The impact of maternal employment characteristics on fathers' participation in child care', *Family Relations*, 39, 20–6.

Dell, P. F. (1989) 'Violence and the systemic view: the problem of power', *Family Process*, 28(1), 1–14.

Dinkmeyer, D. and Carlson, J. (1984) *TIME for a Better Marriage*, Circle Pines, MN: American Guidance Service.

Diogenes, L. (1925) *Lives of Eminent Philosophers*, translated by R.D. Hicks, New York: G.P. Putnam.

Edwards, J. and Williams, J. (1980) 'Sex-trait stereotypes among young children and young adults', *Canadian Journal of Behavioural Science*, 12, 210–20.

Ehrensaft, D. (1987) *Parenting Together*, New York: Free Press.

Emerson, R. W. (1951) *Friendship*, New York: Thomas Crowell.

Evatt, C. (1992) *He and She: 60 Significant Differences Between Men and Women*, Berkeley, CA: Conari Press.

Falbo, T. and Peplau, L. (1980) 'Power strategies in intimate relationships', *Journal of Personality and Social Psychology*, 38, 618–28.

Fendrich, M. (1984) 'Wives' employment and husbands' distress: a meta-analysis and a replication', *Journal of Marriage and the Family*, 46, 871–9.

Freeman, D. (1992) *Family Therapy with Couples: The Family-of-Origin Approach*, New Jersey: Jason Aronson.

Gilbert, A. L. (1988) *Sharing it All: The Rewards and Struggles of Two-career Families*, New York: Plenum.

Glass, L. (1992) *He Says, She Says: Closing the Communication Gap Between the Sexes*, New York: Putnam.

Glasser, B. and Strauss, A. (1967) *The Discovery of Grounded Theory: Strategies for Qualitative Work*, New York: Aldine Publishing Co.

Goodrich, T. J. (ed.) (1991) *Women and Power*, New York: W. W. Norton.

Goodrich, T. J., Rampage, C., Ellman, B. and Halstead, K. (1988) *Feminist Family Therapy: a Case Book*, New York: W.W.Norton & Company.

Gordon, L. and Frandsen, J. (1993). *Passage to Intimacy: Key Concepts and Skills from the Pairs Program which have Helped Thousands of Couples to Rekindle their Love*, New York: Simon and Schuster.

Gottman, J. (1979) *Marital Interactions: Experimental Investigations*, New York: Academic Press.

Gottman, J. and Krokoff, L. (1989) 'Marital interaction and satisfaction: a longitudinal view', *Journal of Consulting and Clinical Psychology*, 57, 817–24.

Gottman, J. M. and Levenson, R. W. (1988) 'The social psychophysiology of marriage', in P. Noller and M. A. Fitzpatrick (eds), *Perspectives on Marital Interaction*, Philadelphia: Multilingual Matters.

Gray, J. (1992) *Men are from Mars, Women are from Venus*, New York: Harper Collins.

Guimond, S. and Dube-Simard, L. (1983) 'Relative deprivation theory and the Quebec nationalist movement: the cognitive emotion distinction and the personal–group deprivation issue', *Journal of Personality and Social Psychology*, 44(3), 526–35.

Gurman, A. and Kniskern, D. (eds.) (1991) *Handbook of Family Therapy: Volume 1*, New York: Brunner/Mazel.

Guthrie, D. M. and Snyder, C. W. (1988) 'Spouses' self-evaluation for situations involving emotional communication', in P. Noller and M. A. Fitzpatrick (eds) *Perspectives on Marital Interaction*, Philadelphia: Multilingual Matters.

Haas, L. (1982) 'Determinants of role-sharing behavior: a study of egalitarian couples', *Sex Roles*, 8(7), 747–60.

Hafner, J. (1993) *The End of Marriage: Why Monogamy isn't Working*, London: Century.

Hall, M. (1992) *Women and Empowerment*, Washington: Hemisphere.

Hare-Mustin, R. T. (1980) 'Family therapy may be dangerous to your health', *Professional Psychology*, 11, 935–8.

Harell, A. (1986) 'Do liberated women drive their husbands to drink? The impact of masculine orientation, status inconsistency and family life satisfaction on male liquor consumption', *International Journal of the Addictions*, 21(3), 385–91.

Hiller, D. and Philliber, W. (1989) *Equal Partners: Successful Women in Marriage*, Newbury Park, CA: Sage.

Hiller, D. V. and Philliber, W. W. (1986) 'The division of labor in contemporary marriage: expectations, perceptions, and performance', *Social Problems*, 33(3), 191–201.

Hochschild, A. (1989) *The Second Shift*. New York: Avon.

Homans, G. (1961) *Social Behavior*, New York: Harcourt, Brace & World.

Jackson, D. (1967) *Personality Research Form Manual*, Goshen, NY: Research Psychologists Press.

Jukes, A. (1993) *Why Men Hate Women*, London: Free Association Books.

Kimball, G. (1983) *The 50/50 Marriage*, Boston, MA: Beacon.

Kingsbury, N. and Scanzoni, J. (1989) 'Process and decision outcomes among dual-career couples', *Journal of Comparative Family Studies*, 20(1), 231–46.

Krausz, S. (1986) 'Sex roles within marriages', *Social Work*, November/December, 457–69.

Lederer, W. (1981) *Marital Choices: Forecasting, Assessing and Improving a Relationship*, New York: W.W. Norton.

Lerner, H. (1985) *The Dance of Anger*, New York: Harper & Row.

Leupnitz, D. A. (1988) *The Family Interpreted: Feminist Theory in Clinical Practice*, New York: Basic Books.

Li, J. and Caldwell, R. A. (1987) 'Magnitude and directional effects of marital sex-role incongruence on marital adjustment', *Journal of Family Issues*, 8(1), 97–110.

Lips, H. (1991) *Women, Men and Power*, Mountain View, CA: Mayfield Publishing Company.

Luecke, D. (1881) *The Relationship Manual: How to Diagnose, Build, or Enrich a Relationship*, Columbia, MD: The Relationship Institute.

McGoldrick, M. C. and Walsh, F. (eds) (1988) *Women in Families: a Framework for Family Therapy*, New York: Norton.

Mace, D., and Mace, V. (1988) *When the Honeymoon's Over*, Nashville: Abingdon Press.

Madanes, C. and Haley, J. (1977) 'Dimensions of family therapy', *Journal of Nervous and Mental Disease*, 165, 88–98.

Marsh, J. and Byrne, B. (1991) 'Differentiated additive androgyny model: relations between masculinity, femininity, and multiple dimensions of self-concept', *Journal of Personality and Social Psychology*, 61, 811–28.

Mason, M. (1988) *The Equality Trap*, New York: Touchstone.

Millar, F. E. and Rogers, E. (1988) 'Power dynamics in marital relationships', in P. Noller and M. A. Fitzpatrick (eds), *Perspectives on Marital Interaction*, Philadelphia: Multilingual Matters.

Miller, S., Nunnally, E. and Wackman, D. (1993) *Talking Together*, Littleton, CO: Interpersonal Communication Programs.

Miller, S., Wackman, D., Nunnally, E., Miller, P. (1988) *Connecting: With Self and Others*, Littleton CO: Interpersonal Communication Programs, Inc.

Minuchin, S. (1974) *Families and Family Therapy*, Cambridge, MA: Harvard University Press.

Mirowsky, J. (1985) 'Depression and marital power: an equity model', *American Journal of Sociology*, 91(3), 557–92.

Mizrachi, S. (1994) *A Qualitative Study of Stable Homosexual and Lesbian Israeli Couples*, Masters Thesis, Tel Aviv University.

Moon, S., Dillon, D. and Sprenkle, D. (1991) 'On balance and synergy: family therapy and qualitative research revisited', *Journal of Marital and Family Therapy*, 17(2), 187–92.

Morris, N. and Sison, B. (1974) 'Correlates of female powerlessness: parity methods of birth control and pregnancy', *Journal of Marriage and the Family*, 36, 708–12.

Nicola, J. S. and Hawkes, G. R. (1985) 'Marital satisfaction of dual-career couples: Does sharing increase happiness?', *Journal of Social Behavior and Personality*, 1(1), 47–60.

Pahl, J. (1989) *Money and Marriage*, London: Macmillan.

Parsons, T. (1954) *Essays in Sociological Theory: Patterns of Aggression in the Western World*, New York: Free Press.

Peplau, L. (1983) 'Roles and gender', in H. Kelley, E. Berscheid, A. Christensen, J. Harvey, T. Huston, G. Levenger, E. McClintock, A. Peplau, and D. Peterson (eds), *Close Relationships*, New York: W. H. Freeman and Company.

Perelberg, R. J. and Miller, A. (eds) (1990) *Gender and Power in Families*, New York: Routledge.

Perlman, D. and Duck, S. (eds) (1987) *Intimate Relationships: Development, Dynamics, and Deterioration*, Newbury Park, CA: Sage.

Pollock, A. D., Die, A. H. and Marriot, R. G. (1990) 'Relationship of communication style to egalitarian marital role expectations', *Journal of Social Psychology*, 130(5), 619–24.

Rabin, C. (1994) 'The egalitarian alternative: concepts and implications for practice', *Journal of Applied Social Sciences*, 18(1), 109–23.

Rabin, C., Tsai, M. and Kohlenberg, R. (in press) 'Targeting sex-role and power issues with a functional analytic approach: gender patterns in behavioral marital therapy', *Journal of Feminist Family Therapy*.

Rapoport, R. and Rapoport, R. (1971) *Dual Career Families*, Baltimore, MD: Penguin.

Raush, H., Barry, W., Hertel, R. and Swain, M. (1974) *Communication, Conflict and Marriage*, San Francisco, CA: Jossey-Bass.

Reinharz, S. (1992) *Feminist Methods in Social Research*, New York/Oxford: Oxford University Press.

Roberts, J. (1991) 'Sugar and spice, toads and mice: gender issues in family therapy training', *Journal of Marital and Family Therapy*, 17(2), 121–32.

Rubin, L. (1983) *The Role of Friendship in Our Lives*, New York: Harper & Row.

Russell, G. and Radin, N. (1983) 'Increased paternal participation: the father's perspective', in M. Lamb and A. Sagi (eds), *Fatherhood and Family Policy*, Hillside, NH: Lawrence Erlbaum.

Safilios-Rothchild, C. (1981) 'Toward a psychology of relationships', *Psychology of Women Quarterly*, 5, Spring, 377–84.

Sanford, L. and Donovan, E. (1984) *Women and Self-esteem: Understanding and Improving the Way we Think and Feel about Ourselves*, London: Penguin Books.

Scanzoni, J. (1972) *Sexual Bargaining: Power Politics in the American Marriage*, Englewood Cliffs, NJ: Prentice-Hall.

Scanzoni, J., Polonko, K., Teachman, J. and Thompson, L. (1989) *The Sexual Bond: Rethinking Families and Close Relationships*, Newbury Park; CA: Sage.

Scharff, D. and Scharff, J. (1991) *Object Relations Couple Therapy*, Northvale, NJ: Jason Aronson.

Schnarch, D. (1991) *Constructing the Sexual Crucible: an Integration of Sexual and Marital Therapy*, New York: W. W. Norton.

Schwartz, P. (1994) *Peer Marriage: How Love Between Equals Really Works*, New York: Free Press.

Silverstein, O. and Rashbaum, B. (1994) *The Courage to Raise Good Men: a Call for Change*, London: Michael Joseph.

Smith, A. and Reid, W. (1986) *Role-sharing Marriage*, New York: Columbia University Press.

Solomon, M. (1989) *Narcissism and Intimacy: Love and Marriage in an Age of Confusion*, New York: W. W. Norton.

Staines, G. and Libby, P. (1986) 'Men and women in role relationships', in R. Ashmore and F. DelBoca (eds) *The Social Psychology of Female-Male Relationships: a Critical Analysis of Central Concepts*, New York: Academic Press.

Stamp, P. (1985) 'Balance of financial power in marriage: an exploratory study of breadwinning wives', *Sociological Review*, 33(3), 546–57.

Steil, J. M. and Turetsky, B. A. (1987) 'Is equal better? The relationship between marital equality and psychological symptomatology', in S. Oskamp (ed.) *Family Processes and Problems: Social Psychological Aspects*, Beverly Hills: Sage.

Steil, J. and Weltman, K. (1991) 'Marital inequality: the importance of resources, personal attributes and social norms on career valuing and the allocation of domestic responsibilities', *Sex Roles*, 24, 161–70.

Storm, C. L. (1991) 'Placing gender in the heart of MFT masters programs: teaching a gender sensitive systemic view', *Journal of Marital and Family Therapy*, 17(1), 45–52.

Strauss, A. and Corbin, J. (1990) *Basics of Qualitative Research*, Newbury Park, CA: Sage.

Tannen, D. (1990) You *Just Don't Understand: Women and Men in Conversation*, New York: Morrow.

Tavris, C. (1989) *Anger: the Misunderstood Emotion*, New York: Simon & Schuster.

Tavris, C. (1992) *The Mismeasure of Women: Why Women are not the Better Sex, the Inferior Sex or the Opposite Sex*, New York: Simon & Schuster.

Thibaut, J. and Kelley, H. (1959) *The Social Psychology of Groups*, New York: Wiley.

Thompson, L. and Walker, A. (1989) 'Gender in families: women and men in marriage, work and parenthood', *Journal of Marriage and the Family*, 51, 845–71.

Traupmann, J., Peterson, R., Utne, M. and Hatfield, E. (1981) 'Measuring equity in intimate relations', *Applied Psychology Measurement*, 5, 467–80.

Uzzell, O. (1986) 'Racial and gender perceptions of marriage roles at a predominantly black university', *The Western Journal of Black Studies*, 10(4), 167–71.

Walters, M., Carter, B., Papp, P. and Silverstein, O. (1988) *The Invisible Web: Gender Patterns in Family Relationships*, New York: Guilford.

Warburton, J., Newberry, A. and Alexander, J. (1991) in M. McGoldrick, C. Anderson and F. Walsh (eds), *Women in Families: A Framework for Family Therapy*, New York: W. W. Norton.

Warmington, E. and Rouse, P. (eds) (1956) *Great Dialogues of Plato*, New York: Mentor.

Watzlawick, P., Beavin, J. and Jackson, D. (1967) *Pragmatics of Human Communication: a Study of Interactional Patterns, Pathologies and Paradoxes*, New York: W. W. Norton.

Weiss, R. (1987) 'Men and their wives' work', in F. Crosby (ed.) *Spouse, Parent, Worker: On Gender and Multiple Roles*, New Haven, CT: Yale University Press.

Wheeler, D., Avis, J., Miller, L. and Chaney, S.(1985) 'Rethinking family therapy training and supervision: a feminist model', *Journal of Psychotherapy and the Family*, 1, 53–71.

White, M. and Epston, D. (1990) *Narrative Means to Therapeutic Ends*, New York: W. W. Norton.

Wile, D. (1981) *Couples Therapy: a Nontraditional Approach*, New York: John Wiley.

Index

abandonment feelings 24, 216
acceptance, therapeutic 4
Adams, J. 41
aggression 204; male 91, 124, 141, 169, 202, 228; women and 42, 169, 202
agoraphobia 119, 136
Aida, Y. 46
alcohol abuse 119
alliances, in therapy 152, 250
alter ego method 184–5, 231
Altrocchi, J. 261n1
Andrew, 256n5
androgyny 26, 81, 87, 97, 173, 191, 210, 236; in communication in equal partner couples 148
anger 43, 102, 162, 182, 223; avoidance/denial 24, 33, 124, 136, 161; female 15, 29, 30, 33, 36, 38, 42, 51, 52, 61, 62, 90–4, 118, 124, 128, 242, 244 (traditional couples 95, 136, 137–9, 198, 199, 200, 210, transitional couples 144, 220, 221, 222); female therapist and 248–9, 251; male 24, 91, 146, 147, 184, 223, 226, 227, 228, 230, 248; trainees and 241, 248
Antill, J.K. 26
apathy, as symptom 136
appreciation 42, 184–5; self- see self-esteem
assertiveness 23, 26, 50, 89, 188, 247
assessment 118–34, 155; areas of

119–21; of couple interaction 121–6; gender/power analysis of low sexual desire 126–34; process of 126
authority 37, 53, 218; of female therapist 247; of supervisor, in training 240; in therapy 152, 156
autonomy see personal autonomy
avoidance of conflict 2, 24, 52, 78–9, 116, 124, 139, 147, 212, 213, 216; reducing men's 104–6; refusal of, in open conflict transitional couple 143; see also withdrawal

Bagarozzi, D. 41, 44, 259n1
Barnett, R. 255n5
Baruch, G. 255n5
Bateson, G. 101
Berman, Ofrit 34
Bernard, Jesse 257n3
Blumstein, P. 49
boundaries, creating 149, 162, 231
Brehm, S. 41, 45
Byrne, B. 26

Campbell, Susan 259n1
Canarton, S. 96
Cancian, F. 33
cases: assessment in couple interaction 123–4; conjoint sessions with focus on individual 181–3; correcting

stereotypes 158, 173; *see also*
gender stereotyping
strategic systems approach
263n6
structural family therapy 251,
252
submission, transitional couple
and 211
subordinate partner/role 169, 171;
empowerment of 160–4; in
therapy 125; women as 50–2,
169, 170–1
successful wife (case) 19–20, 27,
31, 32–4; gender/power analysis
23–5
supervision: equal partnership
themes 239–42; integrating
equal partnership goals 251–3;
issues in 234–53; learning
process 242–6; utilizing training
group dynamics 235–7
support 81, 110, 207; female 102,
104–5
survival mechanism, denial as 225
sympathy, for rejection 112
symptoms: and assessment 118,
119, 120; developing 44–5, 91,
119; mental health 257n3,
259n1; in traditional couple
136, 192; in transitional couple
133
systemic perspective 251, 262n5,
263n6

Tannen, D. 102
Tel Aviv University School of
Social Work 5
therapeutic methods/interventions
159, 251–3; *see also* couple
sessions; individual sessions
therapeutic system, egalitarian
151–7
therapist: and communication 103;
confusion 219–20, 233;
correcting power imbalance by
taking sides 1–4; dealing with
gender and power 12–13, 233,
234–5; and equality 233, 243–4;
female 25, 247–53; gender

ambivalence and fear of change
158; need for equality in own
lives 151; overfocusing on or
allying with one partner 125,
152, 245, 250; result of lack of
attention to gender/power
17–20; self-disclosure 151; and
social change 16, 118–19; values
7–8
therapy *see* assessment;
therapeutic; therapist; treatment
Thompson, L. 101, 255n4
Tiedje, B. 49
traditional couple 49, 118, 135–9,
142, 156, 157, 165; treatment
192–210
traditional family 256n1
traditional marriage 60; indirect
control strategies 39
traditional men 63, 67; and
empowerment 88; lack of
respect 27
traditional power balance 89
traditional roles 15, 61, 63, 66, 67,
118
traditional women 160, 192, 216,
217
training 4; equal partnership
themes in 239–42; exercises on
gender and power 237–9;
female therapist 247–53;
integrating equal partnership
goals 251–3; issues in 234–53;
learning process 242–6;
utilizing group dynamics
235–7
transitional couple 27, 133,
139–47; parallel lives 212–13;
treatment of 211–33
treatment: empirically based 4–9;
goals of 100, 115, 116–17;
noncompliance in 127, 130
treatment model 158–78, 254n2;
education towards equality
173–8; empowerment of each
partner 160–8;
metacommunication to shift
power patterns 168–73;
preparation for sharing 183–91